Individual Rights and Government Wrongs

Brian Phillips

BEP Enterprises Incorporated
Houston, Texas

Published by BEP Enterprises Incorporated, Houston, Texas

Visit IndividualRightsGovernmentWrongs.com for more information.

ISBN: 978-0-578-09795-4

Acknowledgements

In the process of writing this book, many people have contributed in a myriad of ways. I could not begin to thank all of them. However, several individuals deserve special mention.

My wife, Elaine, was a source of continual encouragement, comments, and much more. Her love and support has made the process of writing this book, and my life, more enjoyable.

My friend and editor, Janet Lee Westphal, made many suggestions and comments that vastly improved the content and readability of the book.

My appreciation and admiration of Ayn Rand, whose ideas form the foundation of this book, cannot be understated. While I agree with and support her philosophy, Objectivism, I do not purport to speak for her or represent her philosophy.

The content, and any errors contained herein, is entirely my responsibility.

Contents

Introduction

This book was written for those who love the United States of America and the principles upon which it was founded.

America was founded on an ideology—the right of each individual to his own life, his own liberty, and the pursuit of his own happiness. As philosopher Leonard Peikoff writes: "America is the only country in history created not by meaningless warfare or geographic accident, but deliberately, on the basis of certain fundamental ideas."[1] The Founding Fathers sought to establish a form of government that, unlike monarchy, theocracy, and the mob rule of democracy, recognizes and protects individual rights.

The Founders were intellectual men, widely read in the ideas of the Enlightenment. They were also practical men, concerned with the problems of life on earth. Their great achievement was transforming the ideas of the Enlightenment into a practical socio-economic system—capitalism.

The recognition and protection of individual rights under capitalism led to the unprecedented achievements of nineteenth century America. The spectacular rise in the standard of living for all Americans, the explosion of consumer goods, and the creation of wealth previously unimaginable were the effect. Capitalism was the cause.

By capitalism, I do not mean the mixed economy of contemporary America, which attempts to combine elements of freedom with elements of government control and regulation. Capitalism means a complete separation of state and economics. Just as you should be free to advocate the ideas that you believe to be true, you should also be free to act on those ideas to produce, trade, and buy the values required to sustain and enjoy your life.

---

1. Leonard Peikoff, "Assault from the Ivory Tower: The Professors' War Against America," in *The Voice of Reason* (New York: Meridian, 1989), p. 187.

Intellectual freedom and economic freedom are inseparable. The only proper purpose of government is the protection of your right to live your life as you judge best, free from physical coercion from others. The mutual rights of others prohibit you from using physical force against them. In a capitalist society, the use of force is banned from human relationships.

Beginning in the nineteenth century, both secular and religious statists attacked capitalism and its implied morality. Secular statists argued that individuals must put aside their own interests and values to achieve the collective good. Religious statists argued that individuals must put aside their personal desires in service to family, country, and God. Both agreed that individuals should not pursue their own self-interest, but should act in the name of the "public interest." Both rejected capitalism's implied morality—the moral right of each individual to his own life, his own liberty, and the pursuit of his own happiness. As the nineteenth century came to a close, both the left and the right agreed that unregulated capitalism is impractical, that government controls will lead to greater freedom, and that government must intervene in order to achieve the "common good." The Progressive Era ushered in an unprecedented expansion of government controls and regulations.

The ideas of the Progressive Era are alive and well today. On both the left and the right, the "solution" to nearly every problem, real or imagined, is government regulations, controls, prohibitions, and mandates. From health care to job creation, from the development of energy resources to the construction of infrastructure, from education to poverty, Americans look to government to provide the solutions. The success of capitalism has been forgotten, ignored, and misrepresented.

The purpose of this book is to shine a light on the morality and success of capitalism, and to demonstrate that contemporary problems are solvable when individuals are free. Indeed, many of today's problems would not exist if America had stayed true to its founding principles. When government intervenes in the economy and the lives of individuals, government is no longer a protector of rights, but their most egregious violator. When government violates individual rights, new problems are created and those that existed are made worse.

While a capitalist society as I advocate has never existed, you will see abundant evidence showing how education, mail delivery, charity, and roads can operate in a capitalist society. You will learn how waterways are kept clean without government regulations. You will read the stories of businessmen discovering new sources of affordable energy without government subsidies. You will discover how capitalism discourages racial discrimination. In every realm that we will examine, from libraries to employment, from land use to taxation, you will see that capitalism is not only practical, but because capitalism is the only system that protects individual rights, it is moral as well. You will learn what is possible when the innovative mind of man is unleashed from the shackles of government controls.

Part 1

Life

Once upon a time, there existed a nation that respected and protected individual rights. In that nation, individuals were free to live their lives as they judged best. Nearly half of the mail was delivered by private companies. Libraries were founded and operated by private associations. There were no public schools, yet individuals were well-educated. Much of the infrastructure—such as sanitation and roads—was provided by private businesses. There was no parasitical "entitlement" state. Government intervention in the lives of the citizens was minimal. This is no fairy tale; it is a matter of historical fact. That nation was the United States of America, as envisioned by our Founding Fathers.

What happened? Why are libraries, schools, and infrastructure now government monopolies? Why do "entitlement" programs threaten to bankrupt our nation? Why does government have an omnipresent impact on our lives?

The answer can be found in another historical fact: America abandoned its founding principle—individual rights. Unrestricted by the principle of individual rights, government has steadily usurped those rights, expanding its power and control over our lives. "There is," wrote Ayn Rand,

> only *one* fundamental right (all the others are its consequences or corollaries): a man's right to his own life. Life is a process of self-sustaining and self-generated action; the right to life means the right to engage in self-sustaining and self-generated action—which means: the freedom to take all the actions required by the nature of a rational being for the support, the furtherance, the

> fulfillment and the enjoyment of his own life. (Such is the meaning of the right to life, liberty and the pursuit of happiness.)[1]

Rights are a moral sanction to freedom of action; that is, rights protect your freedom to live your life as you judge best, as long as you respect the mutual rights of others. As we will later see, rights are not a claim to an object, but the freedom to take the actions necessary to produce or earn that object. For example, you have the right to build a house, but you do not have a right to have shelter given to you. You have a right to earn the money to buy a car; you do not have a right to have transportation provided for you. What can stop you from producing or earning the values that you want? What can prevent you from acting as you judge best for your life?

Only physical force, or the threat of force, can prevent you from acting as you choose. If someone ties you up, or hits you with a club, or threatens you with a gun, you cannot act as you would freely choose. Morally, you may not initiate force to interfere with the actions of others, just as they may not initiate force to interfere with your actions. (Self-defense is the use of force in response to those who initiate its use and is therefore moral.) This boundary on the initiation of force includes government, no matter how "noble" the cause, no matter the intentions, no matter the "public interest" that will allegedly result, no matter how many citizens insist upon restricting your actions.

James Madison recognized the threat posed by an uncontrolled majority. In a letter to Thomas Jefferson, he wrote:

> Wherever the real power in a Government lies, there is the danger of oppression. In our Governments the real power lies in the majority of the Community, and the invasion of private rights is *chiefly* to be apprehended, not from acts of Government contrary to the sense of its constituents, but from acts in which the Government is the mere instrument of the major number of the constituents.[2]

---

1. Ayn Rand, "Man's Rights," in *The Virtue of Selfishness* (New York: New American Library, 1964), pp. 93-94.

2. James Madison, "Letter to Thomas Jefferson," *Constitution Society*, accessed May 27, 2011, http://www.constitution.org/jm/17881017_tj.htm.

To Madison, the primary threat to individual liberty under the American system is government acting at the behest of the majority. A government unrestricted by the principle of individual rights is inimical to freedom, whether it is guided by a tyrannical king or the "will of the people."

Unfortunately, most Americans today believe that government must provide certain services, such as education, mail delivery, parks, welfare, and infrastructure. They think that it is proper to force you to pay for these services through taxes, regardless of your own desires and values. Most Americans accept the premise that the ends—education, parks, and roads—justify the means—coerced payments. They argue that you must be compelled to put aside your self-interest to promote the "public interest." They believe that you will somehow be better off if you are forced by government to act contrary to your own judgment.

As we will see, these coercive government institutions are impractical. The results are higher costs, fewer (if any) choices, and poor service. They seldom, if ever, deliver the promised results. Postal patrons must endure long lines and surly clerks. Public schools do an increasingly poor job of educating our children. The welfare state has not conquered poverty. Our roads and bridges are crumbling. These government services are *impractical* because they are *immoral.* They prohibit you—and all Americans—from living your life as you judge best.

As we will also see, capitalism is practical. The results are lower costs, more choices and opportunities, greater economic progress and innovation, and a higher standard of living for all. These practical benefits are possible only in a social system that recognizes and protects individual rights. Capitalism is *practical* because it is *moral.* Capitalism provides the social environment in which you—and all Americans—are free to live as you choose, as long as you respect the mutual rights of others.

America can again be the nation that it once was. America can again be the land of the free. America can again respect and protect individual rights. And that is no fairy tale.

1

A Walk in a Private Park

To meet budget shortfalls, a growing number of municipalities and state governments are considering some form of privatization for their parks. These proposals are usually met with indignant opposition. Private companies, it is claimed, would despoil the parks by building condos on the rim of the Grand Canyon. Motivated by profit, they would erect a Starbucks in front of Old Faithful. They would raise prices and turn parks into the playgrounds of the rich, leaving the poor and middle-class with few opportunities to enjoy outdoor recreation. And, as the acting director of the National Recreation and Park Association stated in 2006, privatizing parks is un-American: "Public parks embody the American tradition of preserving public lands for the benefit and use of all."[1]

Public libraries are similarly defended. "Public libraries invoke images of our freedom to learn, a cornerstone of our democracy," said one supporter of public libraries.[2] Without public libraries, it is claimed, the poor would not have access to books. Private libraries will focus only on their profits and cut needed services. They will neglect patrons and hire unqualified staff.

These positions are widely held, but are they true? Will private parks be filled with fast-food restaurants and commercial activities? Will businesses cut services in the pursuit of profit? Are public

---

1. Richard J. Dolesh, "Advocacy Update: Top Ten Reasons Parks are Important: the Values of Public Parks and Recreation in America," *CBS Interactive Business Network* (January 2006), accessed January 5, 2011, http://findarticles.com/p/articles/mi_m1145/is_1_41/ai_n26742947/?tag=content;col1.

2. David Streitfeld, "Anger as a Private Company Takes Over Libraries," *New York Times*, September 26, 2010, accessed January 5, 2011, http://www.nytimes.com/2010/09/27/business/27libraries.html?pagewanted=all.

parks and libraries really a part of America's heritage? To begin, let us look at the arguments in favor of these public institutions.

Because they operate for the "benefit and use of all," public parks and libraries are guided by different considerations than private businesses: public parks and libraries are meant to serve the "public interest." As one advocate for public libraries claims:

> Generally there isn't enough money to buy every new book, so the librarian has to decide not only what's going to be popular with their readers, but *what will serve the greatest number of patrons. That often means buying books they know won't get more than three or four uses a year....*
>
> This is important because the distinction between a bookstore and a public library is that the bookstore exists to serve those who pay whereas a library exists to serve all [emphasis added].[3]

It is true that a bookstore exists to serve those who pay. Isn't that what a private business does? It must provide the products or services desired by its customers—those who pay—or else it will not stay in business for long. If a bookstore refuses or neglects to stock a book that its customers want, consumers will go elsewhere. A profit-seeking business tries to "serve the greatest number of patrons" because, that is the means by which it will earn a profit.

In contrast, a public library attempts to satisfy the desires of everybody. Of course, this is impossible. It would mean purchasing every book and periodical published, which no library could afford. In practice, it means purchasing books that are popular and in high demand, as well as unpopular, infrequently read books. But libraries have limited budgets, and the purchase of infrequently read books necessarily reduces the funds available for more popular works. In other words, fewer copies of a best-seller, which is in demand by dozens of patrons, are purchased so that the library can buy a book that three or four want to read. A waiting list forms for the most recent book from Stephen King, while *An Introduction to Fluid Dynamics* collects dust on the shelf. Three or four patrons are happy, while dozens are disappointed. And this, we are to believe, serves

---

3. Nat-Wu, "Privatizing Libraries," *Three Wise Men* (Blog), October 5, 2007, accessed January 5, 2011, http://threewisemenblog.com/2007/10/05/privatizing-libraries/.

the "greatest number of patrons." Divorced from market demand, public libraries are reduced to the absurd claim that serving the "greatest number of patrons" has nothing to do with numbers.

The attempt to serve the "public interest" really means that the interests of some take precedence over the interests of others. Whose interests will prevail and by what standard? A bookstore must necessarily seek to satisfy your interests or it will not get your business; you are free to spend your money on the books that you want. In the public library, your interests are largely irrelevant; through taxation, you are forced to pay for books that you do not want to read. In the private sector, each consumer is free to find solutions to fulfill his personal interests. In the public sector, those who make the most noise or have the proper connections have their interests fulfilled. That is, the squeaky wheel usually gets the grease, or in this case, the books. Why should you be forced to pay for books that you do not want? Do you have a better use for *your* money?

The demand for products and services is virtually unlimited. All rational and productive people seek a better life—a nicer car, a bigger home, a more exotic vacation, or similar values. But our resources, such as time and money, are finite, and we must choose how we use them. Those choices are made on the basis of our personal values, with each of us acting in accordance with our own needs, desires, goals, and financial resources.

For example, you might choose to use your money to attend baseball games, while others will attend the ballet. Some will invest their money in bonds, while you might prefer the stock market. You might choose to drive an older car in order to save for a down payment on a house, while others prefer to drive a newer vehicle and live in an apartment. Since there is no right or wrong that is applicable to all individuals, each of us must make such decisions based on the benefits that we think we will derive. However, the defenders of public parks and libraries claim otherwise.

Parks and libraries are desirable and beneficial, they argue. The nature of these goods is such that private companies will not provide them in the quantity or quality that members of the community desire. If such goods are not readily available, all of us would be worse off. Therefore, it is proper for government to compel us to provide financial support through taxation, regardless of our own personal choices, desires, and values.

While it is certainly true that many people value parks and libraries, it is also true that many people don't. Just as some prefer baseball over football, some prefer window shopping over walks in the park. Just as some prefer rock music over classical music, some prefer bookstores over libraries. Public parks and libraries force individuals to pay for goods they do not value and would not choose to otherwise support. What "justifies" such actions?

The defenders of public parks and libraries argue that such goods provide a valuable service to the community, and that fact alone "justifies" using coercive taxation to fund them. Chicago Public Library Commissioner Mary A. Dempsey defended the use of taxation for libraries: "Public libraries are more relevant and heavily used today than ever before, and public libraries are one of the better uses of the taxpayers' dollars."[4] Better uses—to whom and by what standard? Dempsey is clear on her answer. She and her cohorts regard their judgment as superior to yours. They believe that they can decide the best use for *your* money. Morally, your money is yours to spend as you choose; politically, you should be free to act on your judgment. In a capitalist society, if Dempsey and her ilk regard libraries as the best use for *their* money, they are free to act accordingly.

Freedom is the absence of government coercion—the recognition of your moral right to act according to your own judgment in the pursuit of your own values. If you value parks or libraries, freedom allows you to support them. And, if you don't value parks or libraries, freedom allows you to spend your money on other values of your own choosing. If a sufficient number of people are willing to pay for parks and libraries, then entrepreneurs, businesses, and others will provide them. This is true of restaurants, cell phones, televisions, and automobiles. It is true of computers, designer jeans, artisan bread, and candy. It is also true of parks and libraries. Developers, businesses, and non-profit organizations recognize the need and desire for outdoor recreation, and consequently, they offer a variety of solutions.

---

4. Mary A. Dempsey, "Chicago Public Library Commissioner Reacts to FOX Chicago News' Story," *Fox Chicago News*, July 2010, accessed January 5, 2011, http://www.myfoxchicago.com/dpp/news/library-taxes-closed-commissioner-reaction-letter-mary-dempsey-20100702.

Developers have long recognized the appeal of parks to home owners. Many include parks, walking paths, and green spaces in their developments as a means to improve attractiveness, and thus, sell more homes. For example, in 1831 Samuel B. Ruggles purchased a tract of land in Manhattan to build approximately sixty homes. He spent $180,000 to construct a two-acre park in the middle of the homes. Ownership of the park was deeded to the property owners, and today, Gramercy Park is one of the few private parks in New York City.

A more spectacular example can be found in The Woodlands, a community north of Houston, Texas. This privately developed community has 125 forested parks and two hundred miles of hike and bike trails, in addition to dozens of lakes and ponds. Encompassing 23.4 square miles, The Woodlands has nearly eight thousand acres of green space.[5] Similarly, developers across the nation frequently include parks, walking paths, and lakes in their developments.

While these parks are for the exclusive use of residents and their guests, other parks and green spaces are owned or operated by non-profit organizations and made available to the public. For example, KiwanisLand in Garden Grove, California, is a three-acre park constructed and maintained by the local Kiwanis Club. The park is made available to local youth groups and has camp sites, an amphitheater, and a lake.[6] New York City's Central Park—though city owned—is managed and operated by a private, non-profit conservancy, as are parks in Atlanta, Boston, and numerous other cities. Supported largely by corporate and individual donations, these parks are free and open to the public.

On a grander scale, Thousand Trails—a for-profit business—owns more than eighty "preserves" in twenty-two states and British Columbia. These family-oriented facilities have a wide variety of activities, including swimming pools, spas, hiking trails, lodges, and community centers. They offer both lifetime and annual memberships. Similarly, KOA operates nearly five hundred

---

5. "The Woodlands Greenspace Map," The Woodlands, accessed May 27, 2011, http://www.thewoodlands.com/nature/greenspace.html.

6. "History Page," Kiwanis Club of Garden Grove. accessed January 5, 2011, http://www.kiwanisland.com/history.html.

camping facilities around the nation with a wide variety of activities and amenities.

Other businesses offer outdoor recreation in the form of hunting and fishing resorts. They provide a variety of packages, including long-term leases and single-visit packages for hunters and fishermen. The owners carefully manage their property for its scenic appeal, and they control hunting and fishing to ensure plentiful game for their clients.

Contrary to the claims of public park defenders, these private, for-profit businesses do not turn their properties into a sea of fast-food restaurants, billboards, and other commercial activities. The mountains, lakes, green space, and forests on their properties are what attract customers, and large-scale commercial activity would diminish that appeal. In other words, the owners know that it makes no economic sense to turn their properties into Disney World, because that is not the experience that their customers want. They know that those who do want a Disney World-like experience can go to… Disney World, or Sea World, or Busch Gardens (all privately owned), or similar amusement parks that offer that type of recreation.

Imagine what amusement parks would be like if, one hundred years ago, it had been decided that private business cannot or will not build such recreational facilities. What if amusement parks were built and managed by politicians and bureaucrats, rather than profit-seeking businessmen? Who do you think is more likely to provide a fun and enjoyable experience? Would you rather spend your entertainment money at a facility built by a visionary like Walt Disney or a curmudgeon like Barney Frank?

As these examples demonstrate, the private sector can and does provide a wide variety of options in regard to parks and outdoor recreation. Whether it is developers, a civic club, a non-profit organization, or a for-profit business, private parks offer the experiences, amenities, and activities that their patrons desire. Those who value parks and wish to voluntarily support them are free to do so, and those who have other values are equally free to use their money for those values.

But what about libraries? Will private companies deny the poor the opportunity to read books? Will the pursuit of profit lead to cuts in services? As we will soon see, private businesses and organizations also offer a variety of reading options for consumers.

The first lending library in America, the Library Company of Philadelphia, was founded in 1731 by Benjamin Franklin. Supported by subscriptions, members were motivated to join the undertaking as a means to pool resources for the purpose of purchasing a collection of books that they could not individually afford. The Library Company continues to operate as a subscription library today.

Similar libraries were established throughout colonial America. For example, the Charleston Library Society was founded in 1748, the Providence Library Company was established in 1753, and the New York Society Library was founded in 1754. These membership libraries were seen as a way for individuals to voluntarily work together to the mutual benefit of all involved. As an example, the Articles of Subscription for the Book Company of Durham, Connecticut, stated that

> being desirous to improve our leisure hours, in enriching our minds in useful and profitable knowledge by reading, [we] do find ourselves unable so to do for the want of suitable and proper books. Therefore that we may be the better able to furnish ourselves with a suitable and proper collection of books. . . . do each of us unite together, and agree to be copartners in company together . . . to buy books.[7]

Recognizing their common interest, members of these libraries found a voluntary and non-coercive solution to their shared problem—the affordability of books. Most of these libraries had an initial fee, along with an annual membership fee. The content of the libraries usually contained titles of general interest, though many focused on specific topics, such as mechanics, history, science, law, medicine, or music. In contrast to public libraries, which seek to meet the interests of everyone in "the community," the content of today's private libraries is determined by the interests of its members. Unlike public libraries, where "membership" is mandatory and administrators attempt to serve the "public interest," the voluntary memberships of private libraries allow a member to decide if a library will serve his interests.

---

7. Elizabeth W. Stone, *American Library Development., 1600-1899* (New York: The H. W. Wilson Company, 1977), p. 131.

Subscription libraries are not the only alternative for those who want to read but cannot afford to purchase books. For example, William Bathoe opened two commercial circulating libraries in London in 1737 to "rent" books for a fee.[8] In America, booksellers and print shops provided a similar service and were very popular until the early nineteenth century, when books became more affordable. While many of these circulating libraries catered to the less serious reader, they provided an important service in making reading affordable and available to all. Today, companies like Chegg.com, BookRenter.com, and BarnesandNoble.com offer textbook rentals. And thousands of non-copyrighted books are available on the Internet through Google Books and similar services.

An interesting example of a circulating library were the *abonnements de musique*, or music circulating libraries, of France. These libraries operated much like private book libraries, but offered music scores rather than books and periodicals. More than one hundred of these businesses operated in Paris alone from the late eighteenth century until about 1950, and they played an important role in disseminating new musical compositions.[9]

Though the number of private libraries has diminished because taxpayers are forced to subsidize their "free" public counterparts, some private libraries continue to flourish today. Many of the subscription libraries founded in colonial America, such as those in Philadelphia, New York, Providence, and Charleston, are still in operation. The nation's largest subscription library—the Boston Athenaeum—has about eight thousand members. Most subscription libraries obtain financing through donations, endowments, and modest membership fees—a family membership at the Boston Athenaeum was $290 a year in 2011.[10] Those who find value in these establishments are free to pay the required fees, and those who do not value them are also free to spend their

---

8. James Raven, "Libraries for sociability: the advance of subscription library," in *The Cambridge History of Libraries In Britain And Ireland* (New York: Cambridge University Press, 2006), p. 251.

9. "Music circulating libraries in France: an overview and a preliminary list," *The Free Library*, accessed January 5, 2011, http://www.thefreelibrary.com/ Music*circulating +libraries+in+France%3A+an+overview+and+a+preliminary...-a0165238532.

10. "Membership Information," *Boston Anathenaeum*, accessed March 24, 2011, http://www.bostonathenaeum.org/node/24.

money as they choose. And these examples are not limited to America.

In India, at least two private companies operate circulating libraries. Eloor Libraries operates five branches and charges 10 percent of a book's cost as its sole source of revenue.[11] Members have a large assortment of titles to choose from, including new releases. Another company, Friends of Books, whose mission is to "make reading an easier, enjoyable experience for book lovers in India,"[12] operates both an online library and an online book selling service. Members can browse the library's catalogue online and have books delivered to their homes. The company offers twelve different membership packages, which allows members to choose the option that best suits their reading habits and budget.

As the examples throughout this chapter demonstrate, individuals voluntarily pay for both parks and libraries. Contrary to the claims made by defenders of coercively financed public parks and libraries, the provision of these goods can be and is provided by the private sector. Unlike public parks and libraries, which force all taxpayers—both users and non-users alike—to provide financial support, private parks and libraries obtain their funds from those who value and use those goods. Everyone—those who provide private parks and libraries, those who value them, and those who don't value them—is free to act according to his own judgment in the pursuit of his own values. We must wonder what parks and outdoor recreation would be like today without government intervention. What experiences might we enjoy if visionaries were free to build great parks without having to compete with taxpayer subsidized parks?

Halting government intervention in our lives means more than demanding balanced budgets and limited government. It means questioning the fundamental ideas that give rise to deficit spending and the growth of government. It means challenging the manifestation of those ideas, in issues large and small. It means recognizing and protecting individual rights completely and consistently. Public parks and libraries are admittedly, in the grand

---

11. "Membership Information," *Eloor Libraries,* accessed January 5, 2011, http://www.eloorlibraries.in/membership.html.

12. "About Us," *Friends of Books*, accessed January 5, 2011, http://www.friendsofbooks.com/about.htm.

scope of things, relatively minor issues. But a principled defense of individual rights is not limited to large issues. Let us now turn our attention to another institution that demonstrates the impracticality of government coercion—the postal service.

2

You've Got Private Mail

Perhaps no government institution is the object of more jokes and frustration than the United States Postal Service (USPS). Long lines, surly clerks, and "going postal" draw the ridicule of patrons and late-night comedians. Yet, despite the complaints and jokes, any suggestion that the USPS be privatized is met with derision and scorn: How will the citizens in isolated towns get their mail? Won't greedy businesses raise prices and put the pinch on the poor? And besides, since virtually every government on earth delivers the mail, who could possibly think that private companies could do it better?

The government's monopoly on mail delivery has existed so long that few can imagine private mail delivery. Yet, there was a time when much of the nation's mail was delivered by private companies. So, what happened to change this? What are the arguments in favor of the government's monopoly on mail delivery? Why are private companies prohibited by law from competing with the USPS? Let us begin by looking at private mail delivery in the nineteenth century.

Prior to the Civil War, private letter carriers flourished throughout the United States. In sparsely settled areas of the country, about three hundred "western expresses" provided mail delivery.[1] The best known of these companies was the Pony Express. This historical fact belies the claim that private companies would not provide mail delivery to sparsely populated areas, which is a common argument for the government's postal monopoly. In

---

1. Richard R. John, Jr., "Private Mail Delivery in the United States during the Nineteenth Century: A Sketch," *Humanities and Social Sciences Online*, accessed January 5, 2011, http://www.h-net.org/~business/bhcweb/publications/BEHprint/v015/p0135-p0148.pdf.

the more heavily populated Northeast, two types of delivery companies operated—"locals" and "eastern expresses." Both the locals and the expresses offered their services for considerably lower rates than the postal service.

The locals were based in the major eastern cities and primarily served local businesses. One of the largest of the locals was Boyd's City Post in Philadelphia, which employed forty-five carriers and delivered up to fifteen thousand letters a day.[2]

The expresses mostly operated between the larger eastern cities, such as Boston, New York, and Philadelphia. As one example, the American Letter Mail Company was founded by Lysander Spooner in 1844. Spooner believed that he could deliver mail anywhere in the country for five cents per letter, versus the twelve cents charged by the postal service. Not surprisingly, the public loved Spooner's company. And why not? His company saved consumers a lot of money. As a result of this competition, the revenues of the postal service plummeted. Congressmen, who often rewarded political supporters with an appointment as the local postmaster, were incensed and responded by lowering the rates of the postal service. Spooner was not to be outdone and countered by lowering his rates even further. Finally, in 1851 Congress flexed its legislative muscles, strengthened the government's postal monopoly, and forced Spooner out of business.[3] It wasn't poor service or outrageous prices that closed the American Letter Mail Company but literally an act of Congress.

At the time, the popularity of the expresses was so great that one United States Senator estimated that at least half of the letters mailed in the country were being delivered by private carriers.[4] The success of the private mail companies prompted one economist to write in the *New York Review* that, even though postal services in all Western nations were a branch of the government, "we might easily imagine it to be carried on by a private association, without its changing in any degree its essential character."[5] However, this would have meant the end of an important tool for political

2. Ibid., p. 138.

3. Lucille J. Goodyear, "Spooner vs. U.S. Postal System," *American Legion Magazine,* January 1981, accessed January 5, 2011, http://www.lysanderspooner.org/STAMP3.htm.

4. John, "Private Mail Delivery," p. 142.

5. Ibid., p. 143.

patronage. Selah Hobbie, the First Assistant Postmaster General in the early 1850s, allegedly cried, "Zounds, sir, it would throw sixteen thousand postmasters out of office."[6] These political considerations, and the legislation that ensued, eventually forced the private letter carriers out of business. When Congress had to choose between government workers and private companies, it chose government workers. When Congress was faced with the choice between government coercion and freedom, Congress chose government coercion. In other words, the postal service couldn't beat the private businesses economically, so Congress beat the entrepreneurs with the threat of fines and imprisonment.

While political patronage played a role in outlawing the private expresses, there is more to the story. Congress forces the USPS to operate in a manner that, as we will soon see, is often contrary to rational business policies. For example, Congress has imposed on the USPS a universal service obligation that includes "geographic scope, range of products, access to services and facilities, delivery frequency, affordable and uniform pricing, service quality, and security of the mail."[7] To enable the postal service to execute this mandate, Congress has also passed a series of laws—called the private express statutes—that limit the activities of private individuals and businesses. This legislation protects the USPS monopoly on the delivery of first-class mail, while other legislation prohibits private companies from having access to mailboxes.

A number of arguments are used to defend the universal service obligation and the resulting limitations on private businesses and consumers; however, they all boil down to one thing: Congress desires universal service, and therefore the ends—delivering mail to all Americans—justify the means—taxpayer subsidies and prohibitions on competition. But why does Congress desire universal service? While the idea of universal postal service dates from the early years of the republic, a recent report from the USPS offers us a contemporary view of the topic.

In 2008, the USPS issued a report titled "Report on Universal Postal Service and the Postal Monopoly." The report argued that

---

6. Ibid., p. 144.

7. United States Postal Service, *Report on Universal Postal Service and the Postal Monopoly* (Washington: Government Printing Office, 2008), accessed January 5, 2011, http://about.usps.com/universal-postal-service/usps-uso-report.pdf, p. 2.

loosening the restrictions imposed by either the private express statutes or the mailbox access rule would adversely impact the USPS's ability to implement the universal service mandate. Therefore, the report concluded, such changes should not be made.

To justify universal service, the report cited a long-held belief that the mail is used "to bind the Nation together through the personal, educational, literary, and business correspondence of the people."[8] The report goes on to acknowledge that alternatives to the USPS exist for every piece of mail that it delivers. These alternatives include private companies such as UPS and FedEx, as well as the Internet. Indeed, the report cites the growing use of the Internet for document delivery and bill payments as a primary reason for declining USPS volume and revenue. In other words, the exchange of ideas and information can and does occur without the involvement of the USPS—the nation is "bound" together and the USPS isn't required for this to occur. So why the continued insistence on universal service?

The report repeatedly argues that relaxing the private express statutes or taking other measures to permit private businesses greater freedom in mail delivery would substantially weaken the financial position of the USPS. As one example, private companies will offer services that draw customers away from the USPS, particularly in more profitable, high volume areas. If the universal service mandate remains in place, this would leave the USPS to service less profitable routes and result in additional financial strain. Thus, repealing the mandate is dismissed as contrary to "social policy" because doing so would jeopardize the very existence of the USPS. In short, both the USPS and Congress regard the universal service obligation as immutable as the law of gravity. Of course, the law of gravity is a fact of nature and must simply be accepted. But the laws of Congress are another matter entirely, particularly when the results are harmful to everyone. Let us now look at the consequences of these policies.

The report acknowledges that differential pricing—pricing based on distance and location—is common among private companies and makes economic sense. Such pricing recognizes the fact that low volume routes and remote locations incur more costs

---

8. Ibid., 39 U.S.C. 101(a), p. 6.

to deliver mail, and that, as a matter of justice, postal patrons should bear the costs associated with the service they receive. But the report rejects differential pricing precisely because of this fact:

> This would put service in danger for areas of the country whose volumes do not justify the costs to serve, namely isolated rural areas and low income urban areas. This is precisely the portion of the America public who could least afford an increase in postal pricing or a decrease in service. Isolated regions of the country currently depend heavily on the Postal Service to transport prescription medicines, educational materials, and other supplies. Cutting off such areas from uniform, affordable service and access could be devastating for these Americans.[9]

In other words, because of where they choose to live, some Americans need the government's postal monopoly in order to afford regular mail delivery. This is the argument for the universal service obligation—the needs of some Americans "justifies" forcing other Americans to subsidize mail delivery. The report goes on to acknowledge the existential results of these policies: the criminalization of certain voluntary economic activities (such as the private delivery of first-class mail), higher costs to other postal customers, and political pressure to keep financially unprofitable post offices open.

As is usually the case when nonsensical policies are defended, the report claims that this serves the "public interest." We hear about the "public interest" all the time, but what does it mean? In practice, it means that some members of the public receive the benefit of lower postal rates, while other members of the public are forced to bear the costs. Some members of the public are protected from the economic consequences of their choices, such as where to live. At the same time, other members of the public are prohibited from acting according to their own rational judgment, such as starting a postal service or using a private carrier. In practice, the "public interest" means that the interests of some individuals supersede the interests of others. Some are to receive unearned benefits, while others are to be forced to pay for those benefits.

---

9. Ibid., p. 81.

As one example of the costs imposed on consumers, postal regulations allow private companies to deliver certain letter mail, but stipulate specific requirements, such as "the amount paid for private carriage of the letter equals at least *six times* the current rate for the first ounce of a single-piece First-Class Mail letter [emphasis added]."[10] In other words, no matter how inexpensively a private company can deliver a letter, it is legally prohibited from doing so—its price is arbitrarily inflated by Congressional decree. Of course, the cost of these mandates is ultimately borne by you and other consumers.

In addition to legal protection from competition, the USPS enjoys a legal monopoly on access to residential and business mailboxes—private companies are prohibited from delivering to mailboxes. Relaxing this monopoly, the report admits, would help private companies lower costs and put further economic pressure on the USPS: "If existing competitors (e.g., UPS or FedEx) gain the ability to deliver to the mailbox, they may be able to offer a more competitive price on certain items...."[11] Again, private companies are legally prohibited from taking actions that would allow them to offer lower prices to you and other consumers.

Why are some members of the public forced to subsidize the mail delivery of other members of the public? Why do public officials and the general public regard this as a good policy? To answer these questions, we must look beyond politics to the science of morality.

Politics is not a primary. Politics defines the proper principles of interaction between individuals; morality defines the proper principles of individual action. For example, if it is morally proper for an individual to pursue his own happiness, then politically he must be free to act on his own judgment without interference from others. Political policies and institutions are derived from the moral principles that a particular society accepts. What then, are the moral principles that underlie the government's postal monopoly?

The dominant morality in America is altruism. Coined by the French philosopher Auguste Comte, altruism means "other-ism." According to altruism, you have a moral obligation to place the

---

10. Ibid., p. 14. Postal regulations also allow private carriers to deliver letters if they weight more than 12.5 ounces or are marked "extremely urgent."

11. Ibid., p. 58.

welfare and needs of others before your own; you have a moral duty to serve others. According to altruism, you must put aside your own self-interest in the name of the "public interest." Altruism, according to Comte,

> only recognises duties, duties of all to all. Placing itself, as it does, at the social point of view, it cannot tolerate the notion of *rights*, for such notion rests on individualism. We are born under a load of obligations of every kind, obligations to our predecessors, to our successors, to our contemporaries. After our birth these obligations increase or accumulate, for it is some time before we can return any service.... Rights, then, in the case of man, are as absurd as they are immoral.[12]

On a daily basis, you hear calls for altruism: We must sacrifice for the "common good," the "general welfare," or the "public interest"; we are our brother's keeper; "Ask not what your country can do for you—ask what you can do for your country."

Altruism holds that the needs of others supersede your rights. Indeed, according to Comte, the notion of rights is absurd and immoral. To speak of your rights is to put your interests before the interests of others. Americans living in remote locations have a need for affordable mail delivery and therefore, according to altruism, it is your obligation to satisfy that need. If you refuse to make such sacrifices "voluntarily," you are being selfish, and it is proper to force you to do so. And the sacrifices demanded by the universal service mandate go beyond consumers and businesses; they apply to the USPS as well.

While the private express statutes and mailbox access monopoly impose additional costs on private companies and consumers, the universal service obligation (USO) also prevents the USPS from operating rationally. The report states:

> The USO is a set of public policy restrictions on the actions of a post that keep it from making its decisions on purely a business-like basis. For example, a post may be required to provide delivery service to a high cost area at the same price as delivery to a low cost area, even though the costs of that delivery exceed its

12. Auguste Comte, *The Catechism of Positive Religion*, trans. Richard Congreve (London: John Chapman, 1876), p. 332.

revenue. A profit seeking business would not provide that service on an ongoing basis at a uniform price.[13]

The result is that political considerations override rational business decisions, all in the name of providing universal service. For example, the USPS "often faces political resistance when it attempts to close or consolidate facilities."[14] On the one hand, the private express statutes and mailbox access rules prohibit individuals and businesses from acting on their own judgment; on the other hand, the universal service mandate prohibits USPS officials from acting on their own judgment. While imposing costly restrictions and mandates on nearly every member of the public—including postal officials—we are to believe that this policy somehow serves the "public interest."

Such regulations are a necessary component of the universal service mandate. If postal officials were legally permitted to act on their own judgment, they would reduce or eliminate service in many areas, abandon uniform pricing, or both. In other words, universal service makes no economic sense and its continuation is possible only because Congress forces postal officials to act contrary to their judgment and rational business policies. This shouldn't be surprising—how often does Congress show an interest in rational economic ideas?

Those same regulations are also a necessary component of the USPS "business model." If private companies were legally permitted to act on their own judgment, they would draw customers away from the USPS, resulting in declining revenues and further threatening the USPS's ability to meet its universal service mandate. Indeed, this is precisely what occurred in the nineteenth century. Even today, when individuals and businesses are free to choose, they overwhelmingly choose private alternatives to the USPS.

While private delivery companies flourish by offering superior value, the USPS is a complete failure. For example, competition is allowed in the overnight delivery market and two companies—UPS

---

13. United States Postal Service, *Report on Universal Postal Service and the Postal Monopoly*, p. 53.

14. "Executive Summary," United States Postal Service, accessed August 21, 2011, http://about.usps.com/future-business-model/executive-summary.pdf, p. i.

and FedEx—control an estimated 80 percent of that market. Even though it has the legal protection of prohibitions on competition—founded on the morality of altruism—the USPS lost $8.5 billion in 2010 and depends on subsidies from taxpayers.[15] In the same year, UPS made a profit of $3.49 billion and FedEx made a profit of $1.2 billion. Even with their hands tied, these companies have been able to outperform the USPS and prosper. We must wonder what innovations and efficiencies these companies might achieve if they did not have to overcome Congressional restrictions and controls. How much better and how much less expensive would mail service be if private companies were free?

As these historical and contemporary examples demonstrate, when businessmen are free to act according to their own judgment, they will find innovative, efficient means to provide the services consumers desire. And when consumers have a choice, they overwhelmingly use private carriers for the delivery of mail and packages. This was true in the nineteenth century and it is true today. When individuals are free to act according to their own judgment in the pursuit of their own self-interest, both businesses and consumers benefit. However, when government imposes restrictions on the actions of individuals and businesses in the name of the "public interest," the choices available to everyone are fewer, prices are higher, and service is appalling. If lower costs, more choices, and better service aren't in the "public interest," then what is?

The argument for these altruistic policies and government interventions is the claim that only government can or will provide mail service throughout the nation. As we have seen, this claim is patently false. And if it is false in regard to mail service, we must ask ourselves if similar claims about other government services are also false. Let us now turn to another service that many believe *must* be provided by government—education.

---

15. While the USPS insists that it does not receive subsidies, the Federal Trade Commission reports otherwise. See *Federal Trade Commission*, "FTC Releases Report Examining Laws That Apply Differently to the U.S. Postal Service and its Private Competitors" (2008), accessed August 21, 2011, http://www.ftc.gov/opa/2008/01/postal.shtm.

3

A Lesson in Private Education

After passage of the 2009 American Recovery and Reinvestment Act (Barack Obama's first economic stimulus), which earmarked more than $100 billion for public education, the White House website listed President Obama's goals for improving America's government schools. "Providing a high-quality education for all children," the site stated, "is critical to America's economic future." To accomplish this,

> President Obama is committed to providing every child access to a complete and competitive education, from cradle through career. ... He will invest in innovative strategies to help teachers to improve student outcomes, and use rewards and incentives to keep talented teachers in the schools that need them the most. President Obama will invest in a national effort to prepare and reward outstanding teachers...[1]

Is more money and expanded government "investment" the answer to America's educational woes? Is public education necessary, as many claim, for the poor to receive an adequate education to compete in today's global marketplace? Is education a human right? Should government even be involved in education? While few would argue about the importance of education, there is great disagreement over the answers to these questions.

Unfortunately, even some of the Founding Fathers were confused on this issue. Thomas Jefferson, for example, once proposed an amendment to the Constitution to provide public

---

1. "Education," *The White House*, accessed June 5, 2011, http://www.whitehouse.gov/issues/education.

education. However, we can forgive Jefferson for his views on the subject. He did not have the benefit of witnessing the history of public education or the horrible condition of government schools today. But for us, the evidence should be clear. If the goal of government schools is a "high-quality education," those schools are an absolute failure. And they are a failure because they rely on government coercion to obtain both funding and "customers."

Today, education is a virtual monopoly of the government. While home schooling and private schools have grown in popularity in recent decades, government schools remain the dominant source of education for most American children. Indeed, approximately 85 percent of America's schoolchildren attend government schools, primarily because these schools are "free."[2] Of course, these schools are not free. Their costs are borne by you and other taxpayers, which includes parents and non-parents alike.

Because they are forced to financially support government schools, most parents cannot afford the expenses associated with private schools or home schooling. However, according to a survey conducted by the National Association of Independent Schools, only 39 percent of those polled would send their children to public schools if cost and proximity were not factors.[3] In other words, while the vast majority of parents send their children to government schools, those schools are not their preference. As we saw with mail delivery, when individuals have a choice, they overwhelmingly choose private companies. Unfortunately, the burden of taxation to support government schools effectively eliminates such a choice for many parents. In 2008-2009, taxpayers spent $10,441 per student to fund government schools. If they were not forced to financially support public education, most parents would choose an alternative to government schools for the education of their children. And this is only one aspect of education in which parents cannot act according to their own judgment.

Public schools are controlled by state, local, and increasingly, federal government officials. Government control ultimately

---

2. "Education in the United States," *Wikipedia,* accessed January 6, 2011, http://en.wikipedia.org/wiki/Education_in_the_United_States#Elementary_and_secondary_education.

3. "Public Knows Features That Make a Quality School", *Council for American Private Education,* January 2000, accessed January 6, 2011, http://www.capenet.org/Outlook/Out1-00.html.

politicizes the process. Government involvement in education makes school boards a magnet for special interest groups seeking to influence the decisions of educational bureaucrats regarding textbooks, curriculum, and other policies. For example, in a controversy that has spanned decades, those who want evolution taught in government schools and those who want creationism included in the curriculum regularly battle over textbook selection for the public schools in Texas.[4] Similar battles regularly rage in other states, on this and other issues, such as history and sex education. Unfortunately, appeasing those who make the most noise and have the most political connections is often more important than truth.

For example, in Tucson, Arizona, to pacify Mexican-American students, the government schools offer an ethnic studies course. The profanity-laced textbook[5] for *third-graders* claims that "hard drugs and drug culture is an invention of the Gringo because he has no culture." The textbook goes on to declare that "you have to destroy capitalism and we have to help five-sixths of the world to destroy capitalism in order to equal all people's lives."[6] Tucson taxpayers—many of whom vehemently disagree with these ideas—are forced to pay for the teaching of such ideas.

If a parent objects to the public school curriculum, but cannot afford a private school or home schooling, he has no choice but to subject his children to ideas he finds wrong or immoral. And he is simultaneously forced to financially support the teaching of those ideas through his tax dollars. Indeed, this is true of all taxpayers, including non-parents. No matter one's views on evolution, school prayer, sex education, history, or any other topic, to force an individual to pay for the teaching of ideas that he regards as false or immoral is a gross injustice. As Isabel Paterson wrote: "If this principle really is not understood, let any parent holding a positive religious faith consider how it would seem to him if his children were taken by force and taught an opposite creed. Would he not

---

4. "Science standards challenging evolution debated in Texas", *CNN*, March 25, 2009, accessed January 6, 2011, http://www.cnn.com/2009/US/03/25/texas.evolution.teaching/.

5. The textbook includes words such as shit, bullshit, and chingado, which is Spanish for fucking.

6. "Excerpts read aloud from third grade textbook in Tucson.flv," *YouTube*, accessed July 3, 2011, http://www.youtube.com/watch?v=Mcegwz17Zb0.

recognize tyranny naked?"[7]

Abolishing government schools eliminates this intellectual tyranny. Private schools offer the curriculum of their choosing, and parents are free to accept that curriculum or find a school with a curriculum that upholds their values. As Paterson explains, when "teaching is conducted by private schools, there will be a considerable variation in different schools; the parents must judge what they want their children taught, by the curriculum offered."[8]

As an example of what is possible, consider the Knowledge is Power Program (KIPP). Started in 1994, KIPP is a nationwide network of college-preparatory schools located primarily in lower-income neighborhoods. Because KIPP schools are charter schools, they are not subject to many of the political regulations and controls of traditional government schools. Even with this small amount of freedom, teachers and administrators are able to structure their curriculums to meet the needs of their students, rather than the dictates of politicians and bureaucrats. What are the results? A multi-year study found that, after three years at KIPP, "student gains are equivalent to 1.2 years of additional growth in mathematics and 0.9 years of extra growth in reading over three years."[9] These are substantial and meaningful gains, and they demonstrate what is possible when schools are freed, even partially, from the bureaucracy and politics of government schools. What would our schools be like if they were entirely free? What choices and opportunities would be available to students and parents?

While some suggest that KIPP should be expanded, the real lesson is that freedom works. Certainly, KIPP schools achieve better results than traditional public schools. The reason is that the administrators and teachers have fewer restrictions and controls placed upon them by politicians and bureaucrats. The solution to the problems plaguing our government schools is not the expansion of KIPP, but the expansion of educational freedom. The solution is to abolish government schools. Nobody—not educational bureaucrats nor other parents nor government—has a right to

---

7. Isabel Paterson, *The God of the Machine* (New Brunswick: Transaction Publishers, 2006), p. 255-256.

8. Ibid., p. 258.

9. "Overview," *Mathematica Policy Research, Inc.*, accessed June 17, 2011, http://www.kipp.org/files/dmfile/KIPP-mathematica-overview-June22-vFINAL.pdf.

compel you to act contrary to your own judgment. Just as this is true in other areas of human life, such as mail delivery, parks, and libraries, it is also true regarding the education of your children.

Many—including the United Nations—believe that compulsion is a necessary component of education. Article 26 of the United Nations' Universal Declaration of Human Rights states: "Everyone has the right to education. Education shall be free, at least in the elementary and fundamental stages. Elementary education shall be compulsory."[10] And compulsory means just that—children will attend school or their parents are subject to fines or jail time. For example, a law enacted in California imposes fines up to $2,000 for the parents of truant children. In Atlanta, more than three hundred parents have been arrested because their children did not attend school.[11]

Many Americans agree that education is a right. Is it? And if it is, what does this mean? A right is a sanction to freedom of action in a social context. It means the freedom to act according to your own judgment without interference from others. A right is not a claim to an object, but the freedom to take the actions necessary to create or earn that object. (Consider the Bill of Rights. It imposes restrictions on the actions of government for the explicit purpose of leaving you free to act as you choose. The First Amendment, for example, guarantees the right of free speech. It does not require others to provide a printing press or a microphone.) To claim that an individual has a "right" to an education is to assert that others have an obligation to provide that education, regardless of their own choices and judgment. This means, if you do *not* pay for public education, you are violating the "rights" of children. In truth, the "right" to an education means that your actual rights—the freedom to spend your money as you choose—are violated. "Any alleged 'right' of one man," wrote Ayn Rand, "which necessitates the violation of the rights of another, is not and cannot be a right."[12]

---

10. "Universal Declaration of Human Rights," United Nations, December 10, 1948, accessed January 6, 2011, http://www.hrea.org/index.php?base_id=104&language_id=1&erc_doc_id=445&category_id=24&category_type=3&group=.

11. Tristan Smith, "Parents of truant kids can face jail time," CNN.com, October 24, 2008, accessed July 3, 2011, http://articles.cnn.com/2008-10-24/justice/truancy.arrests_1_anti-truancy-programs-parenting-classes-school-engagement?_s=PM:CRIME.

12. Rand, "Man's Rights," p. 96 (see Part 1, n. 1).

Further, to declare that education is a right and that it "shall be compulsory" is a blatant contradiction. A right cannot be exercised under government compulsion. A right is the freedom to act according to your judgment; compulsion negates your judgment. If you are forced to send your children to school, you are not acting as you choose. You are forced to act according to the demands and dictates of government officials, which is precisely what rights prohibit. Isabel Paterson pointedly asks educational bureaucrats: "Do you think nobody would *willingly* entrust his children to you to pay you for teaching them? Why do you have to extort your fees and collect your pupils by compulsion?"[13]

So, what have these coercive measures given us? What have our tax dollars bought? Despite decades of government intervention and the expenditure of hundreds of billions of dollars each year on public education, America's government schools remain an abysmal failure. And the solution, despite the claims of many, is not more money. Between 1962 and 2009 the amount spent per pupil increased from $2,808 to $10,441 in constant 2008-2009 dollars.[14] The results of this massive increase in spending are alarming: An estimated forty-five million adult Americans are marginally illiterate (read at an eighth-grade level or lower) and twenty-one million cannot read at all.[15] In other words, nearly 30 percent of adult Americans cannot read this book. Philosopher Andrew Bernstein notes that this is a trend that extends back for years:

> Since 1983, 10 million Americans have reached twelfth grade without learning to read at the basic level. In 1986, the national test score average for eleventh graders taking the NAEP literature and history test was 54.5 percent correct on the history portion, and 51.8 percent correct on the literature portion. In 1995, a nationally administered history test found that only one student in ten was grade-level proficient in the subject; the majority failed to reach a basic level. In 1996, U.S. high school seniors scored near the bottom on an internationally administered math exam. According to a study published in 1999, a "nationwide

13. Paterson, *God of the Machine*, p. 261.

14. "Fast Facts", *National Center for Educational Statistics*, accessed January 6, 2011, http://nces.ed.gov/fastfacts/display.asp?id=66.

15. Andrew Bernstein, "The Educational Bonanza in Privatizing Government Schools," *The Objective Standard 5*, no. 4, (Winter 2010-11): p. 21.

> assessment of math skills found that 'only 14 percent of eighth graders scored at the seventh-grade level or above'" and "fewer than half of twelfth-graders can do seventh-grade work in mathematics." In 2000, math students in America ranked below those in Malaysia, Bulgaria, and Latvia.[16]

And this trend has continued. In 2009, the Program for International Student Assessment was taken by students in sixty-five countries. American high school students ranked thirty-first in math and twenty-third in science, trailing Estonia and Slovenia in both categories.[17] Further, a study released in 2009 found that only half of all American adults can name all three branches of government. Perhaps more distressing: 43 percent of those who have held elective office could not name the function of the Electoral College.[18] (Some actually thought that the Electoral College is a school for training politicians!)

Poor test scores and ignorance of basic civics are only a part of the story. Nationally, about 30 percent of high school students do not graduate on time. A report released in 2008 found that, in seventeen of the nation's fifty largest cities, the graduation rate is below 50 percent. In Detroit, less than 25 percent of students graduated in 2003-2004.[19] Apparently, many high school students see no benefit to attending government schools. And, given the poor quality of the education provided by those schools, it is little wonder.

Clearly, America's public education system is not producing the results that have been promised. If a "high-quality education" is the goal of government education, it has been a resounding failure. While educational bureaucrats continue to demand more money for their latest "reform," they refuse to identify why America's educational system is producing illiterates. They refuse to

---

16. Ibid., pp. 21-22.

17. "Comparing Countries' and Economies' Performance," *Organisation for Economic Co-operation and Development*, accessed June 5, 2011, http://www.pisa.oecd.org/dataoecd/54/12/46643496.pdf.

18. "Study: Americans Don't Know Much About History," *NBC Los Angeles*, accessed June 5, 2011, http://www.nbclosangeles.com/news/local/Study-Americans-Dont-Know-About-Much-About-History.html.

19. "High School Graduation Rates Plummet Below 50 Percent in Some U.S. Cities," *Fox News*, April 1, 2008, accessed June 5, 2011, http://www.foxnews.com/story/0,2933,344190,00.html.

acknowledge that the problem is government control of education. However, it hasn't always been that way. There was a time when most education in America was provided by the private sector.

Prior to the Civil War (which children should be taught began in 1861), public schools were virtually non-existent. As educator Robert Peterson writes, most young children were taught at home: "Home education was so common in America that most children knew how to read before they entered school."[20] Compare that to the literacy rate achieved by our government schools. It wasn't necessary for public officials to dictate the curriculum, compel school attendance, or force citizens to pay for government schools. Parents recognized their responsibility for educating their children and acted accordingly. For those who desired additional education, private schoolmasters offered an abundance of choices. Peterson writes:

> Historical records, which are by no means complete, reveal that over one hundred and twenty-five private schoolmasters advertised their services in Philadelphia newspapers between 1740 and 1776. Instruction was offered in Latin, Greek, mathematics, surveying, navigation, accounting, bookkeeping, science, English, and contemporary foreign languages. Incompetent and inefficient teachers were soon eliminated, since they were not subsidized by the State or protected by a guild or union. Teachers who satisfied their customers by providing good services prospered. One schoolmaster, Andrew Porter, a mathematics teacher, had over one hundred students enrolled in 1776. The fees the students paid enabled him to provide for a family of seven.[21]

These schools allowed colonial Americans to receive the education they desired without government intervention. The pursuit of profit motivated educators to provide the types of classes and the content that their customers wanted, not that demanded by public officials or pressure groups. The freedom of students permitted them to

---

20. Robert A Peterson., "Education in Colonial America", *The Freeman 33*, no. 9 (September 1983), accessed August 21, 2011, http://www.thefreemanonline.org /columns/education-in-colonial-america/.

21. Ibid.

choose the schools that offered the courses they wanted, not those dictated by politicians and bureaucrats.

Even the poor, blacks, women, and immigrants had an abundance of educational opportunities. Peterson writes: "In 1767, there were at least sixteen evening schools, catering mostly to the needs of Philadelphia's hard-working German population.... There were also schools for women, blacks, and the poor. Anthony Benezet, a leader in colonial educational thought, pioneered in the education for women and Negroes."[22] In short, if an individual—any individual—in colonial America desired an education, he or she had many options from which to choose. What happened? Why do government schools now dominate the educational system?

Despite the success of these private educational services, in the mid-nineteenth century many intellectuals began to demand government schools. Educational reformers, such as Henry Brown, argued for compulsory, state controlled education:

> No one at all familiar with the deficient household arrangements and deranged machinery of domestic life, of the extreme poor, and ignorant, to say nothing of the intemperate—of the examples of rude manners, impure and profane language, and all the vicious habits of low bred idleness—can doubt, that it is better for children to be removed as early and as long as possible from such scenes and examples.[23]

Brown did not approve of the lifestyle and parenting skills of some individuals and sought to use the coercive power of government to impose his views upon the poor and their children. Poor parents may have been uneducated. They may have been rude and used profane language. But, to take their children from them by force and deliver them to arrogant educators who think they know best is far more obscene and immoral than any words those parents might utter. This paternalistic attitude continues to this day: A common argument for the continuation of government schools is that the poor need them. That is, without public schools the children of the poor would not be properly educated, and thereby trapped in a

---

22. Ibid.

23. Robert P. Murphy, "The Origins of the Public School," *The Freeman 48*, no. 7 (July 1998), accessed August 21, 2011, http://www.thefreemanonline.org/featured/the-origins-of-the-public-school/.

cycle of poverty and ignorance. (Ironically, and sadly, that is precisely what government schools are doing today.)

According to altruism, the needs of poor children constitute a claim on you and other taxpayers. But are the poor really helpless? Do they really need government usurping their parental responsibilities?

In practice, the poor can and do have ways to educate their children without government assistance or coercion. In colonial America, for example, education was a favorite form of philanthropy for Quakers, and "the poor, both Quaker and non-Quaker, were allowed to attend without paying fees."[24] Such educational philanthropy is not limited to colonial times: Oprah Winfrey has donated $1.5 million to the Ron Clark Academy in Atlanta[25] and $1 million to Providence St. Mel in Chicago.[26] Both schools serve poor, inner-city children. Winfrey also established the Oprah Winfrey Leadership Academy for Girls in South Africa. The academy's mission is to "provide a nurturing educational environment for academically gifted girls who come from disadvantaged backgrounds."[27] Further, thousands of businesses, trade associations, foundations, and other organizations offer scholarships for students. Such examples demonstrate that those who are concerned about education for the poor can simply provide voluntary financial support. In a free society, each individual can act according to his own judgment and values, and he must respect the mutual rights of others to do the same.

A study by James Tooley, a professor of education policy at the University of Newcastle in England, provides an even more compelling example of education for the poor. Tooley conducted a two-year study of education among the poor in Nigeria, Kenya, China, Ghana, and India. His study focused on differences between public and private schools in the poorest areas of his selected

---

24. Peterson, "Education in Colonial America."

25. "Oprah gives $1.5 million to Ron Clark Academy," Access Atlanta, December 2009, accessed January 6, 2011, http://blogs.ajc.com/the-buzz/2009/12/17/oprah-gives-1-5-million-to-ron-clark-academy/?cxntlid=thbz_hm.

26. "Inner-City School Founder: No Miracle, Just Teaching," NPR.com, December 2009, accessed January 6, 2011, http://www.npr.org/templates/story/story.php?storyId=113683847&ft=1&f=1013.

27. "Mission," Oprah Winfrey Leadership Academy for Girls, accessed June 5, 2011, http://www.owla.co.za/mission.htm.

cities—areas that lacked indoor plumbing, running water, electricity, and paved roads. What he found was remarkable.

For example, in Hyderabad, India, 76 percent of all school children attend private schools. Despite the fact that public education is available, most of the city's poorest parents choose to send their children to private schools, even when they have to pay tuition. Even by Indian standards, the students come from poor households: The students in private schools in Hyderabad have a monthly income of less than $30 per working household member; this is one-third the average income of $46 per month in Hyderabad. Tooley reported similar findings in the other cities and concluded: "[T]he poor have found remarkably innovative ways of helping themselves, educationally, and in some of the most destitute places on Earth have managed to nurture a large and growing industry of private schools for themselves."[28] Tooley's findings dispel the myth that the poor need paternalistic government assistance in order to educate their children.

As we have seen in regard to mail delivery, parks, libraries, and now education, coercive government programs and policies are impractical and immoral. As we have also seen, freedom is practical, because freedom is moral. Freedom delivers "the goods," whether it is mail delivery, libraries, or education. Freedom provides the social context in which you can live your life as you deem best. And *that* is a lesson well-worth learning.

In each of the public institutions we have examined so far, private alternatives are relatively well-known. For example, we are familiar with UPS, FedEx, Disney World, and private schools. We can see, often on a daily basis, the practical benefits of the free market. But what about an area of life that has fewer and less evident examples? What about infrastructure, such as roads and sanitation? Can these be supplied by private businesses? It is to these questions that we will now turn our attention.

---

28. James Tooley, "Private Schools for the Poor," *Catholic Education Resource Center*, accessed January 6, 2011, http://www.catholiceducation.org/articles/education/ed0319.htm.

4

On the Private Road to Freedom

Even among advocates of limited government and free markets, it is commonly believed that government must provide the nation's infrastructure, such as roads, bridges, and sanitation systems. It is believed that if private businesses provided such "public goods," costs would skyrocket because of redundancies, such as the need for multiple sewer mains for competing companies. The nature of such services, it is argued, may often result in a single provider. What if a private road owner decided to charge outrageous prices or close his road entirely? Wouldn't the cost of building such goods prohibit competition and allow private companies to charge monopoly prices? Would private companies even bother to build infrastructure? These objections and questions are plausible; however, we can find historical and contemporary examples of private companies building and maintaining infrastructure. Before we examine these non-government solutions, let us first look at the current state of America's infrastructure.

If you spend much time listening to politicians and pundits, you are likely to hear that America's infrastructure is in shambles. (Infrastructure, according to Wikipedia, "typically refers to the technical structures that support a society, such as roads, water supply, sewers, electrical grids, telecommunications, and so forth."[1]) In 2009, the American Society of Civil Engineers (ASCE) released its assessment of the nation's infrastructure, giving it a grade of "D" and estimating that the nation must spend $2.2 trillion over five

---

1. "Infrastructure," *Wikipedia*, accessed June 9, 2011, http://en.wikipedia.org/wiki/Infrastructure.

years to raise the quality of America's infrastructure.[2] Among the items noted by the ASCE:

- Leaking pipes lose an estimated seven billion gallons of clean drinking water per day.
- More than $200 billion is needed through 2035 to improve the nation's rail system.
- An estimated $186 billion is needed annually to substantially improve the nation's highways.
- The National Education Association's best estimate to bring the nation's schools into good repair is $322 billion. (Schools are often considered part of a society's infrastructure.)

Whether these numbers are accurate, or simply the exaggerated claims of those with a vested interest, it is generally agreed that massive amounts of money are needed to repair and modernize the nation's infrastructure. Who will pay for this? Politicians are quick to answer that question: you and your fellow taxpayers. Is this really the solution?

The general decay and disrepair of the nation's roads, bridges, water and sanitation systems, and other infrastructure demonstrates the impracticality of government owned infrastructure. Yet, given the importance of infrastructure, why do Americans tolerate such poorly maintained systems? Thomas Jefferson provided a clue in the Declaration of Independence when he wrote that "all experience hath shown that mankind are more disposed to suffer, while evils are sufferable, than to right themselves by abolishing the forms to which they are accustomed." While Jefferson was speaking to the outrages of a tyrannical king, the same principle applies in regard to other human activities. Americans suffer a government monopoly in infrastructure (as well as mail delivery and education) because that is the form to which they are accustomed. Why has government established and maintained such a monopoly?

Many reasons are given why government must provide infrastructure. Some result from economic ignorance. For example,

---

2. "Report Card 2009 Grades," *American Society of Civil Engineers*, accessed January 26, 2011, http://apps.asce.org/reportcard/2009/grades.cfm.

in his second State of the Union address, President Obama called for the federal government to rebuild America's infrastructure, saying that doing so will "put more Americans to work repairing crumbling roads and bridges."[3] While many Americans share the President's view that such spending creates jobs, this is actually an economic fallacy. As Henry Hazlitt pointed out in 1946, "There is no more persistent and influential faith in the world today than the faith in government spending. Everywhere government spending is presented as a panacea for all of our economic ills."[4] Hazlitt went on to explain that government expenditures must eventually be paid for through taxes, inflation, or both. And the money taken from taxpayers, including business owners and corporations, is money that they would have spent on other items—items of their own choosing, rather than those mandated by politicians. As Hazlitt concluded, "Therefore, for every public job created by the bridge project a private job has been destroyed somewhere else."[5]

Others believe the government *must* provide infrastructure for ideological reasons. For example, some believe that it is government's responsibility and proper function to provide basic services, such as roads, water, and sanitation. Such services are needed by all citizens, but private companies may not provide adequate and affordable service to everyone. Therefore, in accordance with altruism, government must satisfy that need.

Still others believe that only government can provide infrastructure because, to the knowledge of most people living today, governments throughout the world have always done these things. But is that really the case? Has government always provided infrastructure? If not, why does it have a monopoly today?

Until the late nineteenth century, most infrastructure in America was provided by private businesses. Even though the demands were lower, the technology less complex, and the size of urban areas much smaller, these differences are a matter of degree. The examples that we will examine demonstrate that private companies

---

3. "Obama's Second State of the Union," *New York Times*, January 25, 2011, accessed January 26, 2011, http://www.nytimes.com/2011/01/26/us/ politics/26obama-text.html ?pagewanted=5&_r=1.

4. Henry Hazlitt, "Public Works Means Taxes," in *Economics in One Lesson* (New York: Arlington House Publishers, 1979), p. 31.

5. Ibid., p. 33.

can and will build infrastructure, if they are free of government controls and regulations.

As one example, for the first one hundred years of the republic's history, most urban Americans used "privy vaults" or similar facilities for the disposal of human waste. Privy vaults were a hole in the ground, usually lined with stone, bricks, or concrete. Waste was collected in the vault and then emptied as the need arose.

During the nineteenth century, these were rather crude contraptions. They were not well sealed, and heavy rains often had a tendency to flush waste from the vaults, resulting in any number of unpleasant and potentially unhealthy situations. In addition, waste could seep from the vaults and pollute the surrounding soil. In the late nineteenth century, municipalities began building sanitation systems and banning privy vaults. The result was that most urban households became captive to their municipality's sanitation system.

Certainly, the privy vault as it was constructed in the late nineteenth century left something to be desired. But the proper solution was not banning the device and forcing individuals to become "customers" of the municipality's sanitation system. The proper solution should have been to recognize and protect property rights.

The right to property is the right of use and disposal—the right to use your property as you choose. If you wish to pollute your land, you have a moral right to do so. However, if you pollute the property of someone else, you are liable for damages. Given the normal migration of water under the soil, and runoff during a heavy rain, it is likely that the owner of a poorly sealed privy vault would pollute the property of another. Rather than banning privy vaults, the government should have simply said, "Privy vault owners are free to use these devices, but if they pollute the property of their neighbors, they will be held liable for damages." Instead, the "solution" to this property rights issue was to further usurp property rights, force property owners to act contrary to their own judgment, and compel everyone to join the capital intensive municipal sanitation system.

It is important to understand that this problem did not arise overnight. Privy vaults did not suddenly start leaking *en masse*. The problem appeared gradually, as urban areas were developed. Had government protected property rights from the first indication of a problem, the issue would not have become widespread.

Exactly how the problem of leaking privy vaults would have been solved is difficult to say. Who can predict what innovations individuals will develop? As we have already seen in regard to mail delivery, parks, libraries, and education, free men find innovative solutions to problems. The protection of individual rights, not government coercion, provides the social context in which such problems can be solved. Individual self-interest, not government prohibitions and mandates, provides the motivation for businessmen and entrepreneurs to seek innovative solutions.

The story of privy vaults did not have a happy ending for private companies. But the reason is not because the private sector cannot and will not provide sanitation services. The reason is government's failure to fulfill its proper function—the protection of individual rights, including property rights. A similar story can be told of the private turnpikes of the nineteenth century.

When the first colonists arrived in America, there were no roads. Those who wished to travel from one settlement to another literally had to blaze a trail. For a substantial period of time, this was not a problem because colonists lived fairly isolated lives and traveled little. But as commerce developed, it became increasingly important to be able to deliver goods to and from the market. With no government money, private companies began building roads to connect communities and towns.

The first private turnpike in America was built between Philadelphia and Lancaster and completed in 1794. The sixty-two mile road cost $450,000 to build—that would be about $21 billion in 2011[6]—and was praised as "a masterpiece of its kind."[7] The success of the road inspired the construction of additional roads, and by the 1830s Pennsylvania had more than three thousand miles of private turnpikes being operated by two hundred different companies.[8] Between 1794 and 1840 more than $22 million—more than $400 billion today—was invested in private roads, and more than eleven thousand miles of turnpikes were built throughout New

---

6. Calculated as a percentage of Gross National Product.

7. "Marker Details," *ExplorePAHistory.com*, accessed January 27, 2011,. http://explorepahistory.com/hmarker.php?markerId=1-A-132.

8. Ibid.

England and the Middle Atlantic States.[9] This vast system of private roads no longer exists. Why? What happened to cause these private roads to become a forgotten relic of history?

While these roads were built, maintained, and operated by private companies, the owners were not free to operate them as they saw best. First, they could not begin operations until authorized by the state legislators. Second, the companies were subject to numerous regulations and controls, including the location of toll houses and the rates that could be charged. At the same time, the legislators often prohibited competition by banning parallel routes. In short, these turnpikes were granted monopoly status by the state government and subjected to the dictates and controls of legislators—not unlike today's regulated utilities.[10] While the details varied from state to state, this was the general approach to the "private roads"—they were private in name only.

Economists have reported that the Eastern turnpike companies were seldom profitable. Indeed, as economist Daniel B. Klein writes, subscribers to the turnpike companies generally did not expect to make money from the roads themselves, but they did expect to benefit from the expanded markets that the roads made possible to their communities and to their businesses. Klein quotes an essay from 1795 that argued that a private turnpike "lays open all the unexploited resources of a country to come forth to daylight, and to a market."[11] This was the general attitude towards the private roads, and those who stood to benefit from improved access to markets, such as farmers, merchants, and landowners, were among the most eager investors in the private turnpikes.

The growth of the railroads, beginning in the 1830s, greatly curtailed use of the private turnpikes and many fell into disrepair. But the demise of the Eastern turnpikes cannot be entirely explained by the railroads. Government regulations prevented the owners from acting on their own judgment, so the turnpike companies could not easily respond to changing market conditions. Further, because of the government granted monopolies, the turnpike owners were often complacent because they had no threat

---

9. Daniel B. Klein, "The Voluntary Provision of Public Goods? The Turnpike Companies of Early America," *Economic Inquiry 28*, (October 1990): pp. 788-812.

10. Ibid., pp. 790-91.

11. Ibid., p. 795.

of competition from other roads. The situation was different in the West, particularly Nevada.

In the mid-nineteenth century, Nevada was similar to the original states in the 1790s—many communities were isolated and transportation between them presented a laborious and sometimes dangerous challenge. In 1861, the Nevada legislature authorized the first franchise for the purpose of operating a private turnpike. Within three years, more than fifty additional franchises were granted and, by 1880 at least 117 private toll roads had been built in the state.[12] The investors in these roads also operated other businesses and were motivated to invest in the turnpikes due to the increased business the roads would bring. However, unlike in the East, most of the roads themselves proved to be profitable ventures. What accounts for the difference between Nevada's private roads and those in the eastern states? Historian David Beito notes that "Nevada's state regulatory regime was not overly restrictive."[13] The turnpike owners "faced fewer burdensome mandates on rates, location of toll booths, upkeep, and other specifics than did their eastern counterparts."[14]

Further, unlike the eastern roads, turnpike franchises were not granted a monopoly, and as a result, competition ensued. As one example, Manly Johnson, a teamster, resented the high tolls charged on one road. He responded by threatening to build a competing road. The owner of the road relented and charged Johnson lower rates. Similarly, a stage coach company owner built his own road to save on tolls charged by a competing road owner. When the market is free, high profits attract investors, which increases competition and decreases prices. And, as Manly Johnson illustrated, even the threat of competition drives down prices. Other entrepreneurs competed with existing roads by offering shorter routes, using better paving materials, providing more amenities such as inns, or a combination of the above.

So what happened? As in the East, the arrival of the railroads greatly reduced business on the private turnpikes. Coupled with a

---

12. David T. Beito and Linda Royster Beito, "Rival Road Builders: Private Toll Roads in Nevada, 1852-1880," *Nevada Historical Society Quarterly 41*, no. 2 (Summer 1998): pp. 73-74.

13. Ibid., p. 84.

14. Ibid.

mining depression in Nevada between 1876 and 1881—mining production fell from $36.7 million annually to just $1.2 million—many of the roads, and the towns they served, were simply abandoned. During this time, attitudes towards private roads were also changing.

Beito notes that in the 1870s both politicians and newspaper editors grew less supportive of private roads. As one example, in his 1871 annual address, Nevada Governor Henry G. Blasdel expressed contempt for the private toll roads: "[T]he records of no civilized State disclose such reckless, inconsiderate and unwise grants of power, or so little consideration returned for the enormous and unprecedented rates of toll authorized to be taken."[15] Consider what this means: recognizing and protecting the moral right of the turnpike owners to act as they judged best was a "reckless, inconsiderate and unwise grant of power." According to Blasdel, individual liberty was not to be tolerated. Left unchallenged, evil ideas and the coercive power of government led to the demise of Nevada's private turnpikes. Within a decade the state began devoting more resources to "public" roads, leading to the eventual collapse of the private road system in Nevada.

As with the privy vaults, the experiences of the private turnpikes might suggest that only government can provide such infrastructure. After all, how many private roads survived competition from the railroads? But we must remember that, while the roads were built and maintained by private companies, they were not operating in a free market. In Nevada, where those controls and regulations were less severe than in the East, the private roads were profitable. However, in the East and in Nevada, the private roads faced competition from taxpayer subsidized railroads, "free" government owned roads, or both, just as today's private schools and private libraries must compete with their taxpayer supported public counterparts. In truth, it was government intervention that drove the private turnpikes into bankruptcy.

What can we learn from these examples? History shows that private businesses can and will provide infrastructure, if government does not intervene through regulations, controls, and subsidies to "favored" industries. Private companies can and will

15. Ibid., p. 88.

build the infrastructure that is vital to human life. But these examples are from a time when demands and needs were much different from today. What of a modern, technologically advanced society? Are there any examples of private companies meeting today's more advanced infrastructure needs?

While Japan has followed Western trends by developing municipal sanitation systems, 30 percent of the country uses an on-site sanitation system called a johkasou. Essentially, a johkasou is a high-tech privy vault that treats waste and discharges clean water. Johkasous range in size from single-family units to industrial sized units for small communities and large buildings. As with privy vaults, the sludge that accumulates in a johkasou must be periodically removed, and the Japanese are finding some creative uses for this renewable material—it is being used as a construction material and as a fuel. The johkasou demonstrates that technological solutions—solutions that respect, rather than violate, property rights—are possible.[16]

But what about other forms of infrastructure? In the second half of the nineteenth century, Saint Louis developer Julius Pitzman built approximately forty-seven "private places." The "private places" were planned communities and many provided water, sanitation, steam (for heating), and road maintenance to property owners through a community association.[17] Each property included deed restrictions that contractually limited the use of the property. For example, businesses were prohibited on the property. Those who broke the restrictions and refused to change their ways usually found their utilities cut off.

A similar and contemporary example can be found in today's master-planned communities. While details vary, master-planned communities typically share three characteristics: deed restrictions that control building and land-use, shared amenities, and a community association to which all property owners belong. These community associations, "according to one development company, 'work to assure that the communities' amenities, public facilities and other areas are supported and maintained.' In essence, they are a

---

16. "History of Sanitation in Japan," *Japan Sanitation Consortium*, accessed January 28, 2011, http://www.jsanic.org/inasia/japanhistoryx.html.

17. David Beito, "The Private Places of St. Louis," in *The Voluntary City* (Ann Arbor: The University of Michigan Press, 2002).

combination public works/parks and recreation department. Funding usually comes from maintenance fees assessed on each property owner."[18] While the exact services vary, in many of these communities, trash collection, water, park maintenance, and other "public goods" are provided by private businesses.

A unique example of privately provided infrastructure can be found in downtown Houston, Texas. Located approximately twenty feet underground, a tunnel system connects about ninety-five city blocks and is filled with restaurants, gift shops, banks, shoeshine services, dentists, florists, and more. The system was built by the owners of the various downtown buildings in cooperation with one another as an amenity for their tenants. The tunnel system allows pedestrians to avoid inclement weather and traffic, while also providing convenience for taking care of routine chores. Businesses rave about the benefits of operating in the tunnel system, such as lower crime (and therefore lower insurance costs), a clean environment, and a built-in, upscale clientele.[19]

The above examples show that private companies can supply infrastructure for a small community, but what about a large city? Can private companies supply the needs of a booming metropolis? We can find the answer in Gurgaon, India.

This city of 1.5 million people barely existed twenty years ago. Motivated by high land prices and rents in the capital of New Delhi, developers began building office buildings in Gurgaon, located thirty miles away. Lured by lower costs, businesses began to relocate and the area has grown by more than *70 percent* in the past decade. The local government was completely overwhelmed and could not build the necessary infrastructure to keep pace with the development. So what happened? If, as many believe, only government can provide infrastructure, how did Gurgaon grow? Motivated by their self-interest, businesses and developers took matters into their own hands:

> To compensate for electricity blackouts, Gurgaon's companies and real estate developers operate massive diesel generators capable of powering small towns. No water? Drill private borewells. No public transportation? Companies employ

18. J. Brian Phillips, "Private Cities," *The Freeman 39*, no. 3 (March 1989): p. 113.
19. J. Brian Phillips, "Subterranean Treasures," *Reason 20*, no. 2 (June 1988): p. 44.

> hundreds of private buses and taxis. Worried about crime? Gurgaon has almost four times as many private security guards as police officers.[20]

And Gurgaon is not an isolated example. In Bangalore, India, many companies operate a fleet of buses to transport workers and use power generators to make up for the weak local infrastructure. In Mumbai, India's financial center, many apartment buildings rely on private companies for water.

While these examples show that private companies can and do find innovative solutions to providing infrastructure, many believe that private infrastructure would lead to chaos and inefficiency. Much of this results from a limited context—from viewing a particular issue from the perspective of how infrastructure is provided today, and then projecting that system onto a free market. For example, government built infrastructure is capital intensive. Water and sanitation services are provided from centralized facilities, resulting in miles of water and sewer lines. Los Angeles, for example, has more than 6,700 miles of public sewer lines.[21] If private companies attempted to duplicate such a system, wouldn't there necessarily be redundant lines? Wouldn't this result in inefficiency and higher costs?

As we have seen with the johkasou, alternatives to a capital intensive system are possible. To make a profit, businesses must seek the most efficient means for providing goods and services. Rather than simply accept the status quo, a private sanitation company would seek more efficient means for delivering its services. Nobody can predict what solutions profit-seeking entrepreneurs will develop, just as thirty years ago nobody could predict the widespread use of smart phones and the Internet today.

But what about roads? Who would want to build roads in rural areas? If roads were privately owned, wouldn't toll booths be omnipresent and traffic slowed to a snail's pace. What would stop a road owner from charging high rates or closing his road entirely?

---

20. Jim Yardley, "In India, Dynamism Wrestles With Dysfunction," *New York Times*, June 8, 2011, accessed June 10, 2011, http://www.nytimes.com/2011/06/09/world/asia/09gurgaon.html.

21. "About the City's Sewer System," City of Los Angeles, accessed June 18, 2011, http://www.lasewers.org/sewers/about/index.htm.

To answer these questions, we must first look at the ways private roads might be owned.

Ownership of private roads would likely take many different forms. Private roads might be owned individually—property owners might own the road abutting their property—or jointly through a civic or business association. In either case, maintenance and other responsibilities could be stipulated through the deed attached to the property. This, in fact, is how maintenance was handled in the "private places" of Saint Louis, where both forms of ownership were used. As a part of their ownership, property owners would pay fees for maintaining roads, just as many now pay fees to a homeowner association for the maintenance of parks and other community amenities. In other words, the road in front of your home would not be owned by someone who could arbitrarily close it or charge outrageous rates. Other roads, such as those in business districts and industrial areas, might be owned by individual businesses or by a business association. Roads such as highways would likely be owned by businesses dedicated to operating such roads. And, as we have seen in regard to mail, education, and sanitation, free men find innovative solutions that we cannot even begin to imagine. With an understanding of how roads might be owned, let us now look at how private roads might be financed.[22]

Certainly, toll booths on every corner would impede traffic and could easily create a nightmare. But the mere fact that something is privately owned does not mean that its owners will necessarily charge for its use. For example, the yellow pages are distributed for free, with the company deriving revenue from advertisers. Similarly for Google—use of its search engine and e-mail is free, with advertisers and users purchasing upgrades and other services providing revenue. In the context of roads, many owners would be motivated to allow for the free use of their roads. Businesses for example, need employees, suppliers, and customers to reach their establishment. If businesses charge for use of their road, they would discourage customers. Similar to the free parking provided by many businesses, it is likely that many would also provide free roads.

---

22. The process of moving from the government monopoly on roads to an entirely private system is beyond the present discussion. However, a number of methods could be used. For example, roads in business districts and residential areas could be deeded or sold to the owners of the adjoining properties. Highways might be sold through auction.

Similarly, those who live in subdivisions would want visitors, deliverymen, contractors, and others to be able to easily reach their homes, and it is unlikely that charges would be assessed for using the roads. Indeed, many of the turnpike owners in the East allowed local landowners to use their roads without paying a toll.

Undoubtedly some roads would have tolls, as the private turnpikes did and as many public roads do today. But modern technology allows for tolls to be paid electronically with a windshield mounted transmitter, thereby greatly reducing congestion at toll booths. And, in a free market, entrepreneurs will develop innovative solutions that nobody can predict.

Because they prohibit or limit competition, coercive government institutions stifle innovation. In a free market, entrepreneurs seek more efficient and cost effective means to deliver goods and services. For example, the first personal computer sold by IBM—with a processor speed of 4.77 MHz, 16 kilobytes of RAM, and a 40 kilobyte "hard drive"[23]—cost more than $1,500 in 1981. That would be $3,600 today. What does a computer cost today? How much more powerful is it? How many choices do you have? Today, you can buy a computer made by Dell, Sony, Toshiba, Hewlett Packard, and dozens of other companies. You can buy a laptop for less than $500 with a processor speed of 2.53 GHz, 4 gigabytes of RAM, a 500 gigabyte hard drive, and a DVD player. In short, today you can buy a computer that is vastly more powerful, is portable, and costs a fraction of IBM's first computer. Such innovations and improvements cannot occur when government imposes restrictions and controls, or simply outlaws a device, such as the privy vault. Why would anyone seek to improve a device that he cannot sell?

Motivated by profit, entrepreneurs such as Michael Dell and Steve Jobs have found innovative ways to improve personal computers. They drove down prices dramatically, while improving performance and expanding options at breath-taking speed. What innovations might be developed if the creativity of a Jobs was applied to the privy vault, roads, or other infrastructure? How efficiently might a Dell manufacture or build such things? Unfortunately, we do not know the answers to these questions

---

23. Hard drives did not exist at the time. The first IBM PC came with forty kilobytes of read-only memory.

because government has prohibited anyone from doing so. Government has essentially declared innovation in infrastructure to be illegal, and the results speak for themselves.

As we have seen, when men are free, they can and do find innovative and voluntary methods for providing the values that others want, need, and desire, including sanitation and roads. As the nation's infrastructure continues to crumble, and the estimates for repairing it climb ever higher, it is time to consider a new alternative—a free market.

So far, we have seen the destructive consequences of government intervention in several areas of life. Let us now turn to arguably the most destructive of all government institutions—the "entitlement" state.

5

The Ambitious Shall Inherit the Earth

The exploding federal deficit has prompted some brave souls to suggest that "entitlement" spending be reduced. Even these meager proposals have been met with hostility and outlandish claims regarding the horrors that will befall the poor, the elderly, and children. We are told that the poor will feel helpless and hopeless, Grandma will be left to die in the street, and children will go hungry. But are these claims true? If "entitlement" programs were abolished, what would happen to the elderly, the infirm, and the destitute? Without government assistance, how would communities overcome disasters, such as hurricanes, earthquakes, or flooding? If individuals weren't *forced* to help the less fortunate, why would anyone do so? The answers to these questions have a huge impact on the size and scope of government, the type of society America will be, and the federal deficit.

Of course, there was a time when government did not provide food, shelter, health care, or any of the other values that life requires. Yet today, many Americans believe that they are entitled to such values. Because of the ideas that dominate America, "entitlement" programs have come to be the largest expenditure of the federal government and threaten to bankrupt the nation. Why?

Conservatives and progressives agree on few things, but they almost unanimously agree that each of us has a moral obligation to help those in need. For example, during his presidency, Bill Clinton said, "Citizen service is the main way we recognize that we are responsible for one another."[1] In his first inaugural address, President George W. Bush said, "Where there is suffering, there is duty. Americans in need are not strangers, they are citizens, not problems, but priorities. And all of us are diminished when any are hopeless."[2] During the debate over health care "reform," President Barack Obama said that arguments against universal health care neglected a moral duty: "These are all fabrications that have been put out there in order to discourage people from meeting what I consider to be a core ethical and moral obligation: that is, that we look out for one another; that is, I am my brother's keeper, I am my sister's keeper."[3] Motivated by altruism, every President since Franklin Roosevelt—including Ronald Reagan—has signed at least one piece of legislation that either created or expanded a government assistance or "entitlement" program.

Since the introduction of Social Security in 1935, the federal government has created and expanded a multitude of social welfare and assistance programs: Medicare, Medicaid, food stamps, Temporary Assistance for Needy Families, School Breakfast Program, Supplemental Security Income Program, the Women, Infants, and Children (WIC) Food Program, Low-Income Home Energy Assistance, and more. Today, there are more than seventy different federal programs that provide assistance to the poor and needy, and an estimated $953 billion—nearly $1,000,000,000,000—will be spent on these programs in 2011.[4] That is more than 25 percent of the projected federal expenditures in 2011.

Each of these programs is based on the altruistic premise that an individual's need constitutes a moral obligation on you, the productive citizen, to assist him. If you do not do so "voluntarily," it is proper to force you to do so through taxation. According to altruism, you have a moral duty to subsidize mail delivery, provide parks and libraries for the poor, and educate children. And the

---

1. President Bill Clinton, "Radio address to the nation," April 5, 1997.

2. President George W. Bush, "Inaugural address," January 20, 2001.

3. "'Talk to neighbors, spread the facts' on health care, says Obama," *CNN*, August 19, 2009, accessed April 12, 2011, http://articles.cnn.com/2009-08-19/politics/obama.health.care_1_health-care-health-insurance-public-option?_s=PM:POLITICS.

4. Kiki Bradley, "Expanding the Failed War on Poverty: Obama's 2011 Budget Increases Welfare Spending to Historic Levels," The Heritage Foundation, accessed January 6, 2010, http://www.heritage.org/research/reports/2010/03/expanding-the-failed-war-on-poverty-obamas-2011-budget-increases-welfare-spending-to-historic-levels.

greatest duty of all: You must provide life's basic requirements—including health care—for the needy. The mere fact that someone has been born obligates you to provide for his basic needs and wants; his existence entitles him to a portion of your money. But "entitlement" programs do not accomplish their stated purpose; they are impractical because they are immoral.

In 1964, President Lyndon Johnson announced the "War on Poverty," declaring, "Because it is right, because it is wise, and because, for the first time in our history, it is possible to conquer poverty, I submit, for the consideration of the Congress and the country, the Economic Opportunity Act of 1964."[5] Despite spending trillions of dollars over the past five decades, government has not conquered poverty; since that time, the percentage of Americans living below the poverty line has fluctuated between 11 and 19 percent.[6] Why has the federal government, even with its vast powers, been unable to achieve its stated objective? Benjamin Franklin provided the answer centuries ago:

> I am for doing good to the poor, but I differ in opinion of the means. I think the best way of doing good to the poor, is not making them easy in poverty, but leading or driving them out of it. In my youth I travelled much, and I observed in different countries, that the more public provisions were made for the poor, the less they provided for themselves, and of course became poorer. And, on the contrary, the less was done for them, the more they did for themselves, and became richer.[7]

Franklin understood that government assistance to the poor and needy did not improve their situation in 1766, and that fact remains true today.

Economists have long noted that if an activity is subsidized, more people engage in that activity. Subsidies shield individuals from the economic consequences of their actions, and thereby remove the incentive to take different actions. For example,

---

5. President Lyndon B. Johnson, "Proposal for A Nationwide War On The Sources of Poverty," Special Message to Congress, March 16, 1964.

6. Jerome R. Corsi and Kenneth Blackwell, "Democrats' War on Poverty Has Failed," *Human Events*, September 6, 2006, accessed January 6, 2010, http://www.humanevents.com/article.php?id=16860.

7. Benjamin Franklin, "On the Price of Corn and Management of the Poor," in *Writings* (New York: Library of America, 1987), pp. 587-88.

unemployment benefits subsidize unemployment, thereby providing less incentive to eagerly search for a job. Professor Robert Barro, writing in the *Wall Street Journal*, states "that generous unemployment-insurance programs have been found to raise unemployment in many Western European countries."[8] In 2010, the Federal Reserve Bank of San Francisco noted that "[e]conomists have long recognized that the availability and value of UI [unemployment insurance] benefits can lengthen unemployment spells. Empirical estimates using data from the United States and other countries confirm this general relationship."[9] The reason is that "the extension of UI benefits, which represents an increase in their value, may reduce the intensity with which UI-eligible unemployed individuals search for work."[10] In other words, unemployment benefits reduce the motivation to find employment. Similarly, "entitlement" programs subsidize poverty—they shield individuals from the actions that create poverty and reduce the motivation to change those actions. Benjamin Franklin understood that government handouts breed dependency, destroy ambition, and undermine self-esteem. And, Franklin was not the only Founding Father who opposed government relief.

Thomas Jefferson asserted that such schemes violate a cardinal principle of a civilized society, writing:

> To take from one, because it is thought that his own industry and that of his fathers has acquired too much, in order to spare to others, who, or whose fathers have not exercised equal industry and skill, is to violate arbitrarily the first principle of association, "the *guarantee* to every one of a free exercise of his industry, and the fruits acquired by it."[11]

James Madison—the Father of the Constitution—regarded government "charity" as unconstitutional. In 1794, when Congress

---

8. Robert Barro, "The Folly of Subsidizing Unemployment," *The Wall Street Journal*, August 30, 2010, accessed June 1, 2011, http://online.wsj.com/article/SB10001424052748703959704575454431457720188.html.

9. Rob Valletta and Katherine Kuang, "Extended Unemployment and UI Benefits," FRBSF Economic Letter, Federal Reserve Bank of San Francisco, April 19, 2010, accessed October 16, 2011, http://www.frbsf.org/publications/economics/letter/2010/el2010-12.html

10. Ibid.

11. Thomas Jefferson, letter to Joseph Milligan, April 6, 1816.

appropriated $15,000 for relief for French refugees, he objected on the floor of the House of Representatives: "I cannot undertake to lay my finger on that article of the Constitution which granted a right to Congress of expending, on objects of benevolence, the money of their constituents."[12] Madison stated his position in unequivocal terms: "Charity is no part of the legislative duty of the government."[13]

Both Jefferson and Madison understood that before government can provide relief to one individual, it must first take money from another. If a private citizen engaged in such an activity, he would properly be considered a thief. Even if he joined with most of his neighbors to rob another neighbor, his actions would still be theft, no matter the beneficiary. The nature of such actions does not change merely because government does the taking, no matter how many citizens may support it. Government "entitlement" programs are immoral. They force you, and other individuals, to act contrary to your own judgment, just as surely as a thief. Government "entitlement" programs operate on the altruistic premise that your life and property do not belong to you, but to the downtrodden and destitute. In truth, the misfortune of one person is not a claim on your life or your property.

You were *not* born with an unchosen obligation to serve others. You do *not* have a responsibility to satisfy the wants and needs of the poor, the elderly, or anyone else. Your life is yours to live as you choose, so long as you respect the mutual rights of others. Your only obligations to others are those you enter of your own choice, such as entering into contracts and having children. To claim otherwise is to assert that your life must be spent satisfying the demands of others. This is precisely what the Founding Fathers rebelled against.[14]

Even though "entitlement" programs have failed to eliminate poverty, welfare advocates continue to defend them. When reform

---

12. James Madison, 4 Annals of Congress 1794.

13. James Madison, "On the Memorial of the Relief Committee of Baltimore, for the Relief of St. Domingo Refugees," United States House of Representatives.

14. Many, particularly progressives, claim that a "social contract" obligates individuals to honor the rules and demands of society, such as financial support for "entitlement" programs. However, a contract implies consent to the terms of that agreement. To claim that individuals are bound by a "contract" in which they had no voice and did not consent is a gross contradiction.

of the system is suggested, they respond by predicting any number of evils. For example, in response to the 1996 Personal Responsibility and Work Opportunity Reconciliation Act (which toughened requirements for "entitlement" programs), one pundit wrote that the bill would do "serious injury to American children.... There will be more malnutrition and more crime, increased infant mortality, and increased drug and alcohol abuse. There will be increased family violence and abuse against children and women."[15] All of this, it was claimed, would result from the despair of increased poverty. Did these dire predictions come true? Interestingly, the Census Bureau reports that the percentage of people living in poverty dropped from 15.5 percent in 1996 to 12.8 percent in 1999.[16] When government did less for the poor, the poor did more for themselves—Benjamin Franklin was right. But such facts are simply dismissed by "entitlement" advocates.

To listen to defenders of the "entitlement" state, you might conclude that without government assistance the streets would be filled with the dead and dying. Without "entitlement" programs, they imply, millions of Americans would have no means of sustaining their lives or overcoming disasters. This may make for good sound bites and evoke sympathy, but it isn't true. What the poor need is opportunity, not handouts. What they need is freedom, not an economy strangled by government regulations. Indeed, this was the case in the nineteenth century.

During the nineteenth century, nearly thirty million people immigrated to the United States. Many came with little more than the clothes on their back and a determination to make their lives better. Many did not even speak English. Yet, they found jobs, worked hard, and improved their lives. They did not rely on government handouts—there were no "entitlement" programs. The streets were not filled with corpses, contrary to the claims of welfare advocates. All that these individuals needed was freedom.

Freedom—the absence of government coercion—creates opportunities. When businesses are free of arbitrary government

---

15. Peter Edelman, "The Worst Thing Bill Clinton Has Done," *The Atlantic Monthly 279*, no. 3 (March 1997).

16. "Dynamics of Economic Well-Being: Poverty, 1996 to 1999 - Highlights," U.S. Census Bureau, accessed January 6, 2010, http://www.census.gov/hhes/www/poverty/publications/dynamics96/highlights.html.

regulations and controls, they create jobs. When individuals are free of arbitrary government mandates and prohibitions, they start businesses. As an example, *National Review Online* reports that Texas—which has no state income tax and fewer regulations than most states—created 119,000 of the 224,000 new jobs in the nation between August 2009 and August 2010. The article goes on to say:

> Texas is a model of governmental restraint. In 2008, state and local expenditures were 25.5 percent of GDP in California, 22.8 in the U.S., and 17.3 in Texas. Back in 1987, levels of spending were roughly similar in these places. The recessions of 1991 and 2001 spiked spending everywhere, but each time Texas fought to bring it down to pre-recession levels.[17]

Further, from January 2001 to June 2010, Texas added more than 850,000 jobs, more than the other forty-nine states combined. During that same period, California lost 827,800 jobs.[18] What accounts for these dramatic differences? While California and the United States government allowed each spending spike to become permanent, Texas fought that trend. Texas understood that lower taxes and fewer regulations provide a greater opportunity and motivation to start or expand a business, that is, create jobs.

In a free society—one without government regulations, occupational licensing, and confiscatory taxes—economic opportunities abound, and thus the need for charity is greatly diminished. Freed from arbitrary government restraints, individuals have few impediments to finding work. Those who choose not to work are free to do so, but they cannot force you, or anyone else, to support them. But what about those who cannot work because of illness or injury?

Certainly there are those who, because of debilitating injury or disease, are unable to work. But in a free society, with an abundance of economic opportunity and the empowerment of technology, the

---

17. Rich Lowry, "The Texas Model," *National Review Online*, October 15, 2010, accessed January 6, 2011, http://www.nationalreview.com/articles/249868/texas-model-rich-lowry.

18. "Gov. Rick Perry says Texas has created more than 850,000 jobs, more than the other states combined," *Austin America-Statesman*, accessed June 12, 2011, http://www.politifact.com/texas/statements/2010/sep/23/rick-perry/gov-rick-perry-says-texas-has-created-more-850000-/.

number of individuals who are truly incapable of performing any meaningful work is miniscule. As author Craig Biddle writes:

> A deaf person might choose to pursue a career in genetics, architecture, or accounting. A blind person might choose to pursue a career in music, radio, or psychology. A paraplegic might choose to pursue a career in law, education, or writing. And today—with the technology made possible by freer markets—even a quadriplegic can learn to support himself; he might pursue a career in finance, economics, or computer programming.
>
> When disabled people are fully free to act on their judgment, there is usually something they can do to compensate for their shortcomings. And capitalism not only leaves them completely free to do so; it also makes available an ever-increasing flow of enabling technology.[19]

Biddle's argument is not mere hyperbole. Countless individuals have overcome their disabilities. As a few examples: Helen Keller, who was blind and deaf; Rick Allen, drummer for the rock band Def Leppard, who lost an arm in an automobile accident; physicist Stephen Hawking, who cannot walk or talk due to amyotrophic lateral sclerosis (ALS); actress Marlee Matlin, who is deaf. Each of these individuals, and many more like them, have not allowed a disability to stop them from being responsible for their own lives.

Those who are truly unable to work must rely on private charity, which many consider demeaning. Critics of private charity imply that receiving assistance that is obtained through the voluntary consent of the donor is demeaning, but receiving assistance that is obtained through coercion is not. To paraphrase Benjamin Franklin, if an individual finds charity demeaning, then he should change the conditions that make charity necessary. His life is his responsibility, and he does not have a moral right to rob others to provide for his needs and wants. Nor does he have a moral right to use government as his proxy to do so.

More important, we must recognize the fact that those who cannot work depend upon those who can. For whom should our society be structured—the few who are unable to work or the many who can? Should the able and productive be shackled because of

---

19. Craig Biddle, "A Civilized Society: The Necessary Conditions," in *Loving Life* (Richmond, VA: Glen Allen Press 2002) p. 124-25.

the small number who are unable to be productive? Shouldn't we seek to maximize production by leaving the able free to do so? As Biddle notes:

> What the helpless need but cannot produce is life-serving values; that's what makes them helpless. Such values can be produced only by able people; hence the term able. But able people can produce values only if they are *free* to act on the very thing that makes them able: their judgment. The basic social condition that makes human life possible is *freedom*—freedom from the initiation of physical force—the freedom of each individual to act on the judgment of his own mind.[20]

Protecting individual rights is the only practical and moral way to help the disabled and the needy.

But what about children? They are often the innocent victims of their parents' irresponsibility. Why should they suffer when they have done nothing wrong? A compassionate society, it is argued, should at least provide relief for children. Certainly, no decent person enjoys watching others—let alone children—needlessly suffer through no fault of their own. However, the taxpayers who are forced to provide relief are no less innocent. Nobody's need, no matter their age, circumstances, or innocence, constitutes a claim on the property or life of others. But this does *not* mean that children should be forced to suffer abusive or grossly negligent parents.

Children, like all individuals, have rights. Government's proper purpose is the protection of individual rights, including those of children. When parents are abusive or are not providing for a child's basic needs, government has a responsibility to step in. Having a child entails certain responsibilities on the part of parents, such as providing adequate food, clothing, shelter, and education. Government should protect the rights of children whose parents cannot or will not fulfill those responsibilities.

What about the victims of natural disasters and other calamities beyond anyone's control? In a capitalist society, would they be left to fend for themselves?

The most obvious solution for the financial burdens of natural disasters is insurance. Those who live in areas prone to hurricanes,

---

20. Ibid.

flooding, and similar natural events, can and rationally should purchase insurance to protect themselves from loss. And for those who do not or cannot purchase adequate insurance, they must rely on the charity of family, friends, and their fellow Americans.

Americans are extremely benevolent, and they demonstrate this year after year in their charitable giving. For example, consider the response to the terrorist attacks on September 11, 2001. In the year after the attacks, more than $2.3 billion was donated to assist the victims.[21] Within six months of the tsunami that struck Asia in 2004, Americans donated $1.7 billion to relief efforts.[22] A study by the Pew Research Center found that 56 percent of Americans made donations to help the victims of Hurricane Katrina in 2005[23], and the Center on Philanthropy estimates that a total of nearly $4 billion was donated.[24] Americans donated more than $1.4 billion to charities in response to the January 2010 earthquake in Haiti.[25] Even with today's onerous taxation and coercive "entitlement" programs, Americans help others when tragedy strikes. How much more might be donated if taxes did not consume such a large portion of our income?

Charitable giving is not limited to terrorist attacks or natural disasters. Across the country, thousands of charities and non-profit service organizations raise money and provide services for those in need. Organizations such as the United Way, the Salvation Army, and the Red Cross provide disaster relief, counseling services, educational programs, and other assistance. The Elks provide scholarships, youth programs, and community grants. Members of Kiwanis International stage 150,000 service projects each year and raise more than $100 million annually for their projects and community development.[26] Similarly, members of Rotary

---

21. "Sept. 11 donations swamp charities," *Associated Press*, September 4, 2002, accessed March 4, 2011, http://www.sptimes.com/2002/09/04/911/Sept_11_donations_swa.shtml.

22. "Philanthropy Matters," The Center on Philanthropy at Indiana University, July 2010, accessed January 29, 2011, http://www.philanthropy.iupui.edu/e- newsletter/philanthropymatters_July_2010.aspx.

23. "Haiti Dominates Public's Consciousness," Pew Research Center, January 2010, accessed January 29, 2011, http://people-press.org/report/580/haiti-earthquake.

24. "Philanthropy Matters."

25. Ibid.

26. "Our Impact," Kiwanis International, accessed January 6, 2011, http://sites.kiwanis.org/Kiwanis/en/discover/ourimpact.aspx.

International work locally, regionally, and internationally to fight hunger, to improve sanitation, and to provide education and job training. Each of these organizations, and thousands more like them, are funded primarily through voluntary donations.

Americans are by far the most generous people in the world, donating nearly $300 billion in 2006.[27] Arthur C. Brooks, a scholar at the American Enterprise Institute, wrote in 2008:

> No developed country approaches American giving. For example, in 1995 (the most recent year for which data are available), Americans gave, per capita, three and a half times as much to causes and charities as the French, seven times as much as the Germans, and 14 times as much as the Italians.[28]

A more recent study in 2006 found that charitable giving as a percentage of gross domestic product is highest in the United States: "The U.S. ranked first at 1.7%. No. 2 Britain gave 0.73%, while France, with a 0.14% rate, trailed such countries as South Africa, Singapore, Turkey and Germany."[29] Why do Americans donate more than twice as much as the British and ten times as much as the French?

The most important reason is that, before anything can be donated, it must first be produced. Free individuals are more productive than those shackled by government controls and regulations. There is a causal connection between freedom and the production of the values that human life requires. As evidence, contrast the abject poverty of communist North Korea and Third World dictatorships with the developed nations of the West. Where the West enjoys material abundance, nations such as North Korea must beg for food to feed its starving people.[30] Without freedom, individuals cannot produce the values that life requires, much less

---

27. "Americans give record $295B to charity," *USA Today*, June 25, 2007, accessed January 29, 2011, http://www.usatoday.com/news/nation/2007-06-25-charitable_N.htm.

28. Arthur C. Brooks, "A Nation of Givers," *The American*, March/April 2008, accessed January 29, 2011, http://www.american.com/archive/2008/march-april-magazine-contents/a-nation-of-givers/article_print.

29. "Americans give record $295B to charity."

30. Chico Harlan, "Starving N. Korea begs for food, but U.S. has concerns about resuming aid," *Washington Post*, February 22, 2011, accessed February 26, 2011, http://www.washingtonpost.com/wp-dyn/content/article/2011/02/19/AR2011021901953.html.

produce enough to donate to others.

We have seen the unparalleled generosity of Americans. Isn't this motivated by altruism? How can helping others be in one's self-interest? There can be many reasons why an individual would want to help others, not as an act of altruistic duty, but because of personal, selfish benefits. For example, an individual might help a friend who is temporarily out of work because of an automobile accident. Or, a business owner might volunteer time to mentor young, aspiring entrepreneurs. Or, a person might donate to a charity that is fighting the disease that killed his mother. In each instance, the individual or charity has personal importance to the donor. His donations of time or money are not motivated by a sense of moral obligation, but rather, a desire to further a relationship or cause that he values.

Unlike government "entitlement" programs, in a capitalist society individuals are able to direct their voluntary donations to charities providing the types of services and relief that they want to support. They are also free to refrain from donating to any charity, if they so choose. Nobody has an obligation to help others, voluntarily or otherwise. If a particular charity does not use an individual's donation for his desired purpose, or spends too much on administration and marketing, or in any way does not use the money as he wishes, he is free to end his donations. In contrast, if government social programs waste money or are used for purposes he does not support, he has no recourse—he must continue to provide financing regardless of his own judgment. This is the crucial moral distinction between private charity and government "entitlement" and relief programs. Private charity is voluntary and consensual, while government programs are coercive and mandatory. Private charity recognizes each individual's moral right to act according to his own judgment; government "entitlement" programs render his judgment irrelevant.

In a capitalist society, you are free to donate to the charities and causes of your choice, or none at all. Just as you should not be forced to subsidize mail delivery for others, or pay for parks and libraries you do not want, you should not be compelled to donate to causes and charities against your own judgment and desires. In principle, this means an end to the "entitlement" state.

For decades, we have heard warnings that programs such as Social Security are heading for insolvency. In response, politicians have "kicked the can down the road," devising various schemes to "save" these programs. Today, we hear new warnings that Social Security and Medicare will soon bankrupt the nation as more baby boomers reach retirement age. And again, politicians are trying to develop new plans to "save" these "entitlement" programs. In truth, they cannot be saved; there is no way to make the immoral work. Any attempt to do so is simply delaying the inevitable, and making the resulting agony worse.[31]

The Founding Fathers held that each individual has an inalienable right to his own life, his own liberty, his own property, and the pursuit of his own happiness. This principle—individual rights—cannot be compromised without devastating consequences. To accept the violation of individual rights in any way, for any purpose, is to reject the principle. Who is to determine when exceptions may be made? The King? The Politburo? "The people"? The violation of individual rights is tyrannical, no matter how many voices support it. If you want to end the threat posed by an out-of-control "entitlement" state, you must defend the sanctity of individual rights. If you wish to defend individual rights, you must defend your moral right to live for yourself. And that means, you must reject the morality that claims otherwise—altruism.

---

31. This does not mean that the "entitlement state" should be ended immediately. It does mean that "entitlement" programs should be phased out. Phasing out "entitlement" programs would provide individuals time to prepare and take responsibility for their own lives.

Part 1

Conclusion

The Founding Fathers were revolutionaries in the most fundamental sense. They rebelled against the idea that the individual exists to serve the demands of the pharaoh, the king, or society. They declared that each individual has an inalienable right to his own life, his own liberty, and the pursuit of his own happiness.

A proper government is dedicated to this proposition. It does not coerce you to live for the benefit of others. It does not compel you to pay for goods and services against your own judgment. It does not force you to sacrifice your self-interest for the "public interest." It protects individual rights, and nothing more. A proper government protects your moral right to live your life as you judge best, so long as you respect the mutual rights of others.

A government that uses force against its citizens places itself above moral law. It asserts that your judgment, choices, and values may be overridden by society. It declares that it may dispose of your life as it chooses. It matters not if the edicts are determined by the whim of a king, a committee of representatives, or a vote of the citizenry. If others may dictate how you live your life, your life is not yours.

We have seen the impracticality of government force in regard to parks, libraries, mail delivery, education, infrastructure, and "entitlements." Such institutions impose additional costs, limit choices, and stifle innovation. They compel you—and other citizens—to act contrary to your own rational judgment. They force you to live your life contrary to your own desires and values.

We have also seen that the protection of individual rights provides a social context in which you—and your fellow citizens—can act on your judgment in the pursuit of your values. In a capitalist society, you are free to spend your money on the values that you need and desire. But you cannot compel others to pay for what you want, just as they cannot force you to pay for their wants and needs. In a capitalist society, you are independent in thought and in action. You are free to choose and pursue your values without interference from others, just as others are free to choose and pursue their values without interference from you.

Some might argue that the modern world is too complex to return to the principles of the Founding Fathers. They might argue that a capitalist society is a fairy tale from the past. But where has government intervention gotten us? The postal service is broke, our schools turn out functional illiterates, our infrastructure is crumbling, and the federal government has unfunded liabilities that some have estimated to exceed $100 trillion. So, who is living the fairy tale? Those who advocate for the moral ideal of freedom and individual rights? Or, those who advocate for the same policies and ideas that have gotten us into this mess?

Part 2

Liberty

Imagine, for a moment, the response if government announced that it would prohibit manufacturers from making more than one type of toothpaste. Such a prohibition, government officials might argue, would protect consumers from the burden of choosing between paste and gel, between a whitening formula and tartar control. Manufacturers would be protected from the burden of packaging many different types of toothpaste, and they would be more efficient if they only had to make one type. And with choices eliminated, manufacturers would not have to advertise their products, so both businesses and consumers would save money. It would be a perfect win-win situation.

Americans would likely howl in protest. They would likely argue that they should be free to choose the type of toothpaste that they will use, and they don't need government dictating such details of their lives. Yet, when it comes to far more important issues than toothpaste, Americans accept government controls and prohibitions. When it comes to their occupation, their wages and benefits, the foods they can eat, the medicines they can take, and the support that they can give to political candidates, Americans accept controls and regulations. When it comes to freedom of association and freedom of contract, Americans accept limitations on their freedom to choose.

Liberty means the freedom to choose and pursue your values without interference or coercion from others, including government. It means the freedom to associate with others as you choose. It means the freedom to trade and contract as you judge best. Liberty recognizes your moral right to act on your own judgment, as long as you respect the mutual rights of others. This is true whether the choices involve the type of toothpaste that you will use, your occupation, your wages, or any other issue. Without the freedom to make these choices, you cannot pursue *your* goals and values. Without the freedom to choose your profession, your spouse, your hobbies, and a myriad of other values, large and small, you cannot pursue *your* happiness.

We have already seen many ways in which government controls and regulations prevent you from acting as you choose. You are forced to support public education, subsidize mail delivery, and provide "charity" for the poor and needy. These government institutions violate your right to contract—the right to voluntarily enter, or refrain from entering, into an economic exchange. But unfortunately, these are not the only ways in which government violates this fundamental right to make your own choices.

As we will soon see, government regulations and controls can prohibit you from contracting and associating with others in many ways. Occupational licensing laws can prohibit you from entering the profession of your choosing, and they similarly prevent consumers from hiring the professionals of their choice. Labor regulations can prevent employers and employees from negotiating mutually acceptable wages, benefits, and other terms of employment. Anti-discrimination laws can compel individuals to associate with others, regardless of their own views and judgment. Food regulations can prohibit you from eating the foods of your choice. Controls on medicine can prevent you from taking life-saving drugs. Why? Why are there so many regulations prohibiting individuals from acting on their own judgment?

Most of these laws have allegedly been enacted to protect Americans. They are based on the premise that you, and other individuals, are not wise enough or rational enough to make decisions regarding wages, food, medicine, and more. Government will protect you by restricting, or eliminating, your freedom to choose. Doing so will reduce your chances of making a poor decision by reducing the choices available to you by limiting your liberty.

Making matters worse, these controls and regulations never meet the stated goals. Government intervention in the job market does not make the workplace safer or create more jobs; instead, it stifles safety improvements and kills jobs. Government intervention in the pharmaceutical industry does not improve our health and safety; instead, it makes drugs outrageously expensive and leads to the deaths of thousands of Americans each year. By every rational measure, government regulations and controls are destructive.

As we will also see, when individuals are free to act on their own judgment in the pursuit of their own values, every rational and productive individual benefits. When individuals are free of occupational licensing laws, they can offer a variety of prices and quality that meet the needs of all consumers. When businesses are not stifled by labor laws, employers and employees can negotiate wages and benefits that are mutually beneficial. When doctors and patients are free to act on their judgment, suffering can be reduced and lives can be saved. By every rational standard, liberty is beneficial to individual human beings. This is true whether you are choosing a doctor, an employer, a political candidate, a medication, or a toothpaste.

6

Will Work for Food, if Permitted by Government

Like many entrepreneurial Americans, Mercedes Clemens wanted to start her own business. However, after doing so, the state of Maryland threatened Clemens with thousands of dollars in fines and criminal prosecution unless she closed her business. What was her crime? Was she selling stolen goods? Was she operating a child pornography ring? No, Mercedes Clemens was massaging horses. The state of Maryland deemed Clemens—who is a licensed human-massage therapist and certified in equine massage—a criminal because she did not meet a state occupational licensing requirement. Maryland law mandates four years of veterinary school for anyone who wishes to massage horses, despite the fact that veterinary schools do not teach how to massage horses.[1]

This bizarre law is not an aberration. Across the nation more than eight hundred professions require some form of occupational licensing.[2] It is estimated that as much as one-third of the American workforce must acquire government permission to enter the profession of their choice.[3] A small sampling of these professions includes rainmakers in Arizona, manure applicators in Iowa, lobster

---

1. Bob Ewing, "The Right to Earn a Living Under Attack," *The Freeman 58*, no. 10 (December 2008), accessed December 28, 2010, http://www.thefreemanonline.org/featured/the-right-to-earn-a-living-under-attack/.

2. Morris M. Kleiner and Alan B. Krueger, "The Prevalence and Effects of Occupational Licensing," The Institute for the Study of Labor, Discussion Paper No. 3675, August 2008, p. 1.

3. S. David Young, "Occupational Licensing," Library of Economics and Liberty, accessed December 28, 2010, http://www.econlib.org/library/Enc1/OccupationalLicensing.html.

sellers in Rhode Island, and mussel dealers in Illinois.[4] Why are such professions licensed? Why is government permission required to spread manure?

The alleged purpose of licensing is to protect consumers from incompetent and unscrupulous practitioners. Licensing, we are told, ensures the public that licensed professions have met certain standards. After all, who wants to discover that his surgeon has no medical training? But this is the Big Lie behind licensing. As we will soon see, occupational licensing does not protect consumers. In fact, licensing has destructive consequences for consumers, licensed professionals, and would-be practitioners of licensed professions.

One consequence of licensing is the creation of "Cadillac" services with no "Yugo" options. That is, licensing tends to create a high quality, high price service that may not fit the needs of all consumers. Because of licensing, highly skilled practitioners are often required to perform routine services that could be performed effectively, safely, and at a lower cost by less skilled individuals. For example, a light fixture can be replaced by a competent handyman, but licensing may require that the task be performed by a licensed electrician. The result of the restrictions imposed by licensing is fewer choices for consumers and higher prices. In 2008, Professor Morris Kleiner, a nationally recognized scholar on occupational licensing, estimated that licensing costs consumers more than $100 billion per year.[5] Overall, it is estimated that occupational licensing increases prices to consumers by an average of 10 to 12 percent.[6]

As a consequence of these higher costs, consumers often do without a desired or needed service, or attempt to do it themselves. Professor S. David Young writes:

> The incidence of rabies is higher, for example, where there are strict limits on veterinary practice, and as Sidney Carroll and Robert Gaston documented, rates of electrocution are higher in states with the most restrictive licensing laws for electricians.

---

4. Adam B. Summers, "Occupational Licensing: Ranking the States and Exploring Alternatives," Reason Foundation (August 2007), p. 43, accessed December 28, 2010, http://reason.org/files/762c8fe96431b6fa5e27ca64eaa1818b.pdf.

5. Lee McGrath, "A Primer on Occupational Licensing," Institute for Justice, April 2008, accessed June 13, 2011, http://www.ij.org/index.php?option=com_content &task=view&id=2057.

6. Summers, "Occupational Licensing," p. 15.

> Apparently, consumers often do their own electrical work in highly restrictive states rather than pay artificially high rates for professionals, with predictably tragic results.[7]

These are just some of the costs that consumers must bear.

A report by the Federal Trade Commission (FTC) found that many consumers do not desire a high quality, high price service—the so-called "Cadillac" service. The report states that the "inability of these consumers to choose a low price, low quality bundle makes them worse off."[8] Even when licensed practitioners identify innovative ways to offer more affordable services, licensing often prohibits them from doing so. Young cites "the efforts of the organized medical profession to inhibit prepaid health plans and of lawyers to ban low-cost legal clinics" as examples.[9] Again, the result is higher costs and fewer choices for consumers. If occupational licensing has such detrimental consequences for consumers—its alleged beneficiaries—why is licensing so widespread?

Numerous studies have found that the most vocal supporters of occupational licensing are not consumers, but those already in the profession. Professors Morris Kleiner and Alan Krueger write that occupational associations have "a significant ability to influence legislation, especially when opposition to regulatory legislation is absent or minimal."[10] A report by the Reason Foundation states:

> As one policy analyst observed: "The dirty little secret about state licensure is that the people who lobby for it are usually the stronger competitors of those who would be licensed. Their goal is not to protect the public, but instead to raise barriers to new competitors who might cut prices and lower profits."[11]

In other words, those in a profession use government coercion to erect legal obstacles to prevent or discourage potential competitors from entering the profession. And often those obstacles are simply absurd.

---

7. Young, "Occupational Licensing."
8. Carolyn Cox and Susan Foster, "The Costs and Benefits of Occupational Regulation," Bureau of Economics, Federal Trade Commission, October 1990, p. 36.
9. Young, "Occupational Licensing."
10. Kleiner and Krueger, "Prevalence and Effects."
11. Summers, "Occupational Licensing," p. 15.

As an example, in Texas a licensing law was passed that requires computer-repair technicians to obtain a criminal justice degree or serve a three-year apprenticeship under a licensed private investigator. The bill's sponsor said, "If you're investigating or analyzing data, then you should need a little more credentials than someone who just repairs computers."[12] But why criminal justice? Why not economics or literature? Wouldn't these provide "more credentials," as the bill's sponsor desires? Regardless, competency in repairing computers is not considered sufficient for repairing computers. And if you think otherwise, that is just too bad.

Consider what this might mean in your life if you live in Texas. Suppose that your teenage neighbor offers to repair your computer. You know he is competent because he has built several computers for himself. You agree to hire him on terms that are mutually acceptable. The state of Texas however, would consider your neighbor a criminal because he has not obtained the required criminal justice degree. Who would be harmed by such a transaction? Not you. Not your neighbor. Not most of the other twenty-five million people who live in Texas and know nothing of your transaction. The only people "harmed" would be those computer technicians who do not want to compete in a free market. Restricting entry into a profession, and the higher incomes that result for those who are licensed, is the real motivation behind occupational licensing.

Despite the demonstrable harm caused by licensing, advocates of licensing continue to insist that such sacrifices are necessary. Consumers, they often argue, do not know how to judge the quality of certain professionals, such as doctors, dentists, lawyers, and accountants. Licensing, it is claimed, ensures consumers that they will receive competent service from qualified professionals. In other words, you are not smart enough to decide who is qualified to fill your cavities, spay your cat, or repair your computer, so the state will save you the trouble of making such decisions. But the actual facts belie these claims.

When most licensing regulations are enacted, existing practitioners are "grandfathered." That is, they are granted a license and are not required to meet the licensing requirements that future

12. Ewing, "Right to Earn a Living."

practitioners must meet. Which means, at its inception, licensing has nothing to do with the qualifications or competency of those receiving a license. The FTC report notes that the "high entry requirements which are purportedly enacted to protect consumers are inconsistent with the process of grandfathering which professionals routinely demand."[13] It is hypocritical and grossly unjust to advocate two sets of standards for those in the very same profession. And the hypocrisy does not end there.

Once licensing is established, most licensing boards are comprised of those already in the profession. After all, how could a layman judge the competency and qualifications of a plumber, lawyer, or doctor? What layman wants to spend his days testing plumbers for their knowledge of solder? But study after study has reached a similar conclusion: licensing boards do little to discipline incompetents, but instead invest most of their effort on prosecuting those who are unlicensed. Young writes:

> A major cause is the reluctance of professionals to turn in one of their own. The in-group solidarity common to all professions causes members to frown on revealing unsavory activities of a fellow member to the public. Going public regarding infractions, no matter how grievous, is often viewed as disloyalty to the professional community.[14]

Harm to consumers—the alleged beneficiaries of licensing—is seldom a cause for disciplinary actions. For example, Public Citizen, a consumer advocacy organization, reports:

> Of 10,672 physicians listed in the NPDB [National Practitioner Data Bank] for having clinical privileges revoked or restricted by hospitals, just 45 percent of them also had one or more licensing actions taken against them by state medical boards. That means 55 percent of them – 5,887 doctors – escaped any licensing action by the state.[15]

---

13. Cox and Foster, "Costs and Benefits," p. 37.

14. Young, "Occupational Licensing."

15. "New Public Citizen Study Questions Ability of State Medical Boards to Protect Patients From Dangerous Doctors," Public Citizen, March 15, 2011, accessed April 13, 2011, http://www.citizen.org/pressroom/pressroomredirect.cfm?ID=3294.

In other words, the hospitals where these doctors worked deemed their behavior sufficient to "fire" them, but the licensing board often turned a blind eye. Incompetence and unethical behavior are routinely overlooked by medical licensing boards.

If operating on the wrong knee won't necessarily cause action by the licensing board, what will? Young states that the most common reason for discipline against licensed professionals is activity that violates rules intended to limit competition, such as advertising restrictions. Being a bad doctor is not necessarily a cause for disciplinary action by the medical board; being a good marketer is.

In fact, restrictions on advertising are common in many licensed professions. Interestingly, a frequent argument in favor of licensing is that consumers often lack information regarding professionals. Yet, the very purpose of advertising is to provide information, whether it is about the services offered, pricing, or anything else regarding the service that might help consumers make informed decisions. On one hand, licensing advocates argue that consumers don't have sufficient information; on the other hand, they argue that information should be withheld from consumers. Why do licensing advocates speak out of both sides of their mouths? Do they think that you won't notice their hypocrisy? Not surprisingly, the answer is "yes."

Underlying licensing is an implied paternalism—you and other consumers are just too stupid to make wise decisions. You must be protected from acting on your own judgment and perhaps making unwise decisions. Instead, individuals who have never met you and know nothing about you—politicians, bureaucrats, and licensing boards—will impose their judgment upon you through government force. They will dictate who you can legally hire to perform rain dances, spread manure, or repair your computer.

Whether you are a consumer or a professional, licensing is a direct assault on your moral right to freely contract with others. Under licensing you can act only with government permission, rather than by right. The injustice of such controls was recognized long ago by James Madison:

> That is not a just government, nor is property secure under it, where arbitrary restrictions, exemptions, and monopolies deny to part of its citizens that free use of their faculties, and free choice

> of their occupations, which not only constitute their property in the general sense of the word; but are the means of acquiring property....[16]

Isn't this a description of licensing? Licensing creates "arbitrary restrictions, exemptions, and monopolies" within a profession; it denies individuals the freedom to earn a living as they choose.

The obvious victim of this injustice is the individual who must overcome these arbitrary restrictions to enter the occupation of his choice. Often, these restrictions are outlandish. We have already seen a Texas law that prevents an entrepreneurial teenager from repairing computers if he does not obtain a time-consuming, and pointless, criminal justice degree. As another example, to legally operate a taxi cab in New York City, a city-issued medallion (license) must be attached to the hood of the car. In July 2009, the cost of a single medallion was $766,000![17] How many would-be taxi drivers can afford such an outrageous price simply to obtain government permission to operate a taxi cab? And how much does the cost of a medallion inflate the price of a taxi ride in New York City?

Thus, consumers are also victims of this injustice. They are forced to pay higher prices, have fewer options, and are legally permitted to do business only with those who have obtained government permission to operate a taxi cab. Who benefits from this? Those who are fortunate enough to obtain a medallion. In fact, one company—Medallion Financial—buys medallions and then leases them to taxi operators. The president of Medallion Financial states that medallion prices have averaged a 15 percent appreciation for the past seventy years.[18] Apparently, it is more lucrative to invest in taxi medallions than to actually operate a taxi.

Defenders of licensing often argue that licensing does not prevent individuals from entering a profession—they must simply meet certain standards, and it is reasonable for a profession to have standards. A doctor, for example, must have knowledge of

---

16. James Madison, "Property," *Papers 14:266—68*, accessed January 7, 2011, http://press-pubs.uchicago.edu/founders/documents/v1ch16s23.html.

17. "Driver competition hot as NYC taxi medallions hit $766,000," *USA Today*, August 7, 2009, accessed June 13, 2011, http://www.usatoday.com/money/industries/travel/2009-08-05-taxi-cab-new-york-city-medallions_N.htm.

18. Ibid.

anatomy, diseases, and treatments. An electrician must know how to properly install wiring and electrical fixtures to prevent fires and similar disasters. Licensing, the argument continues, just ensures that these standards are met.

While it is true that every profession has standards, there is a crucial moral difference between those that are mandated and enforced by law and those that are accepted and practiced by voluntary consent. For example, if you live in Arizona and do not meet the criteria mandated by the licensing board, you are legally prohibited from performing rain dances. If you defy the licensing board, you are subject to fines, imprisonment, or both. In contrast, if you cannot meet the standards established by an orchestra, you are not legally prohibited from becoming a musician. You remain free to play music, start your own orchestra, or make records.

In a capitalist society, individuals have no restrictions on entering a profession. Practitioners are free to offer options regarding quality and pricing. They are free to offer products and services of their choosing, including those that are outside of the mainstream or rejected by their colleagues. Consumers are free to purchase those products and services according to their own judgment. Consumers have more options regarding the products and services that are available, including those considered unconventional, and they are free to choose the price/value options that meet their needs and budget. In a capitalist society, producers and consumers are free to contract with others as they judge best.

Does this mean that consumers will be left to the mercy of unscrupulous and incompetent professionals? Does this mean that anyone can practice medicine? No, because nobody has a right to engage in fraud. Anyone who intentionally misrepresents his qualifications, skills, or expertise should be prosecuted. In a capitalist society, anyone would be free to offer medical services. However, anyone doing so could not claim to have training, expertise, or skills that he does not have. At the same time, consumers must take responsibility for the professionals they hire. They must perform their due diligence, such as verifying credentials or speaking to other customers. In a free society, there are a myriad of private, non-coercive means for consumers to obtain information on professionals and service providers.

One well-known example is the Better Business Bureau (BBB)—a private non-profit organization. Members of the BBB are held to a code of conduct that includes:[19]

- **Advertise Honestly.** Adhere to established standards of advertising and selling.
- **Tell the Truth.** Honestly represent products and services, including clear and adequate disclosures of all material terms.
- **Honor Promises.** Abide by all written agreements and verbal representations.
- **Be Responsive.** Address marketplace disputes quickly, professionally, and in good faith.
- **Embody Integrity.** Approach all business dealings, marketplace transactions and commitments with integrity.

Members who refuse or fail to honor this code of business ethics have their membership terminated. The BBB also offers mediation and arbitration services to help businesses and consumers resolve disputes. For businesses, the BBB provides credibility and a means to assure consumers that they will be dealing with a reputable company. For consumers, the BBB provides an independent resource for evaluating businesses.

Similarly, Angie's List—also a private company—provides consumers with a means for finding service providers and sharing their own experiences and recommendations online. The company's website states that "Angie's List is where you'll find thousands of unbiased reports and reviews about service companies in your area. Our members share their experiences with each other so that you can choose the service company that's right for your job the first time around."[20] Among the categories of service providers are doctors, dentists, auto services, child care providers, hair salons, and contractors of every sort. Both the BBB and Angie's List allow consumers to obtain third-party information on companies and respect the rights of both businesses and consumers to act as they judge best. With the popularity of the Internet, a growing number

---

19. "BBB Standards for Trust," Better Business Bureau, accessed December 28, 2010, http://www.bbb.org/us/bbb-standards-for-trust/.

20. "What is Angie's List?" Angie's List, accessed December 28, 2010, http://www.angieslist.com/angieslist/visitor/faq.aspx#whatis.

of websites, such as Amazon.com, B4UEat.com, and TripAdvisor.com, offer consumers a means to review books, restaurants, hotels, and virtually any consumer product or service. And who knows what other methods of consumer education might be developed when men are free of government intervention?

Certification programs also provide a means by which consumers can evaluate businesses. For example, the American Automobile Association (AAA) provides certification for auto repair shops. The certification program "was established in 1975 to address one of the most frequent consumer complaints: unsatisfactory automobile repairs." Certification requires the business to meet stringent requirements, including technical training, customer satisfaction surveys, and financial background checks.[21] Similarly, the National Institute for Automotive Service Excellence (ASE) provides training and certification for automotive repair technicians. The institute explains that

> car-owners can easily find ASE-Certified Technicians who have proven themselves to be knowledgeable professionals. Repair shops can get additional visibility in their markets by qualifying for the Blue Seal of Excellence Recognition program. And certified auto professionals can get the respect and recognition they've worked so hard to earn.[22]

The Institute also has a program—the Blue Seal of Excellence Recognition Program—which identifies shops with a large percentage of ASE-certified professionals.

Many product manufacturers offer certification programs for users of their products. GAF—a manufacturer of roofing products—offers several different levels of certification for roofing contractors. Cisco, which manufactures routers and other computer-related equipment, offers a variety of certification programs that "bring valuable, measurable rewards to network

---

21. "Vehicle Maintenance," AAA Texas, accessed December 28, 2010, http://www.texas.aaa.com/en-tx/buy-maintain-vehicles/vehicle-maintenance/Pages/approved-auto-repair-explained.aspx.

22. "ASE At a Glance," National Institute for Automotive Service Excellence, accessed October 1, 2011, http://www.ase.com/About-ASE/ASE-at-a-Glance.aspx.

professionals, their managers, and the organizations that employ them."[23]

Certification programs differ from licensing in that they are voluntary. Practitioners are free to obtain certification and the benefits that come with it, such as verification of competency and potentially higher wages, or forgo certification and lessen the chances of obtaining higher wages. Consumers are also free to choose certified professionals and pay higher prices, or employ uncertified, lower priced practitioners. Both producers and consumers are free to act on their judgment—to contract as they choose—according to their needs and values. Even the Federal Trade Commission states that:

> One of the most important benefits of certification, as opposed to licensing, is that it would allow consumers greater freedom of choice. An individual could choose either a lower priced, noncertified professional or a higher priced, certified one. [Economist Milton] Friedman states that "[i]f the argument is that we are too ignorant to judge good practitioners, all that is needed is to make the relevant information available. If, in full knowledge, we still want to go to someone who is not certified, that is our business.[24]

Indeed, this is the heart of the matter—each individual has a moral right to make decisions regarding his own life, including which professionals he wants to hire and with which to do business. Freedom of contract is liberty in action.

The right to do business with others is a corollary of an individual's right to act according to his own judgment. As we have seen, a free market can and does provide individuals with the information they need to make intelligent decisions when hiring professionals and service providers—whether doctors, plumbers, or rain dancers. However, consumers must take responsibility for their decisions. If individuals want the freedom to live as they choose, they must accept the responsibility that comes with making choices. If they give up that responsibility, they also give up their freedom.

---

23. "Introduction," Cisco, accessed January 7, 2011, http://www.cisco.com/web/learning/le3/learning_career_certifications_and_learning_paths_home.html.

24. Cox and Foster, pp. 44-45.

If individuals are free to act as they choose, won't some choose to be irrational? Won't some choose to discriminate on the basis of race or gender? Let us now turn to these questions.

7

The Cure for Racism

During the 2008-2009 season, 82 percent of the players in the National Basketball Association (NBA) were black. In a highly competitive business, the owners and managers of professional basketball teams do not care about the skin color, ethnicity, or nationality of their players. They care only about the talent of their players. They want to succeed, and that means focusing on the relevant criteria. Why would any rational business owner think differently?

However, according to the criteria used for other businesses, the owners of NBA teams are guilty of racial discrimination. The percentage of black players is completely out of proportion to the black population of America. But only a fool would claim that white NBA owners are discriminating in favor of black players. Any sensible person knows that they hire the best players that they can find. Yet, when it comes to other businesses, and capitalism in general, many believe that business owners will engage in irrational discrimination. Capitalism, many believe, promotes racism, sexism, and similar irrational ideas. For example, Bobby Seale, a co-founder of the Black Panther Party, once said, "The very nature of the capitalist system is to exploit and enslave people, all people."[1] Similarly, Malcolm X claimed, "You can't have capitalism without racism."[2] Are these claims true? Is racism an inherent characteristic of capitalism?

---

1. Ramy Khalil, "The end of the American Dream — Class struggle on the agenda," SocialistAlternative.org, accessed June 17, 2011, http://www.socialistalternative.org/news/article20.php?id=432.

2. Ibid.

To answer this, let us consider the NBA. If, according to Seale and Malcolm X, capitalism is a system of racism against blacks, why are the players overwhelmingly black? If the capitalist owners are racist exploiters, why do they pay black players millions of dollars per year? The reason is simple: They seek to put together the best team that they can, and the race of the players is irrelevant. To select players on the basis of their skin color, and not their basketball talent, would result in an inferior team.

It would be naïve, irrational, or both, to claim that racism, sexism, homophobia, and similar irrational ideas do not exist. There are some individuals who hold such ideas. But in a free society—one in which the initiation of force is prohibited—those who hold irrational ideas ultimately suffer for it. Or, to state the point positively, capitalism rewards rationality. This is true in the NBA, and it is true of any business.

If racism does exist, don't we need government to intervene to promote equality? Without anti-discrimination laws, why wouldn't a retail chain refuse to hire blacks? What would stop an oil company from erecting a "glass ceiling" and preventing women from advancing? Don't we need government to prohibit workplace discrimination on the basis of gender, race, color, religion, national origin, age, disability, or genetic information, as federal law now does?[3]

The irrational cannot be eliminated by legislative fiat. A mind cannot be forced to accept or reject a particular idea. Just as it is impossible to force a Boston Red Sox fan to become an eager supporter of the New York Yankees, it is impossible to force a racist or sexist or homophobe to reject his ideas. Nor is it a proper function of government to determine which ideas are rational or acceptable and which are not. The proper purpose of government is the protection of individual rights—the moral right of each individual to act according to his own judgment, so long as he respects the mutual rights of others.

The rights of others place a boundary on each individual's actions—a person may not use force (or threaten to use force) to compel others to act contrary to their judgment. An individual can believe any idea he desires, but he cannot act on that idea if it

3. "Overview," U.S. Equal Employment Opportunity Commission, accessed June 17, 2011, http://www.eeoc.gov/eeoc/index.cfm.

involves violating the rights of others. This is true whether those others are black or white, male or female, gay or straight. A person has a right to believe that blacks are inferior to whites; he does not have a right to lynch blacks. An individual has a right to believe that women should be barefoot and pregnant; he does not have a right to steal a woman's shoes and rape her. A person has a right to believe that homosexuality is immoral; he does not have a right to assault gays. Individual rights apply to each individual, no matter his race, gender, or sexual orientation. In short, each individual has a right to hold irrational ideas, but he does not have a right to act on those ideas if doing so involves using force against others.

Government cannot compel anyone to be rational; it can only create the social conditions in which individuals can be rational and enjoy the consequences when they are. In a free society, those who hold irrational ideas cannot impose their choices on others, nor can they force the consequences of their choices on others. A drug addict cannot force others to provide his next fix; a deadbeat cannot compel others to pay his bills. In a capitalist society, each individual is free to act according to his own judgment, and he, as well as those who voluntarily associate with him, is responsible for the consequences.

But what of the victims of racism (or sexism or homophobia)? What of those who are refused service or are denied a job because of their race, gender, or sexual preference? Aren't their rights being violated?

A right, as previously noted, pertains to freedom of action. It is a sanction to act without interference from others, to act according to your own best judgment. The mutual rights of others prohibit you from interfering with their actions. In a capitalist society, all human interactions must be based on the voluntary consent of those involved. This includes the customers a business chooses to serve and the employees it chooses to hire. Freedom of association and freedom of contract apply to business owners as well as to all individuals.

There is no such thing as a "right" to a job or a "right" to be served. There is only the right of the business to offer a job, a product, or a service and the right of employees and consumers to accept or reject that offer. There is only the right to contract as one deems best, and that requires the voluntary consent of each party involved. Just as it is immoral for government to force a consumer to patronize a particular business, it is equally immoral for government to force a business owner to serve or hire a particular group of individuals, such as minorities, women, or gays. The initiation of force is wrong, no matter the intentions. An individual's right to associate with whom he chooses does not cease when he opens a business. Economist Walter E. Williams notes that "the true test of one's commitment to freedom of association doesn't come when he permits people to associate in ways he deems appropriate. It comes when he permits people to voluntarily associate in ways he deems offensive."[4]

If, in a capitalist society, individuals are free to be offensive, why would a business owner shun racism or sexism? A rational businessman is in business to make money. His self-interest—the desire for profit—will motivate him to hire employees with the talents and skills that his business requires, regardless of their race, gender, or sexual orientation. His self-interest will motivate him to attract as many customers as possible, no matter their skin color, genitalia, or sexual partner. However, if he uses irrational criteria, such as refusing to hire blacks or refusing to serve gays, he arbitrarily restricts his labor pool, his customer base, or both. More rational competitors—those who do not use such irrelevant standards—will have better employees and more customers. This is true in the NBA and it is true in any business. Rational consumers will shun his business, either because of the inferior quality of his products and services, his discriminatory practices, or both. In the end, as long as individuals are free to act on their own judgment, irrational business practices will cause a businessman to suffer economically. If he does not adopt rational standards, his business will continue to suffer. But what of past wrongs? Don't we need programs such as affirmative action to correct past discrimination?

A result of the civil rights movement of the 1960s was affirmative action, which "calls for minorities and women to be given special consideration in employment, education and contracting decisions."[5] What does "special consideration" mean? It

---

4. Walter E. Williams, "The Right to Discriminate," TownHall.com, accessed January 29, 2011, http://townhall.com/columnists/WalterEWilliams/2010/06/02/the_right_to_discriminate/page/2.

5. Dan Froomkin, "Affirmative Action Under Attack," *Washington Post*, October 1998, accessed June 17, 2011, http://www.washingtonpost.com/wp-srv/politics/special/affirm/affirm.htm.

means that race and gender *are* to be considered when making decisions regarding hiring and promotion. It means that qualifications other than those relevant to the job are to be considered. What if this were applied to the NBA? What if short, middle-aged, white men were to be given "special consideration"? After all, there is a complete absence of such players in the NBA. Obviously, if NBA teams implemented affirmative action and gave consideration to anything other than talent, the quality of play would greatly decrease.

Ironically, affirmative action has actually caused harm to those it is intended to benefit. As an example, in his book, *Reflections of an Affirmative Action Baby*, black Professor Stephen L. Carter writes that "every professional who is not white is subjected to that extra degree of scrutiny that attaches to those who are suspected of having benefited, at some point in the development of their careers, from a racial preference."[6] In other words, the qualifications of non-white, non-male professionals are eyed with suspicion because of affirmative action. Colleagues wonder: Was he hired because of his race? Was she promoted because of her gender? Such suspicions do not promote good-will and collegiality among co-workers. A prospective employer might raise similar questions, wondering if "special considerations," rather than talent, is the source of the candidate's career development. The solution to past wrongs is not to repeat those wrongs in another form. The solution to discrimination *against* minorities and women is not discrimination in *favor* of minorities and women.

So, what is the solution to racism? How do we achieve the dream of Martin Luther King, Jr., that is, a nation where individuals "will not be judged by the color of their skin but by the content of their character"?[7] The solution to racism, sexism, and every form of irrational discrimination is capitalism—the freedom to contract and associate with others according to one's own judgment. And this is not just theory. History shows us that capitalism promotes rational ideas; history also shows us that it is government force that actually promotes racism.

---

6. Stephen L. Carter, *Reflections of an Affirmative Action Baby* (New York: Basic Books 1991), p. 3.

7. Martin Luther King, Jr., "The I Have a Dream Speech," U.S. Constitution Online, accessed June 17, 2011, http://www.usconstitution.net/dream.html.

Consider slavery. Prior to the Civil War, every Southern state passed "slave codes" that made it illegal to teach slaves to read or write, that prohibited slaves from testifying against whites, and that severely restricted the freedom of slave owners to free their slaves. If an individual inherited slaves but was opposed to slavery, he could not act on his conscience or his judgment. Rather than protect individual rights, the Southern legislatures made it illegal to treat slaves as human beings and thereby violated the rights of both slaves and slave owners. And these violations didn't end with the emancipation of slaves.

Following the Civil War and the end of slavery, Southern plantation owners suddenly found themselves with great uncertainty regarding the labor they required. The agriculturally based economy of the South was heavily labor intensive, and slavery had provided the plantation owners with a known labor force, since the slaves had no options. With the emancipation of the slaves, plantation owners did not know if they would have the workers that they required. The newly freed slaves faced a similar problem. They had few resources or skills and needed employment. These problems were addressed as free men solve problems—by mutual consent to mutual gain—and a number of solutions developed. Some plantation owners simply hired laborers as they were needed. This solution created a new issue for the plantation owners. The planting and harvest seasons created a high demand for labor, which meant that some owners had difficulty obtaining the workers they needed at those times. They were also bidding for that labor against other plantation owners at a time of high demand, which drove wages up.

Another solution that developed was share-cropping. The details varied, but under this arrangement the plantation owner essentially leased his land to a tenant, who would farm the land. The crop was then shared between the landowner and the tenant, hence the term share-cropping. This, too, had certain disadvantages to the landowner, as his profit relied on a successful crop. However, the tenant had a motivation—his own profit—to work the land efficiently and effectively and thus provide a profit for the landowner.

Unfortunately, some tenants purchased seed, fertilizer, and other supplies on credit from the plantation owners, who in turn charged exorbitant interest rates. Many times the tenants could not repay their loans, and in time, they became so indebted that they were economically dependent on the plantation owner. While it is unfortunate that some tenants lacked the economic knowledge to make better decisions, these new arrangements were certainly better for the former slaves. They now had choices and the freedom to act on their judgment. But what about the plantation owners? How did the former slave owners respond to these new relationships?

The plantation owners were not particularly happy with these voluntary, contractual solutions. Many, if not most, were overt racists, and while they were willing to put aside their racism to negotiate with the black laborers, they still believed in the supremacy of whites. Further, and not surprisingly, the plantations were not as profitable as when the owners had slaves to do the work. Throughout the South, it was urged that the landowners collude to keep wages down. As Jennifer Roback, an economist who has studied the Jim Crow laws,[8] writes: "Throughout the Jim Crow period, they pleaded with one another to hold the line on black wages. 'White men must stick together' was the common theme, expressed in the newspapers and magazines of the time."[9] Such attempts at collusion always fail, and this attempt was no exception.

The self-interest of the individual planters—their desire to plant and harvest their own crops—caused them to ignore the pleas for collusion. They concluded that it was better to pay higher wages and earn some profit, rather than risk losing their entire crop and earn no profit. The supporters of collusion had no means to enforce its provisions, since participation was voluntary. What could they do? How could they get individual landowners to put aside their self-interest to promote the "public interest"? We have seen that freedom provided the former slaves with more options and motivated racists to put aside their irrational ideas. We will now examine what happened when government intervened.

Following Reconstruction and the withdrawal of federal troops from the South, Southern Democratic legislators began to

---

8. The Jim Crow laws were state and local laws enacted in the South for the purposes of racial segregation. The origin of the term is attributed to a song and dance, "Jump Jim Crow," that was used to satirize President Andrew Jackson's policies. "Jim Crow" soon became a pejorative term for blacks.

9. Jennifer Roback, "Exploitation in the Jim Crow South: The Market or the Law?" *Regulation*, September/ December 1984, p. 37, accessed June 17, 2011, http://www.cato.org/pubs/regulation/regv8n5/v8n5-6.pdf.

implement state laws that disenfranchised blacks. Literacy tests and poll taxes were among the most common methods used. By 1890, very few blacks were eligible to vote in the Southern states. The voting requirements also excluded many poor whites, but an exception was made for them. Anyone who had been eligible to vote or who was related to someone eligible to vote—such as a grandfather—prior to the Civil War was not subject to the new voting rules (this is the source of the term "grandfather clause"). This provision excluded blacks, whose ancestors had been slaves and therefore ineligible to vote. Most whites, however, met the terms of the provision and were eligible to vote.

With blacks now prohibited from voting, the Southern Democratic legislatures began to enact the Jim Crow laws. While the specifics varied from state to state, they generally contained four key provisions:

> 1. Labor contracts had to be negotiated at the start of the year. This allowed the plantation owners to negotiate when labor demands were low and also provided them with greater certainty that their labor needs would be met during planting and harvesting seasons. Further, it was made a criminal (rather than a civil) offense to break a labor contract or to "entice" laborers to break a labor contract. For landowners, these laws helped reduce competition for labor at the times of peak demand, which drove down wages. For the laborers, these laws greatly decreased both their bargaining power and their wages.
>
> 2. It was made illegal to recruit laborers for work in another state or county. Prior to Jim Crow, employment agents had thrived. These agents advertised and recruited for plantation owners willing to pay higher wages. This was beneficial for the laborers, who could easily find better opportunities, but it created labor shortages in areas with lower wages. As an example, by World War I, so many laborers were leaving Montgomery, Alabama, that the city passed an ordinance making it illegal to entice laborers to take employment outside

of the city. The penalties were a $100 fine, up to six months of hard labor, or both.[10]

3. Vagrancy laws essentially made it illegal to be out of work, even temporarily. This made it almost impossible for laborers to seek higher paying work, as they were subject to arrest if they were "strolling about."[11]

4. Those who were unable to pay the fines for vagrancy or for breaking a labor contract were often sentenced to chain gangs, which were then leased to plantation owners. The mortality rate on the chain gangs was often as high as 45 percent,[12] which meant that the penalty for breaking a labor contract or vagrancy statute was often a death sentence.

Combined, these laws essentially put black laborers into virtual slavery. The laborers were legally prohibited from negotiating on equal terms or acting on their own judgment. They could no longer contract freely. The penalties for breaking a contract or for vagrancy greatly discouraged blacks from seeking better employment. What the plantation cartel could not achieve through voluntary means was achieved through government force. The plantation owners had the steady source of labor that they needed and at more profitable prices.

Prior to the Jim Crow laws, plantation owners competed against one another for labor. Though there were informal agreements to refrain from such bidding wars, individual plantation owners ultimately acted in their own self-interest and competed for labor. Of course, this increased wages to the benefit of laborers and the perceived detriment of the plantation owners. Some plantation owners responded by using government force in the form of Jim Crow laws to impose restrictions on everyone—neither plantation owners nor laborers could act as they judged best.

When the market was free, plantation owners had a motivation—their desire to plant and harvest crops—to put aside their racism and negotiate with black laborers. Those who valued

10. Ibid., pp. 38-39.
11. Ibid., p. 38.
12. Ibid., p. 39.

their racist views more than their profit were free to act accordingly and they suffered the consequences. But they couldn't force blacks or other plantation owners to accept their terms. It was only through Jim Crow laws, that is, government coercion, that racists were able to form a "successful" cartel and impose their racism on others. They could not do this when the market was free. Nor was this the only example of government—not businesses or private individuals—promoting racism.

Throughout the South, city governments passed ordinances mandating a separation of the races on streetcars. In virtually every instance, the streetcar companies resisted, arguing that such mandates imposed additional costs and alienated black customers (who often boycotted the streetcars, which then depressed company revenues). Jennifer Roback concluded: "Many streetcar companies refused to enforce the law because they believed it would be too expensive. There is little indication that streetcar companies initiated legislation or that they would have segregated in the absence of legislation."[13] In short, private businesses had no desire or intention to segregate on the basis of race; they had to be forced to do so by government mandates.

Unfortunately, the streetcars companies did not oppose the ordinances on moral grounds—their right to operate their businesses according to their own judgment. Instead, their opposition focused on practical (i.e., economic) matters. They accepted government intervention as morally legitimate. Legislators regarded the fact that the private businesses would suffer economically as simply the price they must pay for the "public interest." After all, according to altruism—which businessmen did not challenge—the streetcar business owners had a moral duty to sacrifice for others. In this case, the "others" were white racists who could not achieve segregation through voluntary means.

Interestingly, prior to these racist ordinances, many of the streetcar companies had segregated customers, requiring smokers to sit at the back of cars. White smokers were among the most vocal critics of the ordinances, as they were prevented from sitting in the back of cars and could no longer smoke as they rode. When a legitimate problem arose—smoking irritated some customers—the

---

13. Jennifer Roback, "*The* Political Economy of Segregation: The Case of Segregated Streetcars," *The Journal of Economic History 46*, no. 4 (December 1986:, p. 916.

streetcar companies voluntarily solved that problem without the need for government intervention. When an illegitimate problem arose—some whites did not like to sit with blacks—the streetcar companies had to be forced to "solve" the problem.

As both the laborer and streetcar examples show, racist policies were not implemented by private individuals and businesses. They were mandated by state and city governments. When the market was free, all parties could contract according to their own judgment, but they could not impose their choices on others. And even when individuals held racist ideas, their self-interest often motivated them to put aside their irrationality. When they didn't, they suffered economically. When the market was free, the racists were at a competitive disadvantage. Only when government intervened and prohibited individuals from freely contracting were the racists protected from the economic consequences of their ideas.

A similar pattern continues today in regard to other forms of irrational discrimination, especially sexual orientation. As principles, freedom of contract and freedom of association are applicable to all individuals, regardless of race, gender, or sexual orientation. If two individuals wish to associate or enter a contract, that is their right, and it is government's responsibility to recognize and enforce the terms of a contract that they enter. This is true of any voluntary agreement between consenting adults, whether that agreement pertains to employment, a business service, or marriage.[14]

The issue of gay marriage—which is a contractual agreement—is a heated political issue. Many conservative politicians have introduced legislation prohibiting certain adults—gays—from entering voluntary contracts with one another. In other words, government coercion is sought as the means to deny gays their moral right to freedom of association and contract. As in the case of the Jim Crow era, private businesses are responding differently.

Motivated by their self-interest, a growing number of companies are offering benefits to gays and their partners as a means of attracting better employees. The Human Rights Campaign Foundation (HRCF), a gay-advocacy organization that rates large

---

14. This discussion pertains to consenting adults who are not suffering from mental disease or handicaps. It is proper to restrict the freedom to contract of children and mentally handicapped adults–they are not capable of understanding the consequences of their choices.

companies for their policies regarding lesbian, gay, bisexual, and transgender (LGBT) people, has found that companies are increasingly LGBT-friendly. The director of the Workplace Project at HRCF explained, "The private sector has realized that treating all of its employees fairly is actually a better way to create a productive workforce and to attract the best and brightest employees, regardless of their background."[15] The self-interest of the business—not the law—is providing the motivation. The self-interest a business motivates it to recognize the rights of gays, even as government seeks to violate their rights by banning gay marriages.

Raytheon, a defense, aerospace, and technology company, is one example. The company actively recruits gays, stressing its anti-discriminatory policies. Said one Raytheon executive: "Over the next ten years we're going to need anywhere from 30,000 to 40,000 new employees. We can't afford to turn our back on anyone in the talent pool."[16] In an industry with intense competition for talented engineers, Raytheon recognizes that its success—its self-interest—is best served by focusing on rational criteria when hiring. That means hiring individuals on the basis of their engineering talent, not on the basis of whom they sleep with. And less rational competitors will be at a distinct disadvantage.

As these examples show, when individuals and businesses are free to act according to their judgment in the pursuit of their own values, they will demonstrate the practical benefits of rational ideas. The self-interest of each individual will motivate him to reject irrational ideas, such as racism, sexism, and homophobia. Those who do not, ultimately suffer the consequences of their ideas, unless they can use the coercive power of government to impose their views on others. In a capitalist society, rational self-interest is rewarded. As we have seen, freedom of contract allows each individual to choose the economic opportunities that he judges best for his life. The mutual rights of others motivates a person to reach

---

15. David Schepp, "People@Work: American Companies Keep Getting More Gay-Friendly", DailyFinance.com, accessed January 29, 2011, http://www.dailyfinance.com/story/company-news/people-work-american-companies-keep-getting-more-gay-friendly/19366942/.

16. Marc Gunther, "Queer Inc.", Fortune.com, November 30 2006, accessed January 29, 2011, http://money.cnn.com/magazines/fortune/fortune_archive/2006/12/11/8395465/index.htm.

agreements that benefit all involved. And, when that cannot be done, each individual is free to seek other opportunities. Let us now examine how this applies to the workplace.

8

Free the Employers

In 1995, Craig Biggio, an All-Star second baseman for the Houston Astros baseball team, was a free agent. He received offers from several teams, but ultimately decided to stay with the Astros for less money. "I want the team to succeed here," Biggio said at the time. "We're going to make it work and win a championship."[1] Some might think Biggio foolish for taking less money to stay with a team that had never been to the World Series. But Biggio's decision wasn't based solely on money; he had other values that he sought, and he made the decision that he thought was best for him. Should he have been prohibited from accepting less money?

In regard to Biggio and other well-paid employees, most Americans would say that employees have a right to accept any wage they deem appropriate. Yet, many Americans, if not most, believe that other workers should not have that same right. Many support the idea that workers should not be free to negotiate the terms of their employment or accept a wage that others think is below market value. Some believe that government must intervene and "protect" workers. After all, without labor laws mandating minimum wages, benefits, and safety standards, wouldn't employees be left to the mercy of their employers? What would stop employers from demanding longer working hours, offering fewer benefits, and taking advantage of workers? Wouldn't employers subject employees to dangerous working conditions in an effort to cut costs

1. Terry Blount, "Birthday Boy Biggio Gives Astros Reason to Cheer," *Houston Chronicle*, December 15, 1995, STAR edition, accessed June 3, 2011, http://www.chron.com/CDA/archives/archive.mpl?id=1995_1313234.

and maximize profits? Aren't some regulations required to "protect" workers?

Certainly, nobody wants to labor under conditions resembling those of a medieval serf. As we will soon see, the self-interest of employers motivates them to provide safe working conditions and treat their employees well. Just as a business cannot attract customers by selling dangerous, over-priced products, it cannot attract employees by offering dangerous, under-paid jobs. In truth, it is government intervention that stifles safety innovations, creates unemployment, and prevents employees from freely contracting their labor for terms that they find acceptable. As we have seen in regard to racism and homophobia, capitalism rewards rational action; government intervention prevents rational action. This applies to every aspect of the employee/employer relationship. To understand how government intervention creates problems in the workplace, let us first briefly look at the history of labor legislation in America.

Until the Progressive Era, employers and employees were generally free to negotiate the terms of employment, including hours worked. In the late nineteenth century a growing number of states began enacting legislation that limited work hours. Many of these statutes were challenged in court, with very different results. For example, in *Holden v. Hardy* (1898), the United States Supreme Court upheld a Utah law limiting miners to an eight-hour work day. Citing the government's "police power," the court ruled that, while it "cannot be put forward as an excuse for oppressive and unjust legislation, it may be lawfully resorted to for the purpose of preserving the public health, safety, or morals."[2] In *Lochner v. New York* (1905), the Court struck down a New York law that limited bakers to a ten-hour work day, finding that the statute "is not a legitimate exercise of the police power of the State, but an unreasonable, unnecessary and arbitrary interference with the right and liberty of the individual to contract in relation to labor..."[3] Though the Court found this particular use of the police power unconstitutional, in principle, it accepted the use of that power to regulate contracts between employers and employees. It wouldn't be long before state and federal legislators began passing laws

---

2. Holden v. Hardy, 169 U.S. 366 (1898).
3. Lochner v. People of State of New York, 198 U.S. 45 (1905)

regulating and controlling the employer/employee relationship with the intention of "preserving the public health, safety, or morals."

While the state laws generally pertained to work hours, the most sweeping labor laws were federal statutes pertaining to labor unions. For example, the Clayton Act in 1914 exempted labor unions from anti-trust laws, which would have otherwise made unions illegal. In 1932, the Norris-LaGuardia Act gave unions further protections, such as prohibiting "yellow-dog contracts." (A "yellow-dog contract" is an "employment agreement whereby a worker promises not to join a Labor Union or promises to resign from a union if he or she is already a member."[4]) The National Labor Relations Act of 1935 made it illegal for employers "to refuse to bargain collectively with the representatives of his employees."[5] These laws, and others like them, grant increasing power to union leaders, compel employers to negotiate with those leaders, and effectively prevent employees from contracting their labor as they judge best. For example, if your workplace is unionized, you are bound by the contract negotiated by the union, and in many instances you must also pay union dues, regardless of your own judgment or desires. If you are hardworking, industrious, and ambitious, it is illegal for your employer to offer you additional responsibilities, or a promotion, or even a raise, if doing so violates the union contract—a contract neither of you voluntarily entered.

As a report by the Cato Institute states, because of pro-union legislation, "workers have lost a substantial amount of their freedom to contract for the terms of their employment" and "employers have lost the ability to negotiate with employees, being required by law to negotiate 'in good faith' with the union leadership."[6] If you are a union member, you are legally prohibited from negotiating your own employment terms, and your employer is legally prohibited from negotiating directly with you. In short, neither you nor your employer can act according to your own judgment. And both of you are likely to suffer the consequences.

---

4. "Yellow Dog Contract," TheFreeDictionary.com, accessed June 22, 2011, http://legal-dictionary.thefreedictionary.com/Yellow+Dog+Contract.

5. National Labor Relations Act, Section 8(a)(5), National Labor Relations Board, accessed June 14, 2011, http://www.nlrb.gov/national-labor-relations-act.

6. Randall G. Holcombe and James D. Gwartney, "Unions, Economic Freedom, and Growth," *Cato Journal 30*, no. 1 (Winter 2010): p. 5, accessed January 8, 2011, http://www.cato.org/pubs/journal/cj30n1/cj30n1-1.pdf.

The Cato report concludes: "Union contracts likely would not contain some of the provisions they do were it not for the bargaining power labor law gives unions relative to the employers of union labor."[7] Those provisions are arguably beneficial—in the short-term—to those who have a union job, for they obtain higher wages while preventing other workers from finding any work at all. But studies have shown that, in the long-term, union labor contracts are harmful to employers, employees, consumers, and the economy in general.

As an example, the bankruptcies of General Motors (GM) and Chrysler were, at least in part, a result of contracts negotiated by the United Auto Workers (UAW) union. The health benefits for UAW members added $1,200 to the price of each vehicle manufactured by GM in 2007. The Heritage Foundation found that additional benefits, "such as full retirement after 30 years of employment and the recently eliminated JOBS bank (which paid workers for not working), added more."[8] In 2008, the *Christian Science Monitor* reported that non-union auto workers made $25.65 an hour compared to $36.34 for union autoworkers, and benefits such as pensions and health care drove the hourly compensation to almost $70 per hour for union workers.[9] These costs made it increasingly difficult for GM and Chrysler to compete with non-unionized automakers and were a major contributor to their eventual bankruptcy, government bailouts, and massive layoffs.[10] The "benefits" of the UAW contract did not last, and Michigan's unemployment rate soared to 14.6 percent in July of 2009. You might think that Detroit is an isolated example, but is it?

The consequences of unionization are not limited to the auto industry. Indeed, for decades the trend in the United States has been that manufacturing companies using union labor have seen a decrease in jobs while companies using non-union labor have

---

7. Ibid., p. 2.

8. James Sherk, "What Unions Do: How Labor Unions Affect Jobs and the Economy," Backgrounder, The Heritage Foundation, No. 2275, May 21, 2009, accessed January 8, 2011, http://www.heritage.org/Research/Reports/2009/05/What-Unions-Do-How-Labor-Unions-Affect-Jobs-and-the-Economy.

9. "Dixie Welcomes Non-union Auto Jobs," UPI.com, December 4, 2008, accessed January 21, 2011, http://www.upi.com/Top_News/2008/12/04/Dixie-welcomes-non-union-auto-jobs/UPI-17151228433854/.

10. Ford was a notable exception among Detroit's "Big Three" automakers and did not require government bailouts.

increased jobs. Heritage reports that "[u]nionized manufacturing jobs fell by 75 percent between 1977 and 2008. Non-union manufacturing employment increased by 6 percent over that time."[11] During the same period, union construction jobs decreased by about 255,000, while non-union construction jobs increased by about four million.[12] The reason for this shift is that companies using union labor are less competitive, less profitable, and have less investment capital.

Heritage found that unionized companies earn from 10 to 15 percent less profit than comparable non-union companies. Lower profits mean that unionized companies have less money for research and development: "One study found that unions directly reduce capital investment by 6 percent and indirectly reduce capital investment through lower profits by another 7 percent. This same study also found that unions reduce R&D activity by 15 percent to 20 percent."[13] These studies clearly show that unionization—as it currently exists in America—is not good for the long-term health of a business. What does this say about unions? Are unions inherently bad?

To be clear, unions *per se* are not the problem. The problem is unions backed with the coercive power of government. Current labor legislation forces businesses to "negotiate" with the unions or be prosecuted for violating labor laws. This is akin to "negotiations" between a banker and a robber—one side can issue ultimatums punctuated with "or else." And "or else" means the threat of force. America's labor laws effectively prohibit business owners with unionized labor from operating as they judge best. Those laws impose similar restrictions on employees. The dramatic difference in union versus non-union job creation clearly demonstrates that these laws are impractical. Further, the voluntary actions of both employers and employees show that when each can act according to his own judgment, the overwhelming choice is non-union. Only government intervention—in the form of labor laws—can prevent employees and employers from contracting with one another as they judge best.

---

11. Sherk, "What Unions Do."
12. Ibid.
13. Ibid.

When government intervention prevents a business from controlling its costs, the business will either go bankrupt—as GM and Chrysler did—or it will move to jurisdictions that allow it to control costs, such as China, Mexico, or states with "right-to-work" laws. (Right-to-work laws prohibit agreements between labor unions and employers that make membership in unions or payment of union dues a condition of employment. Such laws are as immoral as those that compel employers to negotiate with labor union leaders. Government should not be involved in the employer/employee relationship.) For example, when foreign automakers such as Kia, Toyota, and BMW wanted to build plants in America, they chose Southern states with right-to-work laws. Since 1986, Detroit automakers have decreased employment by six hundred thousand jobs, while foreign automakers have created thirty-five thousand jobs.[14] As another example, when Boeing wanted to build an additional plant, it chose a right-to-work state—South Carolina. Frequently plagued by union strikes, one Boeing executive said that the company "cannot afford to have a work stoppage… every three years."[15] Labor strikes cost money and prevent a company from meeting its contractual obligations to customers. (Shortly before the plant was to open in June 2011, the National Labor Relations Board declared the plant illegal. The issue was not resolved as this book went to publication.)

If employees choose to bargain collectively, that is their right as individuals. Simultaneously, the employer has a right to refuse to bargain with a union or any other group of employees. He also has a right to act on his judgment. Neither party can morally use coercion to make the other act differently than he thinks is best. Government has no prerogative in the relationship between employer and employee, other than enforcing the contracts that are freely entered.

While pro-union legislation kills jobs, minimum wage laws are weapons of mass destruction. First enacted with the Fair Labor Standards Act of 1938, minimum wage laws have destroyed millions

---

14. Patrik Jonsson, "America's 'Other' Auto Industry," *The Christian Science Monitor*, December 5, 2008, accessed June 22, 2011, http://www.csmonitor.com/Business/2008/1205/p01s04-usec.html.

15. Stephen Greenhouse, "Labor Board Tells Boeing New Factory Breaks Law," *The New York Times*, April 20, 2011, accessed June 22, 2011, http://www.nytimes.com/2011/04/21/business/21boeing.html.

of jobs. By making it illegal to pay a wage below the minimum, minimum wage laws price many workers—particularly those with few job skills and less education—out of the labor market. Simply because Congress mandates a particular wage as a legal minimum does not miraculously endow workers with the skills that businesses need. If this were the case, then why doesn't Congress mandate a minimum wage of one hundred dollars per hour and legislate the nation into prosperity? The reason is simple: few, if any, businesses could afford to pay such wages and jobs would be destroyed. The consequences of a minimum wage set at five dollars an hour, or eight dollars, or any other amount, is only a matter of degree. If a teenager's labor is only worth five dollars an hour, does it make economic sense for an employer to pay him eight dollars an hour? Then again, when has Congress done anything that makes economic sense? The fact is, if a business is forced to pay a worker more than he is worth, it will likely pay him nothing—he won't be hired for the job. Congress may not be rational, but most business owners are; as Congress makes it increasingly difficult to operate a profitable business in the United States, companies are moving jobs to nations that are more business friendly, thus creating fewer jobs here.

One example of the job-destroying nature of minimum wage laws occurred in July 2009 when the minimum wage was increased from $6.55 to $7.25. A month before the increase, economist David Neumark wrote in *The Wall Street Journal*: "The best estimates from studies since the early 1990s suggest that the 11% minimum wage increase scheduled for this summer will lead to the loss of an additional 300,000 jobs among teens and young adults."[16] Nine months later, another economist, Casey B. Mulligan, wrote in *The New York Times*, that "part-time employment would have been about 500,000 greater in the last couple of months of the year if it hadn't been for that last increase in the federal minimum [wage]."[17] One doesn't need to be an economist to know that these numbers are significant.

---

16. David Neumark, "Delay the Minimum-Wage Hike," *The Wall Street Journal*, June, 12, 2009, accessed January 8, 2011, http://online.wsj.com/article/SB124476823767508619.html.

17. Casey B. Mulligan, "Did the Minimum Wage Increase Destroy Jobs?" *The New York Times*, March 10, 2010, accessed January 8, 2011, http://economix.blogs.nytimes.com/2010/03/10/did-the-minimum-wage-increase-destroy-jobs/.

While labor laws and minimum wage laws are perhaps the most visible and destructive government interventions in the workplace, they are hardly the only ones. For example, the Equal Employment Opportunity Commission (EEOC) enforces federal anti-discrimination laws, which govern hiring and promotion practices. Businesses must document virtually every human resources practice in order to comply with these laws and to defend against potential discrimination lawsuits. These costs can be significant for smaller companies. Businesses must also defend themselves against complaints of discrimination, most of which are found to be baseless. For example, in 2010 nearly one hundred thousand complaints were filed with the commission. In 64.3 percent of those cases, the EEOC found "no reasonable cause to believe that discrimination occurred based upon evidence obtained in investigation."[18] In other words, the businesses were compelled to waste time, money, and resources to defend themselves against charges that were deemed to have no merit. And if the company took any action against the employee making a baseless claim, it could be subject to a new charge of discrimination. Which means, employees can make arbitrary claims with impunity, while businesses are forced to tolerate employees who make such claims. There is no practical benefit to be derived from such policies.

Similarly, the Occupational Safety and Health Administration (OSHA) also imposes onerous costs on employers, with no practical benefit. Established in 1970, the purported purpose of OSHA is to promote safety in the workplace. In 1995, an article in *Regulation* magazine reported that the cost of meeting OSHA mandates was eleven billion dollars per year (nearly sixteen billion in 2010 dollars).[19] Despite these expenditures, the authors found that "the pre-OSHA drop in the frequency of workplace fatalities from 1947 to 1970 was 70 percent larger than the post-OSHA drop from 1970 to 1993."[20] In other words, workplace fatalities were declining

---

18. Statistics obtained from the EEOC website at http://www.eeoc.gov/eeoc/statistics/enforcement/all.cfm. Definition of "no reasonable cause" obtained from EEOC website at http://www.archive/eeoc.gov/stats/define.html. Both accessed January 21, 2011.

19. Thomas J. Kniesner and John D. Leeth, "Abolishing OSHA," *Regulation*, 1995, p. 50, accessed January 8, 2011, http://www.cato.org/pubs/regulation/regv18n4/v18n4-5.pdf.

20. Ibid., p. 49.

before OSHA was established, and the rate of that decline actually slowed after OSHA began issuing mandates. What accounts for this? The *Regulation* article goes on to state: "The leading causes of work-related deaths are now highway motor-vehicle accidents and murders by customers and coworkers, which are difficult to control using workplace safety standards. A disproportionate share of work-related deaths occur among the self-employed, who are ill-suited for OSHA's inspection/fine approach."[21] In short, OSHA's threats and fines do little to improve worker safety, while imposing needless costs and regulations on businesses.

As another example of the costs imposed by government intervention, the Americans with Disabilities Act of 1990, signed into law by President George H. W. Bush, forces businesses to accommodate those with disabilities. The removal of barriers, building ramps for wheelchairs, installing signs with Braille, and making other accommodations are among the costs imposed on business owners. And when they fail to do so, they can be forced to pay huge financial penalties. For example, a New Jersey doctor was ordered to pay $400,000 because he failed to provide an interpreter for a deaf patient.[22]

The mandates, regulations, and controls imposed by the EEOC, OSHA, and other government bureaucracies add to the cost of doing business, prevent employers (and often employees) from acting as they deem best, and provide no practical benefit. In a capitalist society, government intervention in the workplace does not exist.[23] Employers and employees are free to enter contracts as each judges appropriate. As we saw previously with black laborers in the South, when individuals have the political freedom to act according to their own judgment, each party can negotiate terms that he finds acceptable and that are mutually beneficial. It is only government intervention—such as regulations, prohibitions, and mandates—that can prevent this from occurring. This is true of

---

21. Ibid., p. 52.

22. "A Legal Spanking for an Internist Who Failed to Provide an Interpreter for Deaf Patient," MedicalJustice.com, February 5, 2009, accessed October 23, 2011, http://www.medicaljustice.com/ads/news-article.asp?article-id=503844222&email=abrooks@scoi.com&email=abrooks@scoi.com.

23. By intervention, I mean regulations and controls. If a business negligently subjects employees to dangerous conditions, or breaks contracts, or engages in fraud, or otherwise violates individual rights, government should step in.

wages, as well as other working conditions. Just as consumers can boycott businesses that practice racism, employees can shun businesses that do not pay well or offer unsafe working conditions.

At the same time that Congress is willfully destroying jobs, it seeks to "create" jobs through boondoggles such as the American Recovery and Reinvestment Act of 2009 (Obama's first stimulus package), which cost taxpayers $862 billion. And, as is usually the case, the government's projected results did not come to pass. Prior to passage of the bill, the chairwoman of the President's Council of Economic Advisors issued a report projecting that unemployment would peak at just under 8 percent.[24] In fact, unemployment peaked at more than 10 percent. At the same time that Congress is imposing mandates and prohibitions that make it increasingly difficult for business owners to create jobs, government is also taking billions of dollars out of the private sector.

While it is clear that government intervention in the employer/employee relationship is destructive, would capitalism be any better? Wouldn't employers seek to maximize their profits by cutting wages and demanding longer work hours? As we saw in the last chapter, the free market rewards rational behavior. This applies to issues such as racial discrimination, as well as wages and benefits. Henry Ford provides an example of an employer who recognized the value of paying employees well. In 1914, Ford voluntarily raised the wages of his employees to the rate of five dollars per day—nearly doubling the prevailing wage. At the same time, he cut the work day from nine hours to eight hours. In 1914, there was no union nor were there laws governing the relationship between Ford and his employees. Ford was not motivated by altruism, but by what he called "enlightened self-interest."[25] What was the result? Years later, he explained what occurred after he raised wages and reduced the work day:

> In 1914, when the first plan went into effect, we had 14,000 employees and it had been necessary to hire at the rate of about 53,000 a year in order to keep a constant force of 14,000. In 1915

24. Christina Romer and Jared Bernstein, "The Job Impact of the American Recovery and Reinvestment Plan," Council of Economic Advisors, January 9, 2009, p. 4, accessed October 23, 2011, http://otrans.3cdn.net/ee40602f9a7d8172b8_ozm6bt5oi.pdf.

25. Henry Ford, *My Life and Work* (Garden City, NY: Garden City Publishing Co., 1922), p. 119.

we had to hire only 6,508 men and the majority of these new men were taken on because of the growth of the business.[26]

Ford recognized that by paying employees a wage that was considerably higher than his competitors, he was able to attract better workers and dramatically reduce turnover. Ford recognized that this served his own self-interest, and he didn't need OSHA, or the EEOC, or any other government bureaucracy to tell him so. Ford benefited by having lower turnover, greater efficiency, and ultimately, higher profits. His employees benefited by receiving higher wages and working fewer hours. Consumers benefited from the lower prices that Ford could charge for his automobiles. Everyone benefited because Ford was free to act as he thought best. By putting his self-interest first, Ford's actions ultimately served the interest of his employees and his customers. There is no conflict when individuals pursue their own self-interest and respect the right of others to do the same.

What about worker safety? Without government oversight, wouldn't employers subject workers to dangerous conditions to cut costs? Ford was not the first employer, nor the last, to recognize that offering better wages, more benefits, safer working conditions, or a combination of the above, is beneficial to both the employer and the employee.

When the railroad industry was in its infancy, worker injuries and fatalities were high. Two innovations in the 1880s led to improved safety:

> George Westinghouse modified his passenger train air brake in about 1887 so it would work on long freights, while at roughly the same time Ely Janney developed an automatic car coupler. For the railroads such equipment meant not only better safety, but also higher productivity and after 1888 they began to deploy it.[27]

Though these devices were soon mandated by the Interstate Commerce Commission (the federal agency regulating railroads),

---

26. Ibid., p. 129.

27. Mark Aldrich, "History of Workplace Safety in the United States, 1880-1970," EH.net, accessed January 21, 2011, http://eh.net/encyclopedia/article/aldrich.safety.workplace.us.

they were initially deployed by the railroads as a matter of their own self-interest. The railroads recognized the benefits to their business and their employees: improved efficiency and greater safety for employees.

Like many businessmen, Westinghouse was an innovator in other ways. He also provided superior working conditions for employees:

> Working conditions at the Westinghouse Air Brake Company (WA&B) were more than proficient and the company had many new developments in effect for its employees. In 1869 it was one of the first companies to institute a 9-hour work day and a 55-hour work week. [A ten-hour work day and six-day work week was common in most industries as late as 1900.] WA&B also got the reputation for being the first industry in America to adopt half holidays on Saturday afternoons. A series of welfare options were also instituted to better the working and living conditions of its employees.[28]

As with Henry Ford, Westinghouse recognized that better conditions for his employees resulted in greater productivity, and therefore, improved profits.

Industrialists are not the only businessmen to recognize the benefits of "enlightened self-interest." In 1842, a French house painter—Edme Jean LeClaire—instituted a profit-sharing program for his employees. Recognized as the "father" of modern profit sharing, LeClaire "was determined to challenge the assumption that profit sharing would not increase efficiency and productivity enough to justify the payments made. He was proved right. His business prospered."[29]

Will every business owner recognize these truths? Will every business owner pay his employees above-market wages and offer greater benefits than competitors? Obviously not. But when employees are free to contract their labor, they can seek better jobs. A rational business owner will seek the best and brightest

---

28. "Westinghouse Air Brake Company," *Wikipedia*, accessed January 21, 2011, http://en.wikipedia.org/wiki/Westinghouse_Air_Brake_Company.

29. "Do You Share the Company's Profits?" *Changing Times*, December 1970, p. 49, accessed January 21, 2011, http://books.google.com/books?id=mwcEAAAAMBAJ&printsec=frontcover#v=onepage&q&f=false.

employees he can find. Such employees are the means by which he will achieve greater profits. A less rational business owner will suffer economically, whether he is engaging in racism or paying below-market wages.

As these examples demonstrate, the pursuit of one's self-interest does not entail a callous disregard for others. It recognizes that cooperative endeavors, such as business, must be mutually beneficial to all parties involved. When individuals are free to contract as each judges best, rather than being forced to follow the dictates of politicians and bureaucrats, employers find innovative ways to achieve their values, including offering higher wages, safer working conditions, and better benefits. As Ford, Westinghouse, and others have demonstrated, an employer's pursuit of his own self-interest also benefits employees and customers.

Morally, you have a right to engage in the economic transactions that you think are best for your life. Right or wrong, it is your life. You have a right to contract with whom you choose and on the terms and conditions that you find acceptable. This is true whether you are a free-agent baseball player, an auto worker, a secretary, an engineer, or a business owner. It is true of all individuals.

Freedom of contract and association is not limited by one's place of birth. Indeed, individual rights apply to all individuals, including immigrants. Let us now see how individual rights apply to immigration.

9

Juan has Rights, Too

If an American wanted to move from Miami to Seattle, a distance of more than 3,400 miles, all he must do is load up his belongings and hit the road. However, if a Canadian wanted to move from Windsor, Ontario, to Detroit, Michigan, a distance of less than one mile, he must first obtain the permission of the United States government. To obtain permission, he must complete a myriad of forms, undergo medical testing, and be interviewed. Even if he is not a criminal, a would-be terrorist, or infected with a dangerous disease, he will be denied permission to move to America if he is not deemed "desirable." If he does not have the proper work skills, or relatives in America, or meet other limited criteria, he is not wanted. Even if he were to meet those criteria, if the quotas for his nationality or job skills have been filled, he may also be denied entry. If you had the good fortune to be born in America, you can freely live anywhere within the nation's borders. But if you had been born just one mile outside of America, you cannot legally move to America without government permission.

For a low-skilled worker with no relatives in America, the chances of gaining lawful entry into the country are about as good as President Obama reading this book—it's *not* going to happen. What is such an individual to do when his native country offers few opportunities? Should he simply waste his life in poverty and despair? Should the place of his birth preclude his pursuit of happiness?

Millions of individuals have chosen to enter America illegally, where they are increasingly unwelcome. A growing number of states and municipalities have passed or are considering legislation aimed at illegal aliens and those who associate with them. For example,

Georgia enacted legislation prohibiting the transportation of illegal immigrants, for any purpose, such as driving an illegal immigrant to the store. The cities of Farmers Branch, Texas, and Hazelton, Pennsylvania, approved ordinances that impose fines on landlords who rent to illegal aliens. Why? Why the hostility towards illegal immigrants and those who associate with them?

Many arguments are offered to justify laws aimed at illegal immigrants: Illegal aliens take jobs from Americans. They burden our social services and public schools. Illegal immigrants are trying to change the American culture. They refuse to learn English or assimilate. Illegal aliens are unleashing a wave of crime. But are these claims true? Are illegal immigrants changing American society? Is the answer to illegal immigration a border fence and fining businesses that employ them? How do individual rights apply to this controversial issue?

To help us answer these questions, let us first examine the Fourteenth Amendment to the Constitution. Ratified after the Civil War, the Fourteenth Amendment prohibits state and local governments from depriving individuals of the rights to life, liberty, and property without due process:

> No State shall make or enforce any law which shall abridge the privileges or immunities of citizens of the United States; nor shall any State deprive any person of life, liberty, or property, without due process of law; *nor deny to any person within its jurisdiction the equal protection of the laws* [emphasis added].

The Amendment recognizes that individual rights apply to all individuals—both citizens and non-citizens. However, the popular conservative website RedState argues otherwise:

> The key thought in the 14th Amendment which along with several other provisions established in the Constitution shows that the intent of the Framers was that only citizens of the United States whether born or naturalized are granted the rights and privileges that are available in America....
>
> This does not mean that those who immigrate legally to The United States are treated as second class people or that the laws that protect our citizens whether civil or criminal do not afford the same protections and freedoms to all whether citizen or legal immigrant.

> But the rights that we have to vote, to speak freely, to worship as we will, to keep and bear arms, protection from illegal search and seizure, all are *rights given by authority of the people* [emphasis added] for the people, the citizens of the land. It then is also established that any of these rights that may be afforded or not afforded to non-citizens are given ONLY by the authority of the people of The United States.[1]

First, it should be noted that the Fourteenth Amendment was ratified in 1868, and the last Framer to die was James Madison—in 1836. Therefore, the intent of the Framers cannot be ascribed to the Fourteenth Amendment. Second, what does it mean that rights are "given by authority of the people"? What does "these rights that may be afforded or not afforded" actually mean?

If rights are "given by authority of the people," if rights may be "afforded or not afforded," then rights are merely permissions which may be revoked by "the people" at any time. If freedom of speech, freedom of religion, and protection against illegal search and seizure are "rights given by authority of the people," then government can impose censorship, mandate religious beliefs, and break into homes whenever "the people" choose. In truth, individuals hold "these rights, not from the Collective ['the people'] nor for the Collective, but against the Collective—as a barrier which the Collective cannot cross; . . . these rights are man's protection against all other men."[2] Your rights put a boundary on the actions of others, including "the people."

Protecting the rights of the minority, and the individual is the smallest minority, is precisely what the Founders sought in the Constitution. James Madison, for example, stated that "on a candid examination of history, we shall find that turbulence, violence, and abuse of power, by the majority trampling on the rights of the minority, have produced factions and commotions, which, in republics, have, more frequently than any other cause, produced despotism."[3] The Founders did not advocate for the unlimited

1. Ken Taylor, "The Constitution is the Rule of Law on Illegal Immigration," RedState, April 28, 2010, accessed July 7, 2011, http://www.redstate.com/ken_taylor/2010/04/28/the-constitution-is-the-rule-of-law-on-illegal-immigration/.

2. Ayn Rand, "Textbook of Americanism," *The Ayn Rand Column*, p. 83, accessed October 1, 2011, http://aynrandlexicon.com/lexicon/individual_rights.html.

3. James Madison, Speech at the Virginia Convention to Ratify the Federal Constitution, June 6, 1788, accessed September 3, 2011, http://www.constitution.org/rc

power of "the people," but rather, a government in which the rights of individuals are protected from the passions of the majority.

Rights pertain to freedom of action—they sanction your freedom to act without coercion, interference, or permission from others, including government. Rights protect your freedom to live your life as you choose, no matter how many of "the people" disagree with your choices. So long as you respect the mutual rights of others, morally, "the people" must respect *your* rights.

Individual rights are not "given by authority of the people," nor are rights subject to a vote or the approval of "the people." Individual rights apply to all individuals. The Declaration of Independence does not say that rights pertain only to those born in America, but rather "that *all* men are created equal, that they are endowed by their Creator with certain unalienable Rights, that among these are Life, Liberty and the pursuit of Happiness." As philosopher Harry Binswanger writes, "One has rights not by virtue of being an American, but by virtue of being human."[4] An individual has the right to speak freely, worship as he chooses, and be protected from illegal search and seizure, whether he was born in Memphis or Mexico City.

As we have seen, government—"the people"—can fail to recognize and protect your rights. Government can force you to subsidize mail delivery, pay for parks and libraries that you do not want, and provide "entitlements" for the poor and needy. Government can enact laws that prohibit you from operating a mail delivery service or require you to obtain permission to enter the profession of your choice. Government can make it illegal to accept a wage that it deems too low or make education compulsory. Government can violate your rights by forcing you to act contrary to your own judgment. Only force can prevent you from associating with those you choose. Only force can prevent you from speaking your mind (or punish you for doing so), worshipping as you choose, or subject you to illegal search and seizure. Only the initiation of force can violate your rights.

Immigrating to America does not violate anyone's rights, nor does seeking employment for lower wages than another worker.

/rat_va_05.htm.

4. Harry Binswanger, "Open Immigration," accessed January 18, 2011, http://www.hblist.com/immigr.htm.

Each individual has a moral right to choose where to live, to choose with whom to contract, to choose his profession or trade, and to accept any wage that he finds acceptable. So long as an individual respects the mutual rights of others, that is, he does not initiate force or engage in fraud, his actions should be of no concern to the government.

Nobody disputes that illegal aliens are breaking the law as it stands today. But, it was illegal to harbor fugitive slaves prior to the Civil War. It was illegal to drink alcohol during Prohibition. If you live in Texas, it is illegal to contract with your teenage neighbor to repair your computer if he has not obtained a government license. We should recognize the fact that laws that criminalize these voluntary, non-coercive actions are unjust and immoral. Such laws violate individual rights. And so do laws that limit immigration. Laws that limit immigration or impose sanctions on businesses that hire illegal aliens violate the rights of both the immigrants and businessmen. Such laws prevent individuals from associating and contracting as they judge best. Rather than demanding that government "crack down" on those who are breaking immoral laws, our efforts should be spent on changing those laws.

America, of course, is a nation of immigrants. Virtually every American has ancestors who immigrated to America. Until the 1920s, immigrants from around the world were welcomed with nearly no restrictions. The descendent of one immigrant wrote: "Passports weren't required, and 98 percent of all immigrants to Castle Garden [a precursor to Ellis Island] in New York Harbor were admitted. Citizenship was not as easy to acquire, but the concept of illegal immigration did not yet exist. Almost anyone who wanted to move to America was free to do so."[5]

One notable exception to this policy pertained to the Chinese. In the later half of the nineteenth century, Chinese began to immigrate to the United States in large numbers. Like other immigrants before them, such as the Italians and the Irish, the Chinese were willing to work for lower wages than other workers, and they were soon seen as an economic threat: "When Irish

---

5. Claire Lui, "How Illegal Immigration Was Born," AmericanHeritage.com, accessed January 18, 2011, http://www.americanheritage.com/articles/web/20070507-chinese-exclusion-act-california-chester-a-arthur-immigration-san-francisco-earthquake-of-1906-paper-sons.shtml.

factory workers in San Francisco went on strike in 1870, demanding an increase in pay from three to four dollars a day, they were quickly replaced by Chinese who accepted only a dollar a day."[6] It wasn't long before non-Chinese began demanding government intervention. In 1879, an editorial in *Harper's Weekly* spoke to the issue, citing comments made by California Representative Horace Davis:

> The new-comers are trained by centuries of want to live in a poverty and to be satisfied with wages which would barbarize our own laboring class. He [Davis] holds that it is no wiser to leave the question to be settled by competition than for the farmer to leave the grain and the weeds to fight it out in the field, and that the California laborer is entitled to protection as much as the sugar-planter of Louisiana, or the iron-worker of Pennsylvania, or the cotton-spinner of Massachusetts. The objects of republican government are not cheap labor and the accumulation of wealth, but the creation of a prosperous, happy, and united people. Mr. Davis contends that if the invasion be not checked, American labor will be driven from the Pacific coast…[7]

If the object of a republican government is "the creation of a prosperous, happy, and united people," how is this to occur with exclusion and racism? Further, how is a nation to be prosperous, if not by the accumulation of wealth? The claims made by Davis are repeated today by opponents of immigration, and these claims are as false today as they were in the nineteenth century.

There is no such thing as a right to a job or a right to a "living wage." There is only the right of employers to offer a job and the right of employees to accept or reject that offer. Rights pertain to freedom of action—the freedom to make choices and act accordingly. If an individual, immigrant or American, is willing to accept a lower wage than other workers, he violates nobody's rights. Other workers remain free to make their own choices and act accordingly. Just as minimum wage laws do not endow workers with skills that will command a higher wage, restrictions on immigration do not give American workers more valuable skills.

6. Ibid.

7. "The Chinese Again," *Harper's Weekly*, October 18, 1879, p. 822, accessed January 16, 2011, http://immigrants.harpweek.com/.

Government intervention, whether through pro-union legislation, minimum wage laws, or limitations on immigration, violate the rights of both the employer and the employee to contract as he chooses.

Sadly, many accepted Davis' arguments, and a few years later the Chinese Exclusion Act of 1882 virtually halted the immigration of Chinese for nearly sixty years. With this exception, there were virtually no restrictions on immigrating to America until the early twentieth century.

In the 1920s, Congress began limiting immigration. Quotas were imposed by nation of origin, based first on the 1910 census and then on the 1890 census. These quotas were imposed to reduce the immigration of southern and eastern Europeans, who were deemed less "desirable" than those from the northern part of the continent. Thus the change in the basis year—the ratio of northern to southern and eastern Europeans was more "favorable" in 1890. Emanuel Celler, a critic of the 1924 Immigration Act, noted:

> If you were of Anglo-Saxon origin, you could have over two-thirds of the quota numbers allotted to your people. If you were Japanese, you could not come in at all. That, of course, had been true of the Chinese since 1880. If you were southern or eastern European, you could dribble in and remain on sufferance.[8]

Similar quota systems exist today, and they serve to greatly restrict the number of legal immigrants. However, the number of people who desire to live in America greatly exceeds those quotas and thus the influx of illegal immigrants. In response to the millions of illegal immigrants in the United States, politicians and pundits are demanding action against illegal aliens and the businesses that employee them. So, are illegal immigrants placing a burden on our social services? Are they taking jobs from Americans?

To the extent that immigrants place additional burdens on social services such as health care and public schools—and studies show that this is not generally the case—the fault does not lie with the immigrants. The fault lies with the "entitlement" state and the morality that supports it. According to altruism, and Barack Obama,

---

8. "1917 Immigration Act," Spartacus Educational, accessed April 14, 2011, http://www.spartacus.schoolnet.co.uk/USAE1917A.htm.

we are our brother's keeper. Illegal immigrants represent new "brothers," and while altruism demands that we satisfy their needs, most Americans also recognize that such a perceived financial burden cannot continue. However, rather than question the morality of altruism and its manifestation in public schools and the "entitlement" state, the blame is placed on illegal immigrants. Rather than look in the mirror and blame the Americans who support the legalized theft that finances these public institutions, they blame the illegal immigrant. The fact is, *nobody* has a moral claim to the property of others, and one's place of birth does not change that fact. Those born in Topeka have no more claim to their neighbor's property than those born in Tampico or Toronto.

But most illegal immigrants do *not* come to America to live on welfare. And they "contribute" far more to the "entitlement" state than they receive. First, the 1996 Personal Responsibility and Work Opportunity Reconciliation Act "disqualified illegal immigrants from nearly all means-tested government programs including food stamps, housing assistance, Medicaid and Medicare-funded hospitalization. The only services that illegals can still get are emergency medical care and K-12 education."[9] Second, illegal immigrants pay sales taxes and property taxes (both directly and indirectly). Approximately 67 percent of illegal aliens pay Social Security taxes, Medicare taxes, and income tax withholding, even though they are ineligible for Social Security and Medicare, and most do not receive any refund of their income tax withholding. In short, it is estimated that illegal alien families "contribute on average $80,000 more to federal coffers than they consume."[10] So, who is the real burden? Illegal immigrants or Americans who live on food stamps, free health care, and other government handouts? The facts are clear: in general, illegal immigrants are not a burden on taxpayers. They are coming to America to make better lives for themselves and their families. And they have a moral right to do so.

What about crime? Are illegal aliens unleashing a violent crime wave and filling our prisons, as some have claimed? While such rhetoric certainly fans the flames of hostility towards illegal

---

9. Shikha Dalmia, "Illegal Immigrants are Paying a Lot More Taxes Than You Think," Reason Foundation, May 1, 2006, accessed October 24, 2011, http://reason.org/news/show/122411.html.

10. Ibid.

immigrants, the facts present a much different picture. According to Bureau of Justice Statistics, in "prisons at the state level, where most violent crime is prosecuted, illegal immigrants account for less than 5 percent of all inmates."[11] A report for the Police Foundation, a non-profit organization that provides research and training for law enforcement officers, found:

> Since the early 1990s, over the same time period as legal and especially illegal immigration was reaching and surpassing historic highs, crime rates have *declined*, both nationally and most notably in cities and regions of high immigrant concentration (including cities with large numbers of undocumented immigrants, such as Los Angeles and border cities like San Diego and El Paso, as well as New York, Chicago, and Miami).[12]

Other reports have reached similar conclusions. For example, the Immigration Policy Center found that "for every ethnic group, without exception, incarceration rates among young men are lowest for immigrants, even those who are the least educated. This holds true especially for the Mexicans, Salvadorans and Guatemalans who make up the bulk of the undocumented population."[13] As with claims about illegals burdening America's "entitlement" system, claims about an illegal alien crime wave are unfounded. If the facts belie these claims, why are they repeated so often? What do the opponents of illegal immigrants want?

As is often the case, when government controls and regulations create problems—and such rights-violating intervention *always* creates problems—the proposed solutions typically involve more government intervention. Conservative talk show host Glenn Beck offers an example of such "solutions." In 2008, Beck responded to claims that businesses hire illegal immigrants to fill jobs that Americans don't want:

---

11. Steve Chapman, "Immigration and Crime," *Reason Magazine*, February 22, 2010, accessed July 8, 2011, http://reason.com/archives/2010/02/22/immigration-and-crime.

12. Rubén G. Rumbaut, "Undocumented Immigration and Rates of Crime and Imprisonment: Popular Myths and Empirical Realities," Police Foundation, p. 124, accessed July 8, 2011, http://www.policefoundation.org/pdf/strikingabalance/Appendix%20D.pdf.

13. Chapman, "Immigration and Crime."

The unspoken truth is that these businesses don't hire illegal aliens because they can't find American workers, they hire illegal aliens because they don't want American workers. And it has nothing to do with wages.

Illegal aliens mean no workers' comp claims, no age, race or sex discrimination lawsuits, no healthcare premiums, no unions, and no demands for raises, vacations or bigger offices. In fact, illegal immigrants are the perfect employees because they're not employees at all; they're corporate slaves.[14]

Note the items on Beck's list that involve government intervention: worker's comp, discrimination lawsuits, and unions. His solution to these interventions is more intervention. He wants "crippling fines on the employers who knowingly hire illegal workers."[15] Further, Beck calls illegal immigrants "corporate slaves," which implies that those who hire illegals are slave masters. How does this differ from the anti-capitalists who claim that capitalism necessarily leads to racism and exploitation?

Like the progressives of the late nineteenth century and early twentieth century, Beck believes that workers have no choice in the conditions of their employment. Where the progressives railed against the "exploitation" of child labor, Beck rails against the "exploitation" of illegal immigrants. For example, in 1906 one progressive reformer wrote, "The textile industries rank first in the enslavement of children."[16] In 1900, socialist and progressive Eugene Debs condemned the employment of both women and children:

Today there is more than three million women engaged in industrial pursuits in the United States, and more than two million children. It is not a question of white labor or black labor, or male labor or female or child labor, in this system; it is solely a question of cheap labor, without reference to the effect upon mankind.[17]

---

14. Glenn Beck, "Commentary: Slavery alive and well in U.S.," CNN.com, May 28, 2008, accessed June 16, 2011, http://articles.cnn.com/2008-05-28/us/beck.immigrantworkers_1_illegal-aliens-work-visas-american-workers/2?_s=PM:US.

15. Ibid., p. 3.

16. Quoted in "Child Labor," Spartacus Educational, accessed June 18, 2011, http://www.spartacus.schoolnet.co.uk/USAchild.htm.

17. Ibid.

Like the progressives, Beck ignores the fact that, for the workers, the alternative is poverty, despair, and often, an early death. He ignores the fact that the laborers are acting on their own judgment, as they think best for their lives. He ignores the fact that, unless physical force is involved, these workers agree to the terms of their employment. (And if force is involved, government should protect the rights of the immigrants.) Illegal aliens take low-paying jobs with no benefits because, in their judgment, it is better than the alternatives that they have. Why should the judgment of Beck or anyone else supersede the judgment and rights of immigrants?

Certainly, some Americans find the conditions in which many illegal immigrants work to be unacceptable for themselves. Some find the wages paid to be insultingly low. So? The fact that some, if not many, Americans would refuse to work under such conditions does not give them a right to prohibit others from doing so. It is immoral for government to interfere in the employee/employer relationship, whether it does so by licensing occupations, by mandating collective bargaining, by setting minimum wages, or by stipulating working conditions. This is true whether the employee is an American or an immigrant. If someone wants to come to America to make a better life for himself, and he believes that taking a low wage job offers a better life than he had, what right does the government have to stop him? Why should the government impede anyone's right to associate?

Of course, if an employer intentionally misleads employees regarding the danger of a job, or claims that he has installed safety equipment when he hasn't, or withholds wages, or otherwise engages in willful neglect, the employer should be held liable. Absent fraud or intentional neglect, government should not be involved. At the same time, employees have a responsibility to determine the danger involved in a job and make decisions accordingly.

Individuals have a moral right to contract with others, whether they are business owners or employees, whether they are Americans or Mexicans, whether they were born in the state of Nebraska or born in the state of Sonora. Author Craig Biddle explains:

> Suppose, for example, a man in Los Angeles wants to work at a local car wash, and suppose the owner of that car wash wants to

> hire him. Should the two men be free to do business? Yes. And the reason *why* they should be free to do business is that each man has a moral right to act on his own judgment, so long as he does not violate the same right of others. In other words, the reason is the principle of individual rights.[18]

What if the prospective employee lived in Mexico? Does that change the principle that "each man has a moral right to act on his own judgment"? No, it does not. Biddle concludes, "A government that prohibits or limits immigration thereby initiates force against would-be immigrants—and against those Americans who want to associate with them—and thus violates the rights of both parties." The principle of individual rights—including freedom of association—applies to all individuals, not just those fortunate enough to be born in America.

Open immigration *does not* mean that anyone who wants to come to America should be free to do so. Those who pose an objective threat to Americans—criminals, would-be terrorists, and those with communicable diseases—should be rightly barred. But those who want nothing more than freedom and the opportunities that freedom provides should be welcomed with open arms and open borders. Nor does open immigration mean automatic citizenship—citizenship is a separate issue.[19] Open immigration means that those who want to live in America have a moral right to do so. Not only is this moral, it is also practical.

Immigrants are vital to economic progress. Despite the rabid (and uninformed) claims of many conservatives, illegal immigrants are not "stealing" jobs from Americans. The Cato Institute reports:

> Studies by the National Research Council and the National Bureau of Economic Research have found that immigration exerts a small negative effect on the wages of the small and declining number of Americans without a high school diploma,

---

18. Craig Biddle, "Immigration and Individual Rights," *The Objective Standard 3*, no. 1 (Spring 2008).

19. The requirements for becoming a citizen are beyond the present discussion. However, the fear of many conservatives that immigrants will overwhelmingly vote for Democrats is unfounded and patronizing. Like all individuals, immigrants possess free will, and we cannot predict how they will vote. Likewise, Democrats who want to ease the requirements for citizenship, in the belief that they will expand their voting base, are equally patronizing.

> while delivering higher real wages to the vast majority of native-born American workers. Enabling and urging young Americans to graduate from high school will do far more to raise the earnings of American workers than barring low-skilled immigrants from the country.[20]

Americans with little education and few job skills must recognize the fact that their labor is not worth much in the market. If they wish to earn higher wages, then they must increase their skills. If they fail to do so, then they must accept the wages that come with the few skills that they possess. Perhaps, writes economist Thomas E. Lehman, those clamoring about immigrants "stealing" jobs really fear "that someone will emerge from the 'immigrant class' who would be willing to work for less than they while producing equal or greater output."[21] The advocates of minimum wage laws believe that the value of low-skilled labor can be raised by legislative decree; Glenn Beck and his ilk believe that the value of low-skilled labor can be raised by barring illegal aliens. The fact is, both are wrong. Wages increase when productivity increases, not through legislative mandates. Violating the rights of business owners and employees benefits neither.

Ironically, while conservatives claim that illegal immigrants "steal" jobs, they regularly fail to oppose policies that actually kill jobs, such as minimum wage laws, occupational licensing, and legislation that forces businesses to negotiate with labor union leaders. They want to round up the pick-pockets while ignoring the murderers. Why? Why don't they spend as much time and make as much noise about polices that demonstrably kill jobs as they do about protecting the borders? Anyone concerned with job creation or freedom must demand an end to all laws that interfere with the right to contract.

Labor competition is a financial benefit to all who participate in the economic system. As Lehman notes, lower labor costs allow businesses "to offer products and services at lower prices as they compete for consumers' dollars. Lower prices in turn increase the

---

20. "Immigration," in *Cato Handbook for Policymakers,* 7th ed., (Cato Institute, 2009) p. 633, accessed January 18, 2011, http://www.cato.org/pubs/handbook/hb111/hb111-60.pdf.

21. Quoted in Thomas E. Lehman, "Coming to America: The Benefits of Open Immigration," Freeman 45, no. 12 (December 1995).

purchasing power of the American consumer, and thus enhance living standards for everyone."[22] And this includes the laborer who is willing to accept lower wages, because "what he loses in terms of lower nominal wages he may well regain in terms of lower prices on the goods and services he purchases as a consumer."[23] This is precisely what occurred during the late nineteenth century.

From 1870 to 1900, real wages—the purchasing power of money—increased approximately 20 percent.[24] During this same period, America absorbed twelve million immigrants. (The population in the United States at the 1900 census was just over seventy-six million, which means that first generation immigrants accounted for more than 16 percent of the population in 1900.) These immigrants did not come to live on welfare—there was no welfare state at the time. These immigrants came to America for the same reason Americans move from New York to Florida, or from California to Texas—the opportunity to make a better life for themselves and their family. Because many possessed few job skills, they took low paying jobs. Yet, despite driving down wages, as did the Chinese workers cited earlier, the unskilled worker's standard of living increased. How could this be? How could a worker make less money yet still improve his standard of living?

Between 1870 and 1889, wages for non-farm labor decreased from $1.57 per day to $1.39 per day, a decrease of 10.2 percent.[25] During the same period, the Consumer Price Index[26] decreased more than 23 percent.[27] Even though wages for unskilled labor fell by more than 10 percent over twenty years, prices fell by two times as much, that is, a dollar bought a lot more. Further, there was much more available: canned goods became widely available in the

---

22. Ibid.

23. Ibid.

24. Clifford Edward Clark, *The American family home, 1800-1960*, (Chapel Hill: The University of North Carolina Press, 1986), p. 121.

25. Stanley Lebergott, "Wage Trends, 1800-1900," National Bureau of Economic Research, 1960, p. 462, accessed June 29, 2011, http://www.nber.org/chapters/c2486.pdf.

26. The Consumer Price Index is a government statistic that tracks consumer price inflation. The price of a specific list of consumer goods is calculated at a specific time; this serves as the baseline price. When prices for those goods are calculated at a later time, the rate of price inflation can be determined by the price difference.

27. "Consumer Price Indexes, Series 135-166," United States Census Bureau, p. 211, accessed June 29, 2011, http://www2.census.gov/prod2/statcomp/documents/CT1970p1-06.pdf.

1880s, which provided a much more varied diet, such as fruits and vegetables that were not in season; refrigerated railroad cars made it possible for urban residents to eat fresh meat, grapes, and strawberries more frequently; improvements in the sewing machine enabled manufacturers to mass produce clothing at low prices; department stores offered consumers wide selections in clothing, household goods, and more. In short, the unskilled worker's life was immensely better in 1889 than it had been in 1870, even though he was paid less. In a free market, this will always be the case.

Furthermore, there is no shortage of work to be done. Government intervention, from occupational licensing to minimum wage laws, prevents the creation of jobs to perform that work. From mowing yards to building computers, from cleaning homes to creating software, human life requires the creation of values. In a developed economy, labor is required at all skill levels. Even in today's technological society, the United States economy continues to create thousands of new jobs each year that require relatively few skills. At the same time, "the supply of native-born Americans who have traditionally filled such jobs continues to shrink as the typical American worker becomes older and better educated."[28] In a free society, job creation does not cease. As Harry Binswanger points out, "Jobs do not exist as a fixed pool, to be divided up. Jobs can always be added because there's no end to the creation of wealth and thus no end to the useful employment of human intelligence."[29] More wealth means better tools for production, improved technology, lower prices, and more "gadgets" for everyone. Which means, everyone can be more productive and enjoy a higher standard of living. Immigrants play an indispensable role in that process.

For example, when the Irish began arriving in America in large numbers in the 1840s, there was a great demand for physical labor to build canals and railroads, and "Irish laborers were the mainstay of the construction gangs that did this grueling work."[30] Similarly, when Italians arrived in America, "they worked jobs such as shoe shining, ragpicking, sewer cleaning, and whatever hard, dirty,

---

28. "Immigration," in *Cato Handbook for Policymakers,* 7th ed.

29. Binswanger, "Open Immigration."

30. "The Irish," Oracle Educational Foundation, accessed June 19, 2011, http://library.thinkquest.org/20619/Irish.html.

dangerous jobs others didn't want."[31] And Chinese immigrants took "jobs nobody else wanted or that were considered too dirty."[32] In each instance, the immigrants arrived with few skills or resources. They took low-paying, physically demanding jobs. The work needed to be done, and the immigrants had few job choices. In contrast, later generations of immigrant families developed more skills and obtained a better education, and therefore they had better job opportunities. The same is true today. Yesterday's Irish, Italians, and Chinese are today's Mexicans, Salvadorans, and Guatemalans.

What of claims that immigrants do not learn English or assimilate into the American culture? Are immigrants trying to change American culture? Certainly, many first-generation immigrants do not speak English and do not bother to learn the language. Many live and work in tight-knit communities with fellow immigrants, where they can speak a familiar language and practice their native customs. So? Whose rights do they violate? The failure to speak English violates nobody's rights. The failure to speak English only harms those who do not speak it—their choices and job opportunities are limited. But this has been the trend throughout American history. First-generation immigrants have often settled into Chinatown, or Little Italy, or some similar ethnic community. But with few exceptions, their children assimilate: they learn English, attend college, and become skilled tradesmen and professionals. The Vietnamese are a typical example. When Vietnamese first immigrated in large numbers after the Vietnam War, most immigrants did not speak English. They settled into Little Saigons where they retained their culture and language. However, in general their children became well-educated and entered professions such as science, medicine, and engineering. Immigrants come to America to make a better life for themselves and their families, and that is precisely what occurs. And they are successful in doing so to the extent that they embrace American culture.

"A nation's culture," writes Ayn Rand, "is the sum of the intellectual achievements of individual men, which their fellow-

---

31. "The Italians," Oracle Educational Foundation, accessed June 19, 2011, http://library.thinkquest.org/20619/Italian.html.

32. "The Chinese," Oracle Educational Foundation, accessed June 19, 2011, http://library.thinkquest.org/20619/Chinese.html.

citizens have accepted in whole or in part, and which have influenced the nation's way of life."[33] What is America's culture? Historically, America's culture has been shaped by the principle of individual rights—the freedom of each individual to live his life in the pursuit of his own personal happiness. Individual freedom—the recognition and protection of individual rights—is what attracts immigrants. Of course, as we have seen, individual rights have been under attack, but that attack has *not* been led by immigrants. That attack has been led by America's intellectuals and politicians. The solution is not further violations of individual rights—limits on immigration and freedom of association—but a principled defense of individual rights for all individuals, including immigrants.

Even when politicians and pundits talk of freedom, they often suggest policies that violate individual rights. For example, conservatives frequently talk about their support for freedom. However, they conveniently ignore the meaning of the word when it comes to immigration (and many other issues as well). Freedom means an absence of government coercion. It means the moral right of each individual to live as he chooses, so long as he respects the mutual rights of others. Yet, conservatives support government restrictions on immigration (and other government interventions as well). They demand sanctions and fines on businesses that employ illegal immigrants. They believe that government should intervene in the voluntary interactions between individuals. If conservatives truly support freedom, they must demand it in regard to every issue, including immigration. They must demand that the rights—including those of association and contract—of each individual be protected, no matter his place of birth.

On the base of the Statue of Liberty is the sonnet "The New Colossus." In part, the poem reads:

> Give me your tired, your poor,
> Your huddled masses yearning to breathe free,
> The wretched refuse of your teeming shore.
> Send these, the homeless, tempest-tost to me,
> I lift my lamp beside the golden door!

---

33. Ayn Rand, "Don't Let It Go," in *Philosophy: Who Needs It* (New York: The Bobbs-Merrill Company, 1982), p. 205.

America was built by the "wretched refuse" of the world. Millions have come to America unarmed with pedigree, education, or job skills. All they have wanted is to breathe and live freely. All they have wanted is to pursue their own happiness. If we violate their right to do so, we will extinguish the lamp of liberty for them as well as for ourselves.

10

It's Your Life

One morning in April 2011, armed members of three federal agencies raided the Pennsylvania farm of Dan Allgyer, culminating a yearlong sting operation. The Amish farmer was not dealing in stolen buggies. He was not manufacturing counterfeit designer handbags. He was shipping milk across state lines. But this was no ordinary milk. It was raw, unpasteurized milk—milk as it comes out of a cow. And the federal government did not like that fact. "It is the FDA's position that raw milk should never be consumed," said a spokesman for the Food and Drug Administration (FDA).[1] The raid prompted an outcry from across the nation. Progressives and conservatives alike denounced the raid, declaring that individuals should be allowed to eat and drink whatever they choose. The FDA disagrees, and when it comes to what you may legally ingest, the FDA has the final word.

Few would dispute the fact that contaminated food and toxic drugs are harmful to human life. But what would happen if government did not set standards for food and drug safety? Wouldn't an absence of government regulations lead to the marketing of unsafe products? If individuals were free to purchase the food and medicines of their choice, wouldn't some jeopardize their well-being by purchasing dangerous products? Don't we need agencies such as the FDA to protect consumers and ensure a safe food supply?

Such questions imply that, without government intervention, private companies would abandon all standards. They imply that,

1. Stephen Dinan, "Feds Sting Amish Farmer Selling Raw Milk Locally," *The Washington Times*, April 28, 2011, accessed May 30, 2011, http://www.washingtontimes.com/news/2011/apr/28/feds-sting-amish-farmer-selling-raw-milk-locally/.

without regulations, private businesses would be willing to jeopardize the safety and health of their customers, and in the process, ruin their business. Or, to ask what is really meant by the above questions: without government regulations, why wouldn't private companies intentionally poison their customers to increase profits? It should be clear that no rational business would do such a thing—providing safe products is in the self-interest of every business. In truth, it is government regulations, and particularly those imposed by the FDA, that threaten consumer safety and health. To understand this, let us look at what the FDA does.

The inception of the FDA can be traced to the Pure Food and Drug Act of 1906, which stated that the act's intention was to prevent "the manufacture, sale, or transportation of adulterated or misbranded or poisonous or deleterious foods, drugs, medicines, and liquors, and for regulating traffic therein, and for other purposes."[2] (Ironically, Dan Allgyer was busted for selling unadulterated milk.) As one commentator put it at the time, "The ultimate value of the national food law depends upon the wisdom of the Bureau of Chemistry [a precursor of the FDA], which body must arbitrarily become food-gods, determining what is good and what is bad."[3] Today, the FDA is much more than an arbitrary "food-god." The powers of the FDA go far beyond merely keeping "poisonous or deleterious" foods and drugs off the market—it controls and regulates not only food and drugs, but veterinary products, cosmetics, tobacco, and medical devices. Its determination of what is good and what is bad is forced upon producers and consumers alike, and sometimes with life or death implications. With such sweeping regulatory powers, the FDA is one of the most powerful agencies of the federal government. Such restrictions imply that your body and your life are not yours, but the government's.

What are the existential consequences of such an abhorrent premise? Do these restrictions and controls provide any practical benefits? While the FDA has likely kept some potentially unsafe

2. The Pure Food and Drug Act of 1906, 34 U.S. Stats. 768 (1906).

3. Dr. Edward A. Ayers, "What the Food Law Saves us From," in *The World's Work, Vol. 14* (New York: Doubleday Page and Co., 1907), p. 9322, accessed January 22, 2011, http://books.google.com/books?id=sojNAAAAMAAJ&pg=RA1-PA9316#v=onepage&q&f=false.

products off the market—even a chronic liar occasionally speaks the truth—it has also done incomputable harm. Until 1962, the FDA was a relatively benign (though still immoral) government agency whose primary purpose was to test new drugs for safety. However, with the passage of the Kefauver Harris Amendment to the Federal Food, Drug, and Cosmetic Act (in 1962), the FDA was charged with the task of ensuring that new medicines are effective, as well as safe. One harmful result of this new government mandate has been an increase in the time for approval of a new drug. Prior to 1962, the approval time was seven months; by the late 1970s, it took more than ten years to get a new drug approved.[4] By the mid-2000s, the time had grown to an average of fifteen years.[5] At the same time, foreign nations are approving drugs much faster. Economist Daniel B. Klein writes: "A 1987 study catalogued 192 generic and 1,535 brand-name tested drugs available abroad but not approved in the United States. Of the drugs approved by the FDA between 1987 and 1993, fully 73 percent had already been approved abroad."[6] In other words, while patients in other countries have access to these life-saving drugs, Americans are forced—by their own government—to endure needless suffering, and many wind up dying before the drug is eventually approved. Unless the FDA grants permission, Americans are prohibited from buying medicines which, in their judgment, will be beneficial.

While it is impossible to calculate the precise number of deaths resulting from the delays imposed by the FDA, some have estimated that more than 200,000 Americans died between 1967 and 1997 because they were denied access to drugs used elsewhere in the world.[7] As one example, Dr. Louis Lasagna, director of Tufts University's Center for the Study of Drug Development, estimated that 119,000 Americans died because of the FDA's seven year delay

---

4. "Theory, Evidence and Examples of FDA Harm," FDAReview.org, accessed December 29, 2010, http://www.fdareview.org/harm.shtml.

5. "Food and Drug Administration," in *Cato Handbook on Policy*, 6th ed. (Cato Institute, 2005), p. 394, accessed December 29, 2010, http://www.cato.org/pubs/handbook/hb109/hb_109-40.pdf.

6. Daniel B. Klein, "Economists Against the FDA," The Independent Institute, accessed December 29, 2010, http://www.independent.org/publications/article.asp?id=279.

7. "Food and Drug Administration," in *Cato Handbook for Congress: Policy Recommendations for the 105th Congress*, (Cato Institute, 1997), p. 340, accessed December 29, 2010, http://www.cato.org/pubs/handbook/hb105/105-32.pdf.

in approving beta blocker heart medicines. A four year delay in approving a clot-busting drug called tissue plasminogen activator cost an estimated 30,000 lives.[8] How do these delays protect patients? What good is promoted by denying patients access to drugs and leaving them to die?

The costs imposed by the FDA are not limited to the lives lost. It is estimated that *85 percent* of the cost of developing a new drug is a result of the mandates imposed by the FDA.[9] With the cost of developing a new drug averaging more than $800 million in 2003, and the cost of a new drug discovered in 2003 reaching nearly $2 billion by the time it gets to the market twelve years later,[10] it is little wonder that the cost of drugs and medicines is soaring. Pharmaceutical companies must recover their investments and the additional costs imposed by FDA mandates, or they will have no motivation to continue such risky ventures. If government regulations add 85 percent to the cost of developing a new drug, it makes sense that those costs are then added to the price of the medicines you buy. Remember this the next time you hear someone complain about the high price of drugs. And because of the arbitrary powers held by the FDA, developing new drugs is extremely risky.

The uncertainty associated with the approval process imposes a huge financial risk on drug companies, as jumping through the FDA's hoops is no guarantee that a drug will be approved. A businessman can invest hundreds of millions of dollars and years of research and testing, only to be told by the FDA that his judgment is irrelevant. Drug companies cannot act by right, but only with the permission of government bureaucrats. With such uncertainty looming, the drug companies' incentive for developing new drugs is greatly diminished. Nor does the uncertainty end with a drug's approval. As Daniel B. Klein writes, the FDA also decides what a company can say about its products.[11]

This control over what may or may not be said can reach absurdity. For example, for years it was known that aspirin is

---

8. Ibid., pp. 340-41.

9. Ibid., p. 341.

10. "Food and Drug Administration," in *Cato Handbook on Policy, 6th ed.* (2005), p. 394.

11. Klein, "Economists Against the FDA."

beneficial for heart-attack victims. But the FDA prohibited aspirin manufacturers from advertising that fact.[12] Similarly, in 1992, the Centers for Disease Control and Prevention (CDC)—another federal agency—recommended folic acid supplements for women of child-bearing age to help prevent some debilitating and deadly birth defects, such as anencephaly and spina bifida. The FDA promptly announced that it would prosecute any food or vitamin manufacturer who advertised this fact. And then, in 1998 (only six years later), it demanded that manufacturers begin fortifying certain products with folic acid![13] Even the most minor issues do not escape FDA mandates; the FDA ordered one company to destroy cookbooks that contained information on stevia, an herb used as a sweetener.[14] Eager to flex its dictatorial muscles, the FDA steadfastly refuses to allow either manufacturers or consumers to act on their own judgment. Whether it is issuing prohibitions or mandates, the FDA has the final word, and acting contrary to their dictates can lead to fines, prison, or both. And the results of actually following their edicts can be even worse.

The perversity of the FDA's policies reaches its pinnacle when it comes to the terminally ill. Often, experimental (and unapproved) drugs are the only hope for terminally ill patients. Yet, the FDA routinely refuses to allow patients to use these experimental drugs. Abigail Burroughs is one example. Shortly after the nineteen-year-old was diagnosed with squamous cell carcinoma, her

> family learned of an investigational cancer drug that showed good response in early trials. Abigail's prominent oncologist at Johns Hopkins Hospital believed the drug had a significant chance of saving her life. But every effort on the part of her family, physician, and supporters to procure the drug for Abigail failed. She was ineligible for a clinical trial and the drug company couldn't provide it for her for compassionate use. The FDA was unmoved by her life-and-death situation.[15]

---

12. "Theory, Evidence and Examples of FDA Harm."

13. Ibid.

14. Dr. Mary J. Ruwart, "Death by Regulation," International Society for Individual Liberty, accessed January 22, 2011http://www.isil.org/resources/lit/death-regulation .html.

15. William Faloon, "The Abigail Alliance: A Relentless Campaign to Reform the FDA," *Life Extension Magazine*, November 2010, accessed January 29, 2011, http://www.lef.org/magazine/mag2010/nov2010_FDA-Delay-of-One-Drug-Causes

After a futile seven month battle with the FDA, Abigail died. Less than five years later, the drug was approved by the FDA for Abigail's type of cancer. The FDA arbitrarily played God, and Abigail lost her life. Why? Who benefited from this? Sadly, Abigail's story is not unique.

Contracting a deadly disease is tragic. When government bureaucrats deny an individual access to potentially life-saving drugs, they amplify the tragedy. What would your attitude be if you were diagnosed with a terminal disease but were denied access to an experimental treatment? How would you feel if the FDA essentially issued you a death sentence? If, in consultation with your doctor, you conclude that a particular medicine is worth trying, why should the FDA stop you from doing so? You have a moral right to take any drug you choose—it is your life. If your judgment is wrong, you will bear the consequences. When the FDA is wrong, you must also bear the consequences, regardless of your own judgment.

In practical terms, what is the worse thing that can happen to a terminally ill patient who takes an experimental drug that proves ineffective? He is already facing near certain death. Further, what is the best way to test experimental drugs, if not on willing patients?

As we have seen, the FDA imposes tremendous, and often deadly, costs on Americans. Scientists, doctors, businessmen, and patients are forced to subjugate their judgment to politicians and bureaucrats. Patients are forced to pay substantially higher costs, endure needless suffering, and even die because of prohibitions and delays. Suffering and death are the ultimate consequences of the FDA's coercive power to deny our freedom to purchase and use life-saving medicines.

Making matters worse, many Americans have placed unreasonable demands on the pharmaceutical industry. Many expect drug companies to be omniscient and infallible, to produce drugs that are safe for all individuals under all circumstances. (As evidence, consider the lawsuits that result whenever an adverse side effect to a drug is discovered.[16]) Meeting such expectations is simply

---

-Lost-Life-Years_01.htm.

16. As one example, Merck paid $4.85 billion to settle lawsuits arising from its painkiller Vioxx.

impossible. As Richard E. Ralston, Executive Director of Americans for Free Choice in Medicine, writes:

> When a new drug comes to market, no one can know all of its side effects, nor the impact on all other medical conditions that a patient might have, nor how it might interact with any dosage of any combination of an infinite number of other drugs—nor the cumulative effect of ten, twenty, or thirty years of use. If omniscience is required, no new drug will come to market.[17]

For a drug company to test a product under every possible condition before releasing it to the public would mean that drug production would come to a grinding halt, which is essentially what happens because of the exorbitant costs imposed by the FDA's regulations. Drug companies must spend enormous sums of money to satisfy the FDA, rather than investing that money in research and development. And these costs aren't the only threat to drug companies.

By the FDA's standards, if a particular drug poses a potential threat to *some* individuals under *some* conditions, approval should be denied. If this standard were applied consistently and literally, there is no drug that could pass such an absurd and arbitrary standard. Economist Walter E. Williams writes:

> There's little or no cost to the FDA for not approving a drug that might be safe, effective and clinically superior to other drugs for some patients but pose a risk for others. My question to FDA officials is: Should a drug be disapproved whenever it poses a health risk to some people but a benefit to others? To do so would eliminate most drugs, including aspirin, because all drugs pose a health risk to some people.[18]

Indeed, virtually everything—including water—can be harmful. As an example, in 2007 a California woman died from water

---

17. Richard E. Ralston, "Finding Alternatives to the Food and Drug Administration," Freedom from FDA, accessed January 29, 2011, http://www.freedomfromfda.org/fdaalternatives.html.

18. Walter E. Williams, "FDA: Friend or Foe?," *The Washington Examiner*, May 31, 2007, accessed January 29, 2011, http://washingtonexaminer.com/node/258656.

intoxication after participating in a water drinking contest.[19] Would the FDA ban water because it poses a risk to some individuals under certain circumstances?

The fact that every drug can pose a risk to someone does not mean that drug companies should introduce new products without adequate research and testing. It does mean that if they follow established scientific protocol, then objective law would not consider the companies negligent or legally culpable for adverse reactions to their products. In other words, drug companies should not be held to an impossible standard. Doing so will simply mean that they will be litigated out of existence. Who would benefit from killing the companies that produce life-saving drugs? At the same time, patients must understand that every drug carries some risk with its use. They must weigh those risks versus not treating their disease or condition. And they should not blame the drug companies every time they experience an adverse reaction.

What of companies that negligently release dangerous drugs? Don't regulations prevent rogue companies from endangering patients? While it is certainly possible for companies to disregard the health and safety of their customers, this is not a very rational business practice. Killing one's customers is not good for business. But when negligence does occur, there are legitimate laws already on the books that protect the rights of patients. Rather than treat businessmen as enemies, the government should protect the freedom of drug companies to develop and market their life-saving products.

In a capitalist society, information about adverse reactions, new uses, and other drug related issues flows freely. Doctors, drug companies, and other interested parties are free to issue reports, discuss test results, and make recommendations without fear of legal prosecution. Not only does this speed the discovery of adverse reactions and unexpected consequences of drugs, it also allows doctors and patients to discover new uses for a drug. As in other areas of consumer "protection," third parties can play a crucial role in educating the public. Numerous organizations—such as Underwriters Laboratories, Good Housekeeping, Angie's List, and Consumers Union—test products, provide recommendations, and

---

19. "Woman Dies After Water-drinking Contest," MSNBC.com, accessed January 29, 2011, http://www.msnbc.msn.com/id/16614865/ns/us_news-life/.

offer other information to consumers. Independent third parties have long been an effective means for consumers to learn about products and services.

There is no reason that these organizations, or others like them, cannot or will not do the same in regard to drugs, medical devices, and food. Indeed, this is the case even in today's heavily regulated medical marketplace. For example, ConsumerLab.com provides "independent test results and information to help consumers and healthcare professionals identify the best quality health and nutrition products."[20]

The United States Pharmacopeia (USP) is a more compelling example of a non-government agency providing information and setting industry standards. Founded in 1820, the USP is

> a non-governmental, official public standards–setting authority for prescription and over-the-counter medicines and other healthcare products manufactured or sold in the United States. USP also sets widely recognized standards for food ingredients and dietary supplements. USP sets standards for the quality, purity, strength, and consistency of these products—critical to the public health.[21]

This private, non-profit organization uses volunteers from academia, healthcare professions, the pharmaceutical industry, food industries, and consumer organizations to oversee its operations and avoid conflict-of-interest. Its strict scientific standards have made it a recognized leader around the world. And, as often happens when men are free, alternatives to the USP have also been developed.

In 1905, a group of physicians met in Pittsburgh to found the Council on Pharmacy and Chemistry of the American Medical Association (AMA). A newspaper article at the time stated that "the immediate object of the council is to examine…the composition and status of medicinal preparations offered to physicians which are not included in the United States Pharmacopeia or in other

---

20. "About Consumerlab.com," Consumerlab.com, accessed July 21, 2011, http://www.consumerlab.com/aboutcl.asp.

21. "About USP," United States Pharmacopeia, accessed December 29, 2010, http://www.usp.org/aboutUSP/.

standard books."[22] Together, the USP and the AMA provided physicians and consumers with independent information on drugs and medicines, without the involvement of the government. (The AMA discontinued the Council in 1972.) However, unlike the FDA, neither the USP nor the AMA have the legal authority to prohibit doctors from prescribing drugs that are not approved by their respective organization. In the absence of the FDA, doctors would be free to act on their own judgment and prescribe remedies that they deem appropriate, and patients would be equally free to select such treatments. And this is precisely the type of activity that has led to countless discoveries in medicine.

When the FDA approves a particular drug, that approval is for a specific use or disease—this is called the "on-label" use. However, doctors often find other uses for a drug—these are "off-label" uses. While not officially sanctioned by the FDA, these off-label uses are not prohibited either. Daniel Klein writes:

> Doctors learn of off-label uses from extensive medical research, testing, newsletters, conferences, seminars, Internet sources, and trusted colleagues. Scientists and doctors, working through professional associations and organizations, make official determinations of "best practice" and certify off-label uses in standard reference compendia such as AMA Drug Evaluations, American Hospital Formulary Service Drug Information, and US Pharmacopoeia Drug Information—all without FDA meddling or restriction.[23]

Klein goes on to point out that off-label uses that later get FDA approval appear in the USP on average two and one-half years before FDA approval. In other words, a private organization following rigorous scientific standards, rather than political whim, recognizes the life-saving benefits of drugs thirty months before the bureaucrats at the FDA. How many lives are saved and how much suffering is reduced during those thirty months?

These off-label uses demonstrate that doctors and their patients can make rational health care decisions without government

---

22. "Council on Pharmacy and Chemistry, American Medical Association," *The Boston Medical and Surgical Journal*, March 19, 1905, p. 288, accessed December 29, 2010, http://www.nejm.org/doi/pdf/10.1056/NEJM190503091521009.

23. Klein, "Economists Against the FDA."

meddling, dictates, or controls. Indeed, they demonstrate that patients benefit tremendously when they are free to act on their own judgment, in consultation with their doctors. In contrast, the FDA believes that you should not be free to eat, drink, or ingest what you choose. According to the FDA, your body and your life belong to the government. And that can have deadly consequences.

Freedom to contract in medicine is moral. And, as we have seen in other areas of life, it is also practical, that is, if what one wishes to practice is the relief of human suffering and saving lives.

Having examined the practical and moral reasons for getting the government out of our pantry and out of our medicine chest, let us now examine the reasons for getting the government out of our economic lives.

11

Let's Make a Deal

In early April 2011, President Barack Obama announced his intention to run for re-election. To finance his campaign, he set a goal of raising $1 billion. This nearly equals the amount John McCain and Barack Obama spent during the 2008 Presidential campaign—McCain spent $333 million and Obama spent $730 million. The role of money in politics is undeniable. Does this shift power to the rich and to those who can afford large donations? Is this anti-democratic? Does this drown out the voices of "the people" in a sea of special interest money? Most politicians, including Obama and McCain, answer a resounding "yes."

For example, Senator John McCain said, "The American people are unanimous that they want their government back. We can do that by ridding politics of large, unregulated contributions that give special interests a seat at the table while average Americans are stuck in the back of the room."[1] When the Bipartisan Campaign Reform Act of 2002 (known as McCain-Feingold) was ruled unconstitutional, Obama said:

> With its ruling today, the Supreme Court has given a green light to a new stampede of special interest money in our politics. It is a major victory for big oil, Wall Street banks, health insurance companies and the other powerful interests that marshal their power every day in Washington to drown out the voices of everyday Americans.[2]

---

1. "Clearer Rules About Campaign Finance; No Soft Money," OnTheIssues.org, accessed January 15, 2011, http://www.ontheissues.org/Economic/John_McCain_Government_Reform.htm#Campaign_Finance_Reform.

2. Erin Geiger Smith, "Quotes of the Day, Campaign Finance Edition: Obama Angry, Abrams Thrilled and Schumer Thinks a Hearing Would Change the "Un-

If we listen to the politicians, money is the problem. But is it? Why does so much money flow to politicians? If these candidates denounce the role of money in politics, why do they eagerly accept so much of it? Before we answer these questions, let us examine attempts to limit campaign donations.

The Tillman Act of 1907, which prohibited corporate donations for political campaigns, was the first attempt by Congress to control campaign donations. Interestingly, Senator "Pitchfork Ben" Tillman, the sponsor of the act, was largely motivated by a desire to silence corporate critics of his segregationist policies:

> Tillman's racial politics also clearly contributed to his interest in controlling corporate spending: Many corporations opposed the racial segregation that was at the core of Tillman's political agenda. Corporations did not want to pay for two sets of rail cars, double up on restrooms and fountains, or build separate entrances for customers of different races.[3]

Like the racist plantation owners who used Jim Crow laws to suppress the wages of black laborers, Tillman used the coercive power of government to silence those who had the audacity to disagree with his policies.

Indeed, the very nature of campaign finance regulations limits political speech and freedom of association. Politicians and pundits quickly denounce associations that support their opponents as "special interests," while arguing that their own supporters are merely fighting for a just cause. For example, when Congress was considering legislation to reduce greenhouse gas emissions—America's Climate Security Act of 2007—energy companies fought back. Common Cause, a progressive organization that supports limits on both greenhouse gases and campaign donations, cried foul: "Coal, oil, and other energy interests launched an expensive lobbying campaign in Washington, outspending environmental

---

American" Decision," BusinessInsider.com, January 21, 2010, accessed January 15, 2011, http://www.businessinsider.com/quotes-of-the-day-the-many-comments-on-the-campaign-finance-ruling-2010-1#ixzz1B7SicLto.

3. Bradley A. Smith, "The Myth of Campaign Finance Reform," *National Affairs*, no. 2, (Winter 2010), accessed June 19, 2011, http://www.nationalaffairs.com/publications/detail/the-myth-of-campaign-finance-reform.

groups 20 to 1 to win influence with Congress."[4] Common Cause is typical. The energy companies were associating for the "wrong" political cause, and their efforts were denounced. But no such complaints were voiced when labor unions spent $400 million on the 2008 election[5] because they were supporting the "right" cause—Democrats.

As with all government interventions, the results of the Tillman Act were different than intended, so Congress has occasionally revisited the issue. Since the Tillman Act, Congress has passed numerous laws to limit or prohibit certain types of campaign donations: the Federal Corrupt Practices Act (1925), the Smith-Connally Act (1943), the Taft-Hartley Act (1947), the Federal Election Campaign Act (1971), and the Bipartisan Campaign Reform Act (2002). In addition, other bills, such as the Hatch Act of 1939, also contained provisions limiting campaign donations. Despite these laws spanning more than a century, money still dominates the political process. Why?

Most politicians claim to support the idea of limiting campaign donations and thus the popularity of campaign finance laws. While these laws, and the sound bites their supporters supply, make for good public relations, few politicians actually practice what they preach. As a $1 billion example, consider the amount Obama set as a goal for his re-election. Common Cause notes that campaign finance laws only limit donations to individual candidates. In an effort to overcome such restrictions, "both parties have set up what are known as 'joint fundraising committees,' which allow individual donors to give well in excess of the normal limits because the contributions are divided up among many different committees, such as national and state party committees."[6] During the last Presidential election, John McCain raised about $221 million and Barack Obama raised $228 million through joint fundraising committees.[7] While denouncing "special interest" money, both

4. "Fair Elections and the Environment," CommonCause.org, accessed July 15, 2011, http://www.commoncause.org/site/pp.asp?c=dkLNK1MQIwG&b=5202213.

5. Jane Sasseen, "Business-Union Fight over Union Voting," BusinessWeek.com, January 15, 2009, accessed July 15, 2011, http://www.businessweek.com/magazine/content/09_04/b4117055424769.htm.

6. "Campaign Finance Reform: A New Era," CommonCause.org, accessed January 15, 2011, http://www.commoncause.org/site/pp.asp?c=dkLNK1MQIwG&b=5424665.

7. Ibid.

candidates were more than willing to accept it. While supporting limits on campaign donations, they did everything that they could to finagle their way around those limitations. If they really want to limit the role of money in politics, why don't they start with their own campaigns?

In time, a new piece of legislation will be drafted to "reform" campaign finance and the entire circus will start again. Politicians will righteously denounce the role money plays in American politics, demand new limitations on donations, and then happily accept millions in donations. Why is so much money donated to political campaigns? Why do politicians denounce the influence of money on elections while eagerly gorging on the buffet of campaign contributions?

The answer is the enormous control politicians and public officials have over businesses and the lives of individuals. Political power is a magnet for special interest groups seeking to influence the use of that power. We have seen this with education, mail, and other issues. These groups have a variety of motivations. Some—such as environmental groups—seek legislation to impose their agenda upon the nation through mandates and prohibitions. Whether it is clean air mandates or fuel efficiency standards or restrictions on greenhouse gases, they want to use the coercive power of government to impose their views and values upon others. For example, when Congress was considering the American Security and Clean Energy Act in 2009, environmental groups lobbied heavily in favor of the bill, spending $4.7 million in a three month period.[8]

Some businesses and groups seek subsidies, price supports, restrictions on free trade, or similar special favors. For example, even low-profile industries such as the sugar industry, which has received price supports since the Presidency of James Madison in the early nineteenth century, contribute large sums to political candidates. In 2008, the industry donated $4.2 million to candidates for the House and Senate. Sugar industry price supports cost American consumers an estimated $4 billion per year through

8 Evan Mackinder, "Pro-Environment Groups Outmatched, Outspent in Battle over Climate Change Legislation," OpenSecrets.org, August 23, 2010, accessed September 5, 2011, http://www.opensecrets.org/news/2010/08/pro-environment-groups-were-outmatc.html.

artificially high prices for sugar and products using sugar. Apparently, "investing" in Congressional campaigns is lucrative. As another example, groups representing farmers and related agricultural interests contributed $10.4 million to federal candidates in 2008.[9] These groups lobby for continuation of agricultural "income supporst" and price guarantees, also known as subsidies. Such handouts to the agricultural industry amounted to $15 billion in 2005.[10] And General Electric, as a part of its "eco-magination" initiative, supported federal legislation that mandated higher energy efficiency standards for light bulbs, which effectively banned incandescent light bulbs. Not surprisingly, General Electric is now touting its more efficient compact fluorescent bulbs. (As another example of how government intervention destroys jobs, General Electric has closed three American plants that made incandescent bulbs. Its compact fluorescent bulbs are made in China.)

We have already seen the power held by union leaders because of federal labor laws. To maintain and strengthen that power, union leaders donate to candidates who support legislation favorable to unions. As one example, unions poured $400 million into the 2008 election, hoping to secure support for the Employee Free Choice Act (often referred to as Card Check).[11] The act, which would eliminate secret ballots on the question of employee unionization, is intended to make it easier for employees to form unions. More union members means more union dues, which union leaders can then use in the next election cycle to elect Congressmen who will pass more legislation favorable to unions.

Some—such as regulated businesses—seek to protect themselves from the onerous and destructive dictates that Congress can impose upon them. Rather than meekly acquiesce to those dictates, many businesses fight back by lobbying politicians and donating to those who support their positions. For such businesses, any money they spend on political campaigns is simply self-defense.

---

9 "Agricultural Services & Products: Background," OpenSecrets.org, accessed September 5, 2011, http://www.opensecrets.org/industries/background.php?cycle=2012&ind=A07.

10. Dan Morgan, Sarah Cohen and Gilbert M. Gaul, "Powerful Interests Ally to Restructure Agriculture Subsidies," *The Washington Post*, December 22, 2006, accessed January 15, 2011http://www.washingtonpost.com/wp-dyn/content/article/2006/12/21/AR2006122101634.html.

11. Sasseen, "Business-Union Fight."

As one example, in 1995 Microsoft spent only $16,000 on lobbying.[12] After the federal government filed anti-trust charges against the company in 1998, it increased its lobbying to nearly $9 million in 2008.[13] Should Microsoft have simply accepted threats to break up the company? Or, consider energy companies that are threatened with huge additional costs under "cap and trade." In 2008, they donated $55 million to candidates for Congress in an attempt to win influence on an issue that could destroy their businesses.[14]

No matter their particular motivation, these businesses and groups seek to influence legislation that can have a tremendous impact on their lives and their livelihood. Some seek to impose controls and regulations on others; some seek to escape those controls and retain their freedom to act as they judge best. This is the cause of the growing amount of money spent on and donated to political campaigns. When the accepted solution to every political issue is government force, then campaign donations become one means of influencing the use of that force. So, who is the guilty party? Those who are openly bribing politicians by making donations in support of their pet cause? Those who are paying "protection money" to defend themselves from the coercive power of government? Or those who eagerly accept campaign donations in exchange for their votes to violate individual rights?

Congressmen denounce the influence of money, while evading their role in the process. They denounce the "corrupting" influence of money, believing that corruption can only occur through bribery and back-room deals. They imply that if they hold an appropriate number of hearings and find that a piece of legislation serves the "public interest," no corruption is involved. They imply that if money changes hands under the table, it is corruption. But if the money changes hands openly and the proper forms are completed, no corruption is involved. In truth, the violation of individual rights is corrupt, whether it occurs on a golf course or on the floor of

---

12. Matt Loney, "Microsoft's Lobbying Efforts Eclipse Enron," ZDNet.com, February 12, 2002, accessed May 29, 2011, http://www.zdnet.com/news/microsofts-lobbying-efforts-eclipse-enron/120716.

13. Clint Boulton, "Google, Microsoft Meet in the Lobby on Capitol Hill," eWeek.com, February 04, 2010, accessed May 29, 2011, http://googlewatch.eweek.com/content/evil_google/google_microsoft_meet_in_the_lobby_on_capitol_hill.html.

14. "Fair Elections and the Environment."

Congress, whether the influence is peddled in a secret meeting or is reported in the appropriate government documents.

The essence of the problem is the absence of political principles. Absent the principle of individual rights, every decision, policy, and program ultimately hinges on the whim of those in power. As Ayn Rand wrote, when the "public interest" supersedes the rights and interests of individuals,

> all men and all private groups have to fight to the death for the privilege of being regarded as "the public." The government's policy has to swing like an erratic pendulum from group to group, hitting some and favoring others, at the whim of any given moment....
>
> All "public interest" legislation (and any distribution of money taken by force from some men for the unearned benefit of others) comes down ultimately to the grant of an undefined, undefinable, non-objective, arbitrary power to some government officials.[15]

If someone desires to obtain the unearned, the cost of a junket or a campaign donation can be a good "investment." If someone seeks to impose his values upon individuals who would not accept them voluntarily, what better way than a campaign donation to those with the power to make his wish a reality? Unfortunately, with Congress holding almost unlimited power to control and regulate producers, and with so many competing claims, it often becomes difficult, if not impossible, to tell who is acting in self-defense and who is pursing the unearned.

And what choice do the potential victims of this power lust have but to fight back? If your product might be banned, or some bureaucrat could force you to make extensive and expensive changes to your manufacturing process, wouldn't you fight back? If your company manufactures lawn darts, what would you do when the Consumer Product Safety Commission considers banning their sale in the United States? (Lawn darts were banned in 1988.) If the future of your business and your life hinged on the findings of some Congressional committee, wouldn't you seek to influence their findings? For example, if you manufacture incandescent light

---

15. Ayn Rand, "The Pull Peddlers," in *Capitalism: The Unknown Ideal* (New York: New American Library, 1967), p. 188.

bulbs, would you passively accept proposals to make them illegal? If Congress threatens to seize the portion of your profits that it deemed "excessive," as Congress has done to oil companies in 2005 and 2011, would you quietly accept those threats?

Campaign finance laws are an attempt to eliminate an effect without identifying or addressing its cause. The effect—the huge sums of money donated to politicians—is caused by the vast government intervention in the economy. That intervention has ever expanding implications regarding the economic life of every individual and business in America. Government regulations—including campaign finance laws—are an attempt to limit the choices available to Americans. Campaign donations are merely one means of purchasing the use of government's coercive powers or to shield oneself from those powers. No matter the issue, many individuals, businesses, and special interest groups seek ways to influence legislators. Campaign finance laws fail to address the underlying problem, and indeed, they are a symptom of that problem. What is the solution? Must we accept the cynical version of the "Golden Rule"—he who has the gold rules?

Some, such as Common Cause, the progressive group that supports campaign finance "reform," would prefer to see elections financed primarily through public funds. This would "amplify the voices of ordinary Americans and enable candidates to break free from endless pursuit—and influence—of wealthy donors."[16] Of course, "public funds" ultimately come from you and other taxpayers, including "wealthy donors." This means that "wealthy donors" are to have limitations on campaign donations while they are simultaneously forced to help finance the campaigns of candidates with whom they may or may not agree. Indeed, this would be true of all taxpayers. Republicans would be forced to finance the campaigns of Barack Obama and Nancy Pelosi, while Democrats would have been forced to finance the campaigns of George W. Bush and Sarah Palin. In short, not only will you be prevented from supporting the ideas you advocate, you will be compelled to support contrary ideas. Thomas Jefferson denounced such measures, writing that "to compel a man to furnish

---

16. "Campaign Finance Reform: A New Era."

contributions of money for the propagation of opinions which he disbelieves and abhors, is sinful and tyrannical."[17]

Lobbyists and special interest groups have existed since the first days of the republic. There have always been those who sought special favors from elected officials, whether it was to build a canal, obtain aid for French refugees, or to institute protectionist tariffs. But if government is limited to its proper purpose—the protection of individual rights—such efforts would have no effect. If government cannot regulate, prohibit, control, tax, and dictate, lobbying becomes moot. If politicians cannot initiate force, the motivation to influence those politicians disappears. Indeed, this was largely the case prior to the twentieth century.

The Presidential election of 1896 is regarded as the birth of modern campaign financing. Mark Hanna, the chairman of Republican William McKinley's campaign, raised between $3.4 million and $7 million.[18] That is $79 million to $164 million in 2011 dollars, but it pales in comparison to the $1 billion that Obama set as a goal for 2012. These donations allowed McKinley to outspend his opponent, William Jennings Bryant, by a margin of twelve to one. Hanna duplicated his efforts for McKinley's 1900 re-election campaign, and after the election "Senator Henry Teller of Colorado complain[ed] that the Republicans had 'plenty of money for purposes legitimate and illegitimate,' while another disgruntled Democrat, Illinois Governor John Peter Altgeld, grouse[d] to Bryan that 'the enemy simply bought the ground from under us.'"[19] Why did the 1896 election herald the era of big-money in politics? And why has it grown so significantly?

The end of the nineteenth century marked the beginning of the Progressive Era. During this period, the federal government began to seize control over businesses and the lives of individuals. Beginning with the Interstate Commerce Act in 1887, the federal government implemented a series of sweeping laws that granted the

---

17. Thomas Jefferson, Bill for Religious Freedom (1779), accessed January 15, 2011, http://candst.tripod.com/statute.htm.

18. "The Hanna Project," The Center for Public Integrity, accessed July 10, 2011, http://www.buyingofthepresident.org/index.php/the_hanna_project/election_year/1896_mckinley_vs_bryan

19. "The Hanna Project," The Center for Public Integrity, accessed July 10, 2011, http://www.buyingofthepresident.org/index.php/the_hanna_project/election_year/1900_mckinley_vs_bryan

government immense powers: the Sherman Anti-Trust Act in 1888 gave government virtually unlimited powers over businesses; a federal income tax was established by the Sixteenth Amendment in 1913; the Federal Reserve was created in 1913; the Federal Trade Commission Act was enacted in 1914; the Clayton Antitrust Act of 1914 expanded government controls over businesses; and the Federal Farm Loan Act of 1916 expanded government involvement in agriculture. These powers became a magnet for special interest groups and campaign donations. The growth of government power preceded the growth of campaign donations. When looters and parasites realized that they could gain immense wealth for the price of a few cocktails, a fancy dinner, or a campaign donation, the race was on to influence politicians and bureaucrats. Government intervention is the cause; campaign donations and lobbying are the effect.

The solution to the problems caused by government intervention is not more government intervention. The solution is to return government to its proper purpose—the protection of individual rights, including the right to associate and to support a political candidate or cause. If Congress, or any legislative body, is serious about reducing special interest groups and the influence of money on elections, then they must begin by reducing their power over businesses and the lives of Americans. Special interest groups will not spend enormous sums of money on political candidates if elections do not have such significant implications for their cause or business. In short, if Congress is limited to its proper purpose, there will be no incentive to seek to influence its members.

To protect individual rights, government has only three legitimate functions—the police, the courts, and the military. The purpose of the police is to protect individuals from those who initiate force—thieves, kidnappers, rapists, murderers, and the like—and thereby prevent an individual from acting according to his own judgment. The purpose of the courts is to determine the guilt of accused criminals, assess punishment to the guilty, and to arbitrate disputes. And the purpose of the military is to protect individuals from foreign threats to their freedom. Any other activity on the part of government necessarily involves the use of force to prevent individuals from acting on their own judgment, and thereby becomes a violation of their rights. And when government has the power to violate individual rights, interest groups will seek to influence government. We have seen the consequences of government intervention in education, mail delivery, the employer/employee relationship, the drug industry, and more. Such intervention prevents individuals from contracting freely and associating with others on terms that the parties involved find mutually acceptable.

The solution is not further government intervention, but ending the motivations that give rise to the large sums donated to political candidates. The solution is a complete separation of government and economics. The solution is complete freedom of association and freedom to contract—the recognition and protection of the moral right of individuals to act according to their own judgment. If we want to end the influence of money on politics, then we must end the influence of politicians on our lives. The solution is capitalism and the protection of individual rights.

It is easy to blame politicians and the role of money in politics for government's ever expanding control over our lives. But as long as voters continue to demand special favors from government, Representatives and Senators will continue to pander to those demands. If Americans want the freedom to pursue their own personal happiness, then they must reject the ideas that give rise to government intervention. More importantly, Americans must defend each individual's moral right to live as he chooses. Only then will voters elect politicians who respect and defend individual liberty.

Part 2

Conclusion

Politicians and pundits frequently speak about freedom. But what does freedom mean? Freedom means the absence of government coercion. Freedom of contract means the absence of government coercion in the realm of producing, buying, and selling values, such as labor, food, and medicine. Freedom of association means the absence of government coercion in the relationships between individuals, such as in the workplace and political campaigns.

We have seen the many ways government intervention takes these freedoms from us. In many professions, you cannot contract your labor without first obtaining the permission of government bureaucrats. You cannot hire and promote employees based on the criteria of your choosing, but instead must give "special consideration" to factors such as race and gender. You cannot produce, buy, or sell the foods and drugs of your choice, but only those approved by government. And if you disobey these government edicts and prohibitions, you face fines, jail, or both. If you dare to act on your own judgment, even though you do not violate another person's rights, you can become a criminal.

Fundamentally, government regulations are about controlling your choices. The judgment and choices of government officials supersede yours, and those officials back their decrees with the coercive power of government. The destructive consequences are clear: massive job loss, unemployment, bankruptcy, suffering, and even death.

The Founding Fathers held that you have a right to your own life, your own liberty, and the pursuit of your own happiness. The examples that we have examined are only a few of the many ways in which government coercion violates your rights.

Force cannot and does not create values. Force can only destroy values. Occupational licensing requirements do not protect consumers; they kill dreams. Labor laws do not protect workers; they kill jobs. Anti-discrimination legislation does not protect women and minorities; they kill benevolence. Campaign finance laws do not protect the voice of "the people"; they kill free speech. FDA regulations do not protect patients; they kill patients.

The solution to unemployment, racism, poor working conditions, immigration, rising health care costs, and the dominance of money in politics is not more government controls and regulations. The solution is freedom of choice and the absence of government coercion. The solution is the recognition and protection of individual rights, including the right to contract and the right of association. In other words, the solution is capitalism.

Part 3

Property

Like many Americans, Chantell and Michael Sackett wanted to build their dream house. They bought a small parcel of land on Priest Lake in Idaho. Shortly after excavation began, the Environmental Protection Agency (EPA) issued a "compliance order" demanding that the couple stop construction and return the land to its natural condition. The Sacketts were threatened with fines of $32,500 per day for non-compliance. The Sacketts were not dumping toxic chemicals into the lake. They were not burning trees on neighboring property. The EPA determined that the property was considered a "wetlands," and therefore subject to provisions of the Clean Water Act, even though the land held no standing water. Without warning or any hearings, the Sacketts were prohibited from building their dream house, and threatened with ruinous fines.[1]

Sadly, the Sacketts are not alone. The Pacific Legal Foundation has found that the EPA has regularly issued up to three thousand "compliance orders" per year.[2] Thousands of Americans are denied the right to use their land as they choose, not because they are violating the rights of others, but because some bureaucrat has deemed their property a "wetlands."

The right to property is the right to own, use, keep, and dispose of material values. It is, like all rights, a sanction to act on your own judgment. It is the freedom to produce or earn the material values that life requires. The right to property is not the right to be

---

1. As this book went to publication, *Sackett v. United States Environmental Protection Agency* was before the United States Supreme Court.

2. Bob Unruh, "Family's Plan for Dream House Halted by Feds Armed with 'Rule'," World Net Daily, June 17, 2011, accessed September 16, 2011, http://www.wnd.com/?pageId=311969.

provided an object, but the right to take the actions necessary to create or earn that object. A person does not have the right to be given a smart phone; he has the right to take the actions necessary to create one or earn the money to purchase one.

The values required to sustain and enjoy life must be created. Automobiles, I-Pads, flat screen televisions, and dream homes are not simply lying around waiting for someone to pick them up. They require thought and effort to come into being. The individual or business who exerts the thought and effort to create those values is the rightful owner. If you grow vegetables in your garden, those vegetables are rightfully yours. If you catch fish in the nearby public lake, those fish are rightfully yours.

Further, ownership means control—the freedom to use and dispose of your property as you choose. "Ownership" without control is a sham; it means that you have the responsibilities of ownership, such as maintenance and upkeep, but you cannot use or dispose of the property as you judge best. For example, the Sacketts must pay property taxes and maintain their land, but they cannot use it as they choose.

We have already seen many ways in which government regulations and controls prevent you from living according to your own judgment. Government regulations and controls also prevent you from using your property as you choose. Whether those regulations take the form of zoning, restrictions on drilling for oil, antitrust statutes, or any other government control on the use of your property, you may use your property only with the permission of government officials, rather than by right.

Restrictions on the use of property are an assault on all of your rights. "The right to life," Ayn Rand wrote,

> is the source of all rights—and the right to property is their only implementation. Without property rights, no other rights are possible. Since man has to sustain his life by his own effort, the man who has no right to the product of his effort has no means to sustain his life. The man who produces while others dispose of his product, is a slave.[3]

---

3. Ayn Rand, "Man's Rights," in *The Virtue of Selfishness*, p. 94 (see Part 1, n.1).

If you cannot use your property, such as land, a factory, or money, as you choose, your property and your life become pawns for the desires and dictates of others.

As with all rights, only physical force can deprive you of your right to property. Only coercion can prevent you from drilling for oil, or erecting a sign, or freely spending your money, or building your dream house. Only physical force can compel you to plant the "right" kinds of trees, or use a particular architectural style, or take any other action that is contrary to your own judgment. Whether it takes the form of theft or extortion, jail or fines, only physical force (or the threat thereof) can violate your right to property.

In a social context, the recognition and protection of property rights is the only means by which to resolve conflicts and disputes. Highly politicized issues such as pollution, "incompatible" land uses, smoking, and energy policy can be addressed by recognizing and protecting the moral right of each individual to use his property as he deems best. Even issues such as discrimination and educational curriculum are removed from the political arena when property rights are recognized and respected. When individuals are free to use their property as they judge best, the owner decides whether to serve gays, whether to hire blacks, whether to teach evolution or creationism. And others are also free to patronize a business or boycott it, to associate with bigots or ostracize them.

A thief does not have the right to take your "stuff" or dictate how you use it. Neither does the government. Let us now see how the recognition and protection of property rights provides affordable housing, clean water, abundant and inexpensive energy, and "fair taxation."

12

The Land of the Free

On February 16, 2001, John Thoburn was arrested by Fairfax County, Virginia, officials. Thoburn was ultimately held for ninety-eight days and fined $1,000 per day. His crime? Refusing to move ninety-eight trees on his driving range. To receive permission from county officials to occupy his land in 1994, Thoburn had planted seven hundred trees at a cost of $125,000. But seven years later, zoning officials decided that *they* didn't like the location of the trees on *Thoburn's* property and demanded that he move some of them. When Thoburn refused to abide by their unreasonable dictates, they had him jailed.[1] Unfortunately, John Thoburn is but one of many horror stories regarding zoning.

Many Americans believe that without zoning, unrestricted land-use will create a myriad of problems. Wouldn't factories be built in residential neighborhoods? Wouldn't such land-uses disrupt neighborhoods and make the roads unsafe? Wouldn't unrestricted land-use result in chaotic development? Don't we need government planning and regulations to make our cities and towns more "livable" and pleasant?

For nearly one hundred years, American cities have used zoning and similar land-use regulations to control development and construction. While zoning laws vary considerably from one locale to another, the purpose of zoning is to control and regulate building and development within a community. Zoning is often used to segregate commercial and industrial land uses from residential areas, to designate a building's distance from the property edge (its "setback"), to mandate architectural styles, and to dictate other

1. John Thoburn, "Rights Are on the Line at Range," accessed February 1, 2011, http://www.freejohnthoburn.com/.

details regarding land use. Even though these controls and restrictions have proven to be destructive in city after city, they persist and grow in scope. Before we examine the destructive results of zoning, let us look at the nature of zoning.

The nation's first zoning ordinance was enacted in New York City in 1916. The ordinance was written in response to the increasing number of skyscrapers in the city, and it "established height and setback controls and designated residential districts that excluded what were seen as incompatible uses."[2] During the next few decades, zoning was adopted by most American cities as a means of preventing "incompatible" land use, with Houston, Texas, being the one notable exception.[3] Since its inception, zoning has grown far beyond simply designating residential areas and segregating land use. It has become a powerful and destructive political tool. As one example, in the late 1980s, developer Albert Ginsberg applied for, and received, the required permits to build a thirty-one-story building in New York City. However, a bureaucratic error failed to discover that the building was in an area limited to nineteen-story buildings. Long after construction had started, the leader of a civic group discovered the error and complained to city officials. After a protracted legal battle, Ginsberg was ordered to remove the top twelve stories of his building.[4]

Zoning boards, like all political bodies in a mixed-economy, are a magnet for special interest groups eager to control the property owned by others. One group may demand Spanish architecture for a proposed development, while another group demands colonial architecture. One group may insist on retail space, while another group insists on more office space. One group may demand "public" art, while another group demands green space. And through all of this, the rightful owner sits by helplessly, while others

---

2. "About NYC Zoning," New York City Department of City Planning, accessed January 31, 2011, http://www.nyc.gov/html/dcp/html/zone/zonehis.shtml.

3. Only two American cities with a population over 100,000 do not have zoning—Houston and Pasadena, Texas, a Houston suburb. Houston voters have rejected zoning in referendums on three separate occasions. The most recent referendum was in 1993.

4. John Taylor, "Pushing the Outer Limits," *New York Magazine*, April 10, 1989, p. 90, accessed July 17, 2011, http://books.google.com/books?id=AekCAAAAMBAJ&pg=PA90&lpg=PA90&dq=Albert+Ginsberg+new+york+city+building&source=bl&ots=BKic9Qxucd&sig=EExaQ5J5KqtLZMNPP7MYAi1u044&hl=en&ei=KwMjTvnTBZCjtgfTloycAw&sa=X&oi=book_result&ct=result&resnum=3&ved=0CC0Q6AEwAg#v=onepage&q=Albert%20Ginsberg%20new%20york%20city%20building&f=false

debate how he may use *his* property. For example, when the owner of the Edgewater Hotel in Madison, Wisconsin, wanted to invest $93 million to redevelop his property, neighboring property owners and preservationists protested. During public hearings on the project, members of civic groups, politicians, labor union leaders, and other non-owners of the property debated the merits of redevelopment, while the hotel owner waited for others to decide his future.[5] Such political pressures inevitably lead to increasingly complex zoning ordinances and, with few exceptions, to an expansion of government control over land-use. As one example, the Indianapolis zoning ordinance of 1922 was eighteen pages long.[6] By 1951 it had grown to forty-one pages.[7] Today it is more than six hundred pages.[8]

Why did a relatively simple ordinance turn into a massive tome? Professor Bernard H. Siegan explains why:

> Small, modest zoning ordinances grow into very complex and complicated ones. One reason is, of course, the change in conditions, building techniques, and thinking that occurs over the years and is reflected in our laws. But there are two other explanations for the uncontrolled growth of zoning. The first is that zoning has been a story of unrealized expectations. It usually does not work as represented....[9]

As we have previously seen, government coercion never delivers as promised. Even when one group is pleased with the results of zoning, others aren't. In response, they seek variances and other

---

5. Kristin Czubkowski, "Controversy Follows Proposed Zoning Change for Edgewater," *The Cap Times*, January 26, 2010, accessed September 17, 2011, http://host.madison.com/ct/news/local/govt_and_politics/article_64ce9350-0ac6-11df-82bd-001cc4c002e0.html.

6. "Zoning Ordinance," City of Indianapolis and Marion County, accessed April 15, 2011, http://www.indy.gov/eGov/City/DMD/Planning/Zoning/ordinances/Zoning%20Ordinance%20%28City%29%20-1922.pdf.

7. "Zoning and Planning Regulations of Indianapolis," City of Indianapolis and Marion County, accessed April 15, 2011, http://www.indy.gov/eGov/City/DMD/Planning/Zoning/ordinances/Zoning%20Ordinance%20%28City%29%20-1951.pdf.

8. "Indianapolis/Marion County Zoning Ordinances," City of Indianapolis and Marion County, accessed April 15, 2011, http://www.indy.gov/eGov/City/DMD/Planning/Zoning/Pages/municode.aspx.

9. Bernard H. Siegan, *Property and Freedom* (New Brunswick: Transaction Publishers, 1997), p. 189.

changes to the zoning plan. As Siegan writes, "Another reason for the proliferation of zoning regulations is that the process is a battlefield for warring interest groups."[10] These interest groups seek to influence zoning officials and use government coercion to shape the community according to their own personal desires. And with many groups doing this simultaneously, zoning boards inevitably expand land-use regulations to accommodate the demands made by the various interest groups.

The growing controls imposed by zoning turn ordinary citizens into criminals, simply because they do not meet the dictates and demands of zoning officials. In Princeton, New Jersey, Irving Urken was threatened with a ninety-day jail sentence after he displayed a few barbecue grills in front of his hardware store, which he had been doing for fifty-seven years. A new zoning ordinance banned anything in front of any store in town—except books, flowers, plants, vegetables, and newspapers.[11] In East Hampton, Long Island, authorities issued a warrant for the arrest of Jerry Della Femina because he had some pumpkins stacked in front of his store—a violation of the local zoning ordinance.[12] And, as we have seen, even when zoning officials grant you permission to use your property, they can later change their mind (at your expense):

> In September 1993, the New York City buildings commissioner bushwhacked Fordham University. Fordham had received permission from the city government to build a 480-foot radio tower at its campus in the Bronx. After the radio tower was almost half finished, the city government reversed its position and revoked the building permit. The government's action cost Fordham over half-a-million dollars.[13]

In these examples, and countless others, legitimate and ordinary activities were criminalized, even when nobody's rights were being violated.

Why are these common activities criminalized? The answer can be found in the morality that underlies zoning—altruism. Zoning

---

10. Ibid.

11. James Bovard, "Zoning: The New Tyranny," The Future of Freedom Foundation, accessed February 1, 2011, http://www.fff.org/freedom/0896d.asp.

12. Ibid.

13. Ibid.

holds that individual property owners must put aside their self-interest—their desired use for their property—in order to promote the "public interest." But who decides what constitutes the "public interest"? The gang that can make the most noise, twist the most arms, and demonstrate the most political clout. If Citizens United Against Pumpkin Displays or the Anti-Grill League yells loud enough and long enough, they can convince zoning officials that they speak for "the public." When individual rights, including property rights, are subservient to the "public interest," anything goes.

For instance, in 2005 the city council of Manassas, Virginia, passed a zoning ordinance that restricts residents living in households to immediate relatives. This excluded aunts, nephews, cousins, and other members of the extended family. The council acknowledged that the ordinance targeted Hispanics. Why? Apparently Hispanics were not wanted in the area and zoning provided the tool to keep them out.[14] Similarly, in Mt. Laurel, New Jersey, zoning was systematically used during the 1970s to drive the town's low income residents (mostly black) out of the community.[15] The zoning ordinance required large lot sizes for single-family homes, which made home ownership unaffordable for low income residents. In both Manassas and Mt. Laurel, zoning was used for purposes that had nothing to do with "incompatible" land uses and everything to do with driving "undesirables" from the community.

While the use of zoning for such exclusionary purposes is certainly rare, these examples demonstrate that zoning can be, and is, used for nefarious purposes. These are not examples of a good law being used for a bad purpose. Rather, zoning is an evil law used for evil purposes—to impose the values of some upon an entire community. Whether those values pertain to race, income, how a parcel of land is used, or the display of pumpkins and grills, by its very nature zoning is a rights-violating institution. And the costs of zoning go far beyond the visible victims discussed above.

---

14. Stephanie McCrummen, "Manassas Defends New Rule On Who Can Live Together," *Washington Post*, December 30, 2005, accessed February 1, 2011, http://www.washingtonpost.com/wp-dyn/content/article/2005/12/29/AR2005122901410.html.

15. "History," The New Jersey Digital Legal Library, accessed February 1, 2011, http://njlegallib.rutgers.edu/mtlaurel/aboutmtlaurel.php.

Numerous studies have found that zoning increases the cost of housing, as well as the cost of doing business. One report by Professors Edward Glaeser and Joseph Gyourko concluded:

> The bulk of the evidence that we have marshaled suggests that zoning and other land-use controls are more responsible for high prices where we see them.... Measures of zoning strictness are highly correlated with high prices. While all of our evidence is suggestive, not definitive, it seems to suggest that land-use regulation is responsible for high housing costs where they exist.[16]

In a 2008 article in *The New York Sun*, Glaeser compared middle-class families in New York City and Houston, Texas. At the time, the median price of a home in Houston was $150,000; in New York City the median price was $496,000, and in Manhattan the median home price was $787,900. Glaeser concluded that home ownership is virtually impossible for the middle-class in New York. Why is housing so much more expensive in Manhattan than in Houston? Glaeser writes: "The permitting process in Manhattan is an arduous, unpredictable, multiyear odyssey involving a dizzying array of regulations, environmental, and other hosts of agencies."[17] This process imposes significant costs on developers and escalates the price of every activity that involves land or a building—which means, virtually everything.

Similarly, in 2008, University of Washington professor Theo Eicher found that land-use regulations imposed by the city of Seattle and the state of Washington increased the cost of a home by $200,000! At that time, the median home price in Seattle was $450,000, which means that land-use regulations increased the cost of a home by 44 percent. As an example of one regulation, in 2005 Seattle imposed a $15-per-square-foot surcharge on developers to

---

16. Edward Glaeser and Joseph Gyourko, "Zoning's Steep Price," *Regulation*, Fall 2002, accessed November 2, 2011, http://www.cato.org/pubs/regulation/regv25n3/v25n3-7.pdf.

17. Edward Glaeser, "Houston, New York has a Problem," *The New York Sun*, July 16, 2008, accessed February 1, 2011, http://www.nysun.com/opinion/houston-new-york-has-a-problem/81989/.

subsidize low-income housing. That regulation alone added $9,000 to the cost of a 600-square-foot downtown condominium.[18]

The costs imposed by zoning and other land-use regulations often make urban home ownership unaffordable for many Americans, and they are among the hidden victims of zoning. Most do not know that zoning and land-use regulations are the reason for unaffordable housing. Many purchase less expensive homes in the suburbs, resulting in long commutes, congested highways, and calls for more government control over transportation. If zoning has such destructive consequences, why is its use so widespread? Why is zoning accepted in so many communities?

These rights-violating interventions and controls are often defended as a necessary tool that allows government officials to plan a community's development. Yet, that planning has resulted in reduced housing choices, outrageous housing costs, and long commutes. If these results are planned, then we must question the motivation of those officials. If these results are not planned, then we must question their competence. Regardless, these destructive consequences are what inevitably occur when government planning is forced upon individuals.

In a capitalist society, you are free to act according to your own judgment. You are free to set goals, determine a course of action, and then take the actions you think best. You are free to exercise your property rights—the right to earn, use, own, keep, and dispose of material values—in the pursuit of your goals. In short, you are free to plan and act on your plan. However, government intervention, including zoning, prevents you from acting on your judgment—your plan. Your plan becomes subservient to the plan of others. You are compelled to sacrifice your self-interest—your goals and dreams—in the name of the "public interest." For example, you might be forced to move trees that you planted years before, or you might be compelled to lop twelve stories off of your building. This is just one more example of how the altruist morality harms the lives of individuals.

---

18. Russell Hokanson, Reagan Dunn and Samuel L. Anderson, "Misguided Land-use Regulations Push Middle Class out of King County," *The Seattle Times*, April 9, 2008, accessed February 1, 2011, http://seattletimes.nwsource.com/html/opinion/2004335618_reagandunn09.html.

Another way that government violates property rights is through eminent domain, which forces you to sacrifice your property for the "public interest." Eminent domain compels you to "sell" your property, regardless of your own choices. And, as we have seen in recent years, the "public interest" can include private development that will expand a tax base. For example, the city of New London, Connecticut, used eminent domain to "buy" ninety acres of land for a redevelopment project. Seven homeowners fought the forced sale of their property, and in *Kelo v. City of New London* (2005), the Supreme Court ruled that eminent domain could be used to "transfer" ownership of land from one private owner to another.

A second stated purpose of zoning and land-use regulations is the elimination of "incompatible" land uses, such as noisy businesses in a residential area. While this is a legitimate concern, the solution is not coercive government policies that violate property rights and reduce housing options. The solution is the recognition and protection of property rights—your moral right to use your property as you judge best, so long as you respect the rights of others.

The right to property does not mean that you can do absolutely anything you choose with your property. As with all rights, property rights are contextual. Rights are not a license to engage in any desire or whim. You cannot use your land in a manner that violates the property rights of others. As one example, this means that you may not create a nuisance for your neighbors.

With roots in common law, a nuisance "is an interference with a person's enjoyment and use of his land. The law recognizes that landowners, or those in rightful possession of land, have the right to the unimpaired condition of the property and to reasonable comfort and convenience in its occupation."[19] You have a moral right to use your land without being subjected to loud noises, nauseating fumes, or similar conditions that interfere with your "comfort and convenience." However, creating loud noises or obnoxious odors does not necessarily violate the rights of anyone, and therefore, nuisance is highly contextual. A property use that constitutes a nuisance in one context may not be a nuisance in

---

19. "Private Nuisance", TheFreeDictionary.com, accessed February 1, 2011 http://legal-dictionary.thefreedictionary.com/nuisance.

another context. For example, burning rubbish in a rural setting is likely to impact nobody, while doing so in a suburban neighborhood could send unhealthy smoke and fumes into the yards of neighbors. Nuisance laws recognize a property owner's right to use his property as he chooses, so long as his use does not interfere with the mutual rights of others.

An important aspect of nuisance is the principle of "coming to the nuisance", which is rooted in the maxim "no legal wrong is done to him who consents."[20] "Coming to the nuisance" holds that prior use establishes one's right to continue that use:

> On this principle, if someone comes to an existing nuisance—say, he builds a house next to a shooting range, or opens a restaurant next to a paper factory—then he has no right to demand that the nuisance of loud noise or nasty smell be eliminated. Conversely, if someone builds a shooting range next to a preexisting quiet residential neighborhood, the residents of that neighborhood have a right to demand that the range either reasonably soundproof its facility or cease operation.
>
> Granted, cases can be more complex than these, but the basic principle still applies. If someone comes to a preexisting nuisance, he has no right to demand that it be eliminated.[21]

Nuisance laws address the issue of factories and similar businesses in residential areas. If the factory existed prior to the residential area, home owners "came to the nuisance," and have no legitimate complaint. If the factory was built after the homes, the factory must reduce its noise or smoke, or cease operations. The principle of nuisance allows for "incompatible" land uses to be addressed while respecting property rights.

Does this mean that your neighbor cannot paint his shutters a color that you find hideous? Does this mean that you cannot decorate your yard with gargoyles and pink flamingos if your neighbors complain? While an individual may find such uses of property to be annoying or to "interfere" with his enjoyment of his property, valid nuisance claims must be objective—a personal

---

20. Timothy Swanson and Andreas Kontoleon, "Nuisance," Sribd, p. 391, accessed February 1, 2011, http://www.scribd.com/doc/239238/Nuisance.

21. J. Brian Phillips, "Houston, We Have a Zoning Problem," *The Objective Standard 4*, no. 1, (Spring 2009): p. 66.

preference or dislike is not a threat to the well-being of persons or property. For example, the color that your neighbor paints his shutters may be ugly, but his color choice poses no threat to your health, safety, or your property. Poor taste does not violate your rights. To claim otherwise means that every petty annoyance is a valid nuisance claim, and thus, all property rights are destroyed. You could make any arbitrary claim against your neighbor, just as he could make any arbitrary claim against you.

Those who do not want to live in a neighborhood where gargoyles and pink flamingos are permitted can choose to live in communities with rights-respecting deed restrictions (also called covenants). A deed restriction is a voluntary, contractual agreement to limit the use of your property. For example, deed restrictions may limit commercial activities, the type and location of fences, architectural styles, and more. While deed restrictions can control virtually every aspect of the property's use, an important distinction exists between deed restrictions and zoning: the former are voluntary and contractual, while the latter are mandatory and coercive. Those who find the deed restrictions in one neighborhood too restrictive can purchase a home in a different neighborhood—nobody is forced to accept the restrictions. As is true of freedom in general, home buyers must take responsibility for their decisions. They must identify what deed restrictions are in place when they consider a home purchase, and this includes nearby land, such as the vacant lot next door or the empty field at the end of the street. If these parcels of land are unrestricted, a home owner might find future uses unappealing.

When land-use decisions are left to the discretion of property owners, land uses reflect the demands of the market, rather than the demands of zoning officials. As one example, in Houston—which lacks zoning—when demand for housing began to increase near the world-famous Galleria shopping mall, home owners in one neighborhood voted to change their deed restrictions to allow for denser land use. Similarly, when demand for housing near the central business district grew, Houston developers responded quickly by converting lots from single-family homes to townhomes. The result is less expensive housing and an abundant variety of housing choices. In addition, in some areas of Houston, the demand has grown for mixed-use developments as home buyers and renters want easier access to shopping, restaurants, and other businesses that are often considered "incompatible" under zoning. In each instance, developers are able to act according to their own judgment, in the pursuit of their own self-interest, and everyone—including their customers—benefits.

Interestingly, in many municipalities, zoning is used to prohibit multi-use development and multi-family housing, such as townhomes and apartments. In other communities, zoning is used to mandate multi-use development. Decisions regarding these land uses are not made by developers responding to the needs and desires of their customers, but by the dictates of government officials in accordance with the latest urban planning fads and the demands of interest groups.

The absence of zoning in Houston is particularly beneficial to lower income families. Many people in Houston, it should be noted, choose to live in non-restricted communities because these neighborhoods offer more abundant housing choices. They don't mind that a convenience store is near their house, because otherwise, they would not be able to afford a house. It is not a coincidence that studies routinely find that Houston has some of the most affordable housing in the nation.[22] This is an example of how the free market provides a wide variety of land uses and housing choices, meeting the individual needs of everyone.

Freedom in land use provides choices to businesses, property owners, developers, home buyers, and tenants. Each is free to use his property as he judges best, whether it is to build a store, convert a single-family home to a duplex, build a deck, or any other activity that does not violate the rights of others. Each can seek housing based on his own criteria, whether it is price, location, or proximity to stores. Each is free to act according to his own judgment in the pursuit of his own self-interest.

The alleged purposes of zoning—preventing "incompatible" land uses and allowing for community planning—are easily addressed with deed restrictions and nuisance laws, both of which respect and protect property rights. Unlike zoning regulations, which can be changed at the whim of zoning officials in response to

---

22. For example, in 2008 Houston ranked number eight in housing affordability among the largest fifty metropolitan areas. See Casey Wooten, "Houston Gets High Marks on Housing Affordability Study," *Houston Business Journal*, accessed March 27, 2011, http://www.bizjournals.com/houston/stories/2008/03/31/story13.html.

noisy pressure groups, deed restrictions are contractual agreements that allow developers and property owners to plan without fear of arbitrary changes. Unlike zoning regulations, which impose standards across a community, nuisance laws recognize the contextual nature of "incompatible" land uses.

Land-use regulations, like all regulations, are founded on the premise that your property—and therefore your life—ultimately belongs to society, to be used for whatever purpose is deemed to be in the "public interest." This is the premise that must be rejected. Morally, your property is yours to use as you choose. And your life is yours to live as you choose.

What about pollution? If individuals and businesses can use their property without restrictions, won't some fill the air and waterways with toxic chemicals? Don't we need controls and regulations to protect the environment? These are the questions we will now answer.

13

Pollute Your Water, not Mine

In October 1948, twenty people were asphyxiated and more than seven thousand suffered illnesses from severe air pollution in Donora, Pennsylvania. In 1969, the Cuyahoga River in Cleveland, Ohio, caught fire (reportedly for the thirteenth time) due to floating debris and chemicals. These incidents, and others like them, are frequently cited as evidence of the damage inflicted to air and water by unregulated private companies. Don't these incidents demonstrate that government must intervene to protect the environment? Don't we need government regulations to ensure that we have clean air and water?

Certainly, polluted air and water are not good. But as we have seen, neither are government regulations and controls. Not only is government intervention immoral, it has proven impractical in every issue that we have examined—mail delivery, "entitlements," occupational licensing, food, drugs, and more. The same is true with pollution.

Despite decades of government regulations and the expenditure of billions of tax dollars, many American waterways are so polluted that they are not safe for human use. For example, a 2004 study by the Environmental Protection Agency (EPA) found that nearly one-fourth of America's rivers and one-third of its lakes were under fish consumption advisories because of polluted waters.[1] After forty

---

Many of the ideas contained in this chapter were originally developed in an article I co-authored with Alan Germani, "The Practicality of Private Waterways," *The Objective Standard*, Vol. 5, No. 1, Spring 2010.

1. Jaime Holguin, "Pollution Overtaking Lakes, Rivers", CBSNews.com, accessed February 1, 2011, http://www.cbsnews.com/stories/2004/08/24/tech/main638130.shtml.

years of regulations aimed at reducing phosphate levels in waterways,[2] it is estimated that two-thirds of the nation's bays and estuaries contain harmful amounts of phosphates.[3] Record numbers of beaches have been closed due to pollution from sewage, despite mountains of regulations controlling the treatment of sewage.[4] Even the EPA, the government agency charged with the task of keeping waterways clean, predicts that by 2016 American rivers will be as polluted as they were in the 1970s.[5]

While failing to curtail pollution, government regulations are also imposing huge costs on businesses, consumers, and taxpayers. As one example, bans on phosphates have forced the manufacturers of detergents and fertilizers to reformulate their products; consumers have been forced to use more expensive and less effective products. And taxpayers have been forced to spend billions of dollars toward efforts to combat and clean up pollution. For example, the Great Lakes and Lake Champlain Act of 2002 spent $250 million of taxpayer money to remove contaminated sediment from the Great Lakes and their tributaries.[6] The state of Florida expects to spend between $44 million and $119 million to clean contamination near Lake Okeechobee.[7] Obama's economic "stimulus" package in 2009 forced taxpayers to spend $600 million to clean up pollution. These amounts are only a small portion of the money taken from taxpayers to clean up rivers, lakes, and other waterways since passage of the Clean Water Act of 1972. Despite these massive expenditures and an expanding array of regulations, a large percentage of the nation's waterways remain polluted. If government force is not working, what is the solution? Or, must we

---

2. Michael Hawthorne, "From the Archives: Banned in Chicago but Available in Stores," *Chicago Tribune*, April 4, 2007, accessed February 1, 2011, http://www.chicagotribune.com/news/local/chi-daley-phosphates,0,2871187.story.

3. "Water Pollution Facts," Grinning Planet, accessed February 1, 2011, http://www.grinningplanet.com/2005/07-26/water-pollution-facts-article.htm.

4. "Testing the Waters 2011," Natural Resources Defense Council, accessed March 1, 2010, http://www.*nrdc.org/water/oceans/ttw/titinx.asp.*

5. Martha L. Noble, "The Clean Water Act at 30—Time to Renew a Commitment to National Stewardship," *Catholic Rural Life Magazine*, accessed March 1, 2010, http://www.ncrlc.com/crl-magazine-articles/vol45no2/Noble.pdf.

6. Great Lakes and Lake Champlain Act of 2002, accessed February 1, 2011, http://www.epa.gov/glnpo/sediment/legacy/Legacy%20Act%20of%202002.pdf.

7. Paul Quinlan, "U.S. Sugar Pollution Cleanup Could Cost Florida $44 Million", PalmBeachPost.com, accessed February 1, 2011, http://www.palmbeachpost.com/state/content/local_news/epaper/2008/11/13/1113sugar.html.

simply accept polluted air and water? Before we answer these questions, let us first understand what is meant by pollution.

One definition of pollution is the "presence in or introduction into the environment of a substance or thing that has harmful or poisonous effects."[8] Pollution can occur through natural events, such as an erupting volcano, or it can occur as a result of human activities.

Waste and contaminants are a by-product of human activity. Transforming the raw materials of nature into human values necessarily creates waste and contaminants, whether it is the water used in a paper mill or the smoke emitted from a factory. Even as a consumer you generate waste, whether it is the containers from the food you buy or old and broken consumer products. In short, the very process of creating the values that we need to live and enjoy our lives results in waste and contaminants. To demand that we produce no pollution is to demand that we stop producing and using the values that we need to sustain and enhance our lives. To demand that we put an end to man-made pollution is to demand an end to the life-serving values that create pollution.

Certainly, nobody wants to drink poisonous water or to breathe toxic air. But clean air and water is not the goal of environmentalists.

> Whenever there is a hydroelectric dam to be built, it is the welfare of the snail darter or the Chinook salmon that is inviolate, and the welfare of man that is dispensable. Whenever there is a choice between cutting down trees for human use and leaving them in place for the spotted owl, it is the bird's home that environmentalists save and human habitation that goes unbuilt.
>
> Huge tracts of Arctic land are off-limits to productive enterprises, in order not to disturb the caribou and the ice floes. Mosquito- and alligator-infested swamps (euphemistically called *wetlands*) are deemed sacred, not to be defiled by man-made drainage.... The most beneficial projects, from housing developments to science observatories, are halted if there is any

---

8. "Pollution," Oxford Dictionaries, accessed October 30, 2011, http://oxforddictionaries.com/definition/pollution?region=us.

> danger—if there is any *allegation* of danger—to some piddling species.[9]

Rather than transform nature into the values that makes human life possible, environmentalists want man to leave nature untouched. In any "conflict" between man and nature, it is man who must sacrifice his values and interests.

This is a logical consequence of altruism. Altruism holds that we are to place the welfare and interests of others before our own. Is this not what occurs when we sacrifice the dam that could run our air conditioning, so that rivers can run "free"? Altruism holds that we must sacrifice our rights to the needs of others. Is this not what occurs when the needs of mosquitoes supersede the rights of a property owner? Altruism holds that we must sacrifice our values. Is this not what occurs when we refrain from drilling for oil, prohibit the construction of new refineries, or deny ourselves other life-enhancing values because of concerns for the environment?

It is rational to want clean water and air for the purpose of sustaining human life. But environmentalists do not want to sustain human life. Environmentalists actually want to extinguish humans from the face of the earth. For example, Ingrid Newkirk, national director of People for the Ethical Treatment of Animals (PeTA), publicly said, "Humans have grown like a cancer. We're the biggest blight on the face of the earth."[10] David Graber, a biologist for the United States National Park Service, writes:

> Human happiness, and certainly human fecundity, are not as important as a wild and healthy planet. I know social scientists who remind me that people are part of nature, but it isn't true…. We have become a plague upon ourselves and upon the Earth.
>
> It is cosmically unlikely that the developed world will choose to end its orgy of fossil-energy consumption, and the Third World its suicidal consumption of landscape. Until such time as

---

9. Peter Schwartz, "The Philosophy of Privation," in *Return of the Primitive* (New York: Meridian, 1999), pp. 219-20.

10. "Ingrid Newkirk," Wikiquote.com, accessed June 28, 2011, http://en.wikiquote.org/wiki/Ingrid_Newkirk.

Homo sapiens should decide to rejoin nature, some of us can only hope for the right virus to come along.[11]

John Davis, editor of *Wild Earth Magazine,* writes about The Wildlands Project, which seeks to depopulate as much as 50 percent of North America. He explicitly states the goal of the project: "Does all the foregoing mean that Wild Earth and The Wildlands Project advocate the end of industrialized civilization? Most assuredly. Everything civilized must go...."[12] While environmentalists would prefer to dismantle civilization by using bulldozers and viruses, they are content to do so by strangling businesses with regulations and controls that impede production.

Are these our only choices? Must we choose between ending civilization on the one hand or living with polluted air and water on the other hand? Is our choice between cell phones, automobiles, and air conditioning, along with burning rivers, polluted oceans, and noxious air, versus living in caves, eating raw meat, and living to the ripe old age of twenty, along with clean air and water? Fortunately, we do not have to choose between the life of a primitive and poisoned water. We do not need to exterminate the human race, dismantle industrial society, or accept polluted waterways. What is needed is the recognition and protection of property rights.

The right to property means the freedom to own, use, keep, and dispose of material values. Just as liberty means that others cannot morally interfere with your freedom to act as you choose, property rights mean that others may not morally interfere with your freedom to use your property as you choose, as long as you respect the mutual rights of others. Your rights place boundaries on what others may morally do. They cannot deprive you of your right to use your property, whether intentionally or through neglect or accident. Most understand this principle as it applies to property such as automobiles, homes, money, and similar values. If you cause an auto accident, you are responsible for the damage done to another's vehicle. If your tree falls on your neighbor's roof, you are responsible for repairing the damage. If you store hazardous

---

11. David M. Graber, "Mother Nature as a Hothouse Flower," *Los Angeles Times,* October 22, 1989, accessed June 28, 2011, http://articles.latimes.com/1989-10-22/books/bk-726_1_bill-mckibben/2.

12. John Stewart, "What is the Dirty Little Secret?" About.com, accessed June 28, 2011, http://4wheeldrive.about.com/cs/drivingtipssafety/a/wildlands_2.htm.

chemicals on your property and they seep onto adjoining land, you must pay for the clean up. While these examples are clear, how do we apply the principle of property rights to a resource that moves, such as air or water. Aren't air and water common to all? Aren't air and water "public property"? For centuries, this has been the view.

Founded on both Roman and English common law, the doctrine of "public trust" holds that certain resources, such as rivers, lakes, and oceans, should *not* be privately owned, but held in trust by government for all to use. In 1892, the United States Supreme Court cited this doctrine, ruling that state governments hold title to resources such as rivers and lakes, "a title held in trust for the people of the state, that they may enjoy the navigation of the waters, carry on commerce over them, and have liberty of fishing therein, freed from the obstruction or interference of private parties."[13]

This "public ownership" results in the well-known "tragedy of the commons." When a resource—whether a pasture, a berry patch, or a river—is owned "in common," its users have no motivation to protect or maintain its long-term value. Instead, they tend to use the resource for their own short-term gain, fearing that others will deplete the resource before they get their "fair share." For example, if a pasture is "publicly owned," each individual will graze his animals frequently, for fear that others will let their animals eat all the grass. The result is that the grass is quickly eaten, and there is no food for any of the animals. When a resource is not privately owned, nobody has a motivation to manage that resource for its long-term value. "Public ownership," which means the absence of property rights, has resulted in polluted air and waterways, and impositions on taxpayers to manage and clean up their "property." The failure of government to recognize and protect property rights is *the cause* of our polluted waters and air.

Certainly, moving resources, such as air and water, present complexities that are not present with other forms of property. But complexity does not negate the principle: others cannot morally interfere with your use of your property.

Let us begin with a simple example and the concept of nuisance. As discussed in the previous chapter, nuisance is highly

---

13. *Illinois Central* R. *Co. v Illinois* (1892) 146 U.S. 387, 452.

contextual. An action that does not interfere with another's use of his property in one context may do so in another. For example, if you use your grill on your back patio, you will generate smoke. But the amount of smoke that you create is unlikely to impact your neighbors. However, if you build a bonfire in your back yard and send plumes of smoke over your fence, your actions could pose a threat to the welfare of your neighbors. But, if you build a bonfire in the middle of your thousand-acre ranch, nobody is likely to be impacted by the smoke. In each instance, you have generated smoke, but your action is a nuisance only when that smoke prevents others from using and enjoying their property. You have a right to use the air that is on your property, just as your neighbors have a right to use the air that is on their property. If you wish to fill your air with smoke, you have a moral right to do so. However, if you fill your neighbor's air with smoke so that he cannot use and enjoy his property, you have violated his right to use that air.

Whether or not an action causes harm (or poses an objective threat) is a matter of context. Government regulations ignore this fact, declaring certain actions illegal, regardless of the context. In other words, regulations criminalize certain actions even when nobody's property rights are being violated. And, as we have seen, those regulations have not lead to clean water.

If the absence of property rights leads to polluted water, how do we apply property rights to lakes, rivers, streams, and oceans? To answer this, let us first examine the meaning of "property."

The concept "property" recognizes the fact that human life requires material values, such as food, clothing, I-Pods, and automobiles, for its sustenance and enjoyment. These values require thought and effort to come into existence, and they rightfully belong to those who exert the necessary thought and effort. John Locke recognized this principle in *The Second Treatise on Government*, writing:

> Though the earth, and all inferior creatures, be common to all men, yet every man has a property in his own person: this no body has any right but himself. The labour of his body, and the work of his hands, we may say, are properly his. Whatsoever then he removes out of the state that nature hath provided, and left in

> it, he hath mixed his labour with, and joined it to something that is his own, and thereby makes it his property.[14]

Locke, of course, was speaking of the state of nature—a time when natural resources were unowned and available for all to use. Once a person has "mixed his labor" with a resource, it becomes his property and others may not morally interfere with his use of that property. When property is privately owned, a person cannot trespass on his neighbor's property, pick his berries or chop down his trees, and then morally claim ownership of those products.

Ayn Rand elaborated on Locke's identification, noting that the effort required to transform nature into property is both mental and physical: "Any material element or resource which, in order to become of use or value to men, requires the application of human knowledge and effort, should be private property—by the right of those who apply the knowledge and effort."[15] Ownership recognizes the causal relationship between human thought and effort, and human values. The former cause the latter. The person who enacts a cause rightly owns the effects of his actions.

If you cause an accident and damage is done to the property of another, you are responsible for—that is, you own—the effects of your actions. If you cause a house or new software or a new gadget to come into existence, you own the effects of your actions. Each individual has a moral right to the consequences of his actions. At the same time, each individual is morally responsible for the consequences of his actions.

Conversely, until an individual (or individuals) has transformed a natural resource into a human value, that resource is unowned—it belongs to no one. Oil under the ocean floor and minerals on the moon are unowned until someone transforms those resources into a value. Thus, that which is unowned remains available for all to use.

In this regard, the Homestead Act of 1862 established the proper principles by which individuals can morally claim ownership of unowned resources. To claim ownership, settlers were required

---

14. John Locke, "Of Property", *Two Treatises of Government and A Letter Concerning Toleration*, Digireads.com Publishing, pp. 79- 80.

15. Ayn Rand, "The Property Status of Airwaves," in *Capitalism: The Unknown Ideal* (New York: Signet, 1967), p. 122.

to improve a plot of land and maintain that improvement for five years. In other words, the settler "mixed his labor" with the land to transform it into a human value and then that land was rightfully his. It is important to understand that ownership extends only to that which has been transformed into a human value. For example, settlers in the American West could not claim ownership over plots of land that they did not improve. Ownership extended only to that area that they improved and maintained.

With a proper understanding of the nature of property, we can begin to identify how ownership of moving resources such as waterways can be claimed. The following are a few examples:[16]

- Those who construct wharves, piers, and ports to provide greater access to the waterway are properly the owners of the portion of waterway immediately surrounding the structures they have built.
- The builder of an offshore oil platform owns the surrounding waterway necessary to run his operation.
- The builder of a beach for purposes of human recreation owns a portion of the adjacent waterway consonant with that use.
- A fisherman who, to increase the fish population, takes measures to improve the habitat within a fishery is the legitimate owner of that portion of the waterway he has improved.

In each of these examples, an individual or business transformed nature into a human value. The oil under the ocean has been there for millennia, but until someone exerted the thought and effort required to extract that oil, it was of no value to human beings. The company that extracts the oil creates a value that did not exist before. Similarly, the ocean floor has remained in a state of nature since its formation. The individual or business that improves the habitat creates a value where none existed.

With the ownership of waterways established, issues such as pollution become a matter of protecting property rights. Just as you cannot damage the automobile, home, or other property of your neighbor with impunity, damaging another's waterway would carry legal penalties. In short, if waterways were privately owned, you

---

16. J. Brian Phillips and Alan Germani, "The Practicality of Private Waterways," *The Objective Standard 5*, no. 1, (Spring 2010): pp. 57-58.

could not morally pollute in such a fashion that the property of others would be damaged.

> If an individual (or a corporation) dumps toxins into a river, thereby killing fish stocks or vegetation, or making the water unsafe for human or livestock consumption or for human recreation, he violates the rights of property owners in or along the waterway. Even in unowned waters, one may pollute only *if* and to the extent that one can do so without (demonstrably) damaging another's property. But, given water's free-flowing nature, the ability of individuals and corporations to pollute a waterway without violating another's property rights is quite limited. Those who do harm another's property—whether on land or in waterways—risk prosecution and punishment by a government dedicated to protecting its citizens' rights.[17]

The recognition and protection of property rights allows individuals to act according to their own judgment and use their property as they judge best. If they take actions that damage the property owned by others, they are held responsible. Recognizing and protecting property rights provides us with the principles required to have clean air and water.

While most waterways are "public property," there are examples of privately owned waterways, and they demonstrate that the recognition and protection of property rights is not only moral, but also practical.

In Scotland, most coastal salmon fisheries have been privately owned for centuries. Many of the fishery owners lease their fishing rights to sports fishermen as a source of income. Owners protect the value of their property against over-fishing, pollution, and other threats. For example, when a hydroelectric dam was built on a salmon stream at the town of Pitlochry, the migration of salmon was threatened, and with it the value of the property of upstream owners. Those property owners had purchased their property largely because of the value brought by the salmon. To prevent the migration of the salmon would be a violation of the prior property rights of the upstream property owners. To protect the rights of those owners, the English Parliament required the construction of a

---

17. Ibid., p. 63.

"salmon ladder" to allow the salmon to make their way past the dam.[18] The practical benefits of private waterways also extend to the problem of pollution: a study by the Fisheries and Aquaculture Department of the United Nations in 1985 found that more than 95 percent of privately owned rivers in Scotland were unpolluted, but less than 67 percent of the "publicly owned" rivers were pollution free.[19]

In England, where common law protects rights to recreational use of rivers, the Pride of Derby fishing club successfully sued the city of Derby, the state-run electricity board, and a business for the discharge of sewage and other waste that damaged their fishing. In a similar case, when Britain's Environmental Agency delayed prosecuting the Anglian Water Company for polluting a river, a private fisherman successfully sued the company. Since the 1950s, the Angler's Cooperative Association—a private association of angling clubs and fishermen in Great Britain—has handled more than fifteen hundred pollution cases, often winning large damage settlements that allow property owners to restore their fisheries.[20]

In the United States, nearly every state *prohibits* the private ownership of streams on the grounds that they should be held in the "public trust," with the result that many streams are polluted, over-fished, or both. One notable exception is Yellowstone Valley in Montana, where many streams begin and end on private property and have *not* been subjected to the "public trust" doctrine. As in Scotland, property owners sell fishing leases as a source of income, and here too, the waters are clean and well-stocked with fish.[21] Property owners voluntarily limit livestock grazing in proximity to the streams to reduce pollution, and they also limit access to their streams to protect wildlife and provide an uncrowded, high-quality fishing experience.

As we have seen, the failure to recognize and protect property rights is *the cause* of polluted air and water. As we have also seen, the

---

18. "Stream of Improvements," Adam Smith Institute, accessed February 1, 2011, http://www.adamsmith.org/80ideas/idea/18.htm.

19. "Inland fisheries of Europe", Fisheries and Aquaculture Department of the United Nations, accessed February 1, 2011, http://www.fao.org/docrep/009/t0798e/T0798E18.htm.

20. "Stream of Improvements," Adam Smith Institute, accessed February 1, 2011, http://www.adamsmith.org/80ideas/idea/18.htm.

21. Ibid.

recognition and protection of property rights can and does lead to cleaner water. The owners of the property have a vested interest to maintain and protect the long-term value of their property. The protection of property rights—not government mandates and prohibitions—has proven practical in keeping waterways clean. It is practical because it is moral.

Bad ideas lead to bad consequences. Ideas contaminated with the poison of altruism lead to polluted air and water. In contrast, the protective power of individual rights provides us with the values we need to live and enjoy our lives, including clean air and water.

We have now seen how the recognition and protection of property rights can be used to address numerous conflicts—"incompatible" land uses, nuisance, and pollution. Let us now examine how these same principles apply to America's energy policies.

14

Government Power versus the Energy Industry

The OPEC oil embargo of the early 1970s sent gasoline prices from a national average of 38.5 cents per gallon in May 1973 to 55.1 cents in June 1974, an increase of more than 43 percent. In response, President Richard Nixon "asked"—and we know what it means when the President "asks" you to do something—gas station owners to refrain from selling gas on Saturday nights and Sundays. When station owners complied, long lines formed at gas stations.[1] During 2000 and 2001, residents and businesses in California suffered rolling blackouts when electricity providers could not meet the state's energy demands. In the summer of 2008, gasoline prices rose to an all-time high—a national average of $4.12 per gallon. Incidents such as these prompt politicians and pundits to demand that government do "something." And "something" usually involves blaming businesses. For example, in 2011 socialist Senator Bernie Sanders said, "The skyrocketing price of gas and oil has nothing to do with the fundamentals of supply and demand, and has everything to do with Wall Street firms that are artificially jacking up the price of oil in the energy futures markets."[2] Similarly, President Obama said, "We are going to make sure that no one is

---

1. "1973 Oil Crisis," *Wikipedia*, accessed June 7, 2011, http://en.wikipedia.org/wiki/1973_oil_crisis.

2. John Stossel, "Gasoline and Onions," Real Clear Politics, May 4, 2011, accessed July 22, 2011, http://www.realclearpolitics.com/articles/2011/05/04/gasoline_and_onions_109746.html.

taking advantage of the American people for their own short-term gain."[3]

America's energy requirements grow each year. Manufacturing, transportation, lighting, cooling, and virtually every human activity create an enormous demand for energy. Don't we need a national energy plan? How do we deal with the nation's dependence on foreign oil? How can energy producers meet the nation's growing demand? Before we answer these questions, let us briefly examine America's energy policies.

For decades, politicians have talked about the need for a national energy plan that includes renewable sources. In the late 1970s, President Jimmy Carter said "that we must start now to develop the new, unconventional sources of energy we will rely on in the next century."[4] More recently, Barack Obama declared that "the transition to clean energy has the potential to grow our economy and create millions of jobs—but only if we accelerate that transition."[5] Both Presidents—along with many others—issued dire predictions of impending disaster if the nation did not adopt a comprehensive energy policy. Yet, they ignore the fact that the nation does have an energy policy. That policy consists of a mish-mash of government controls, regulations, and subsidies. It is a policy that imposes restrictions and mandates on energy producers, drives up costs, and results in shortages. It is a policy that has proven to be both impractical and immoral.

Consider the fact that, despite "deregulation," electricity companies remain heavily regulated. As one example, in Texas—which allegedly has deregulated electric companies—the Public Utilities Commission regulates, among other things, the frequency and format of electric bills, how electric meters must be read, standards for transmitting electricity, infrastructure for the electrical grid, a myriad of reporting requirements (such as service quality, transmission construction, and retail reliability), and pricing.[6] While

---

3. Ibid.

4. Jimmy Carter, "Televised Speech," April 18, 1977, accessed February 2, 2011, http://www.pbs.org/wgbh/amex/carter/filmmore/ps_energy.html.

5. Barack Obama, "Energy & Environment," White House, accessed February 2, 2011, http://www.whitehouse.gov/issues/energy-and-environment.

6. "Electric Substantive Rules," Public Utility Commission of Texas, accessed September 21, 2011, http://www.puc.state.tx.us/agency/rulesnlaws/subrules/electric/Electric.aspx.

details vary from state to state, electric companies are subject to price controls, prohibitions on vertical integration (some states prohibit a single company from producing, distributing, and delivering electricity), onerous regulations regarding new power plants, and prohibitions on long-term contracts between producers and distributors.[7] In fact, this last regulation was the cause of the rolling blackouts in California in 2000 and 2001—retail prices to consumers were capped while wholesale prices were not subject to controls. When wholesale prices increased, electricity providers were forced to sell power for less than they were paying for it. Not surprisingly, California's electric companies suffered massive financial losses, leading to the energy crisis. This is just one example of how regulations prohibit energy producers from supplying the energy that Americans need.

Oil companies are also subject to a plethora of regulations and restrictions. For example, the federal government has prohibited drilling in the Arctic National Wildlife Refuge (ANWR), an area that is bigger than the states of Maryland, Vermont, and New Hampshire combined. The area of ANWR in question "is completely flat and barren with no trees, hills, or mountains. Nine months of the year [it] is covered with snow and ice and practically void of life."[8] Though inhospitable to life, it is estimated that the coastal plain of ANWR could produce 1.5 million barrels of oil per day—nearly 25 percent of America's current production.[9] But those numbers are only estimates because Congress has prohibited any drilling in this vast barren wasteland. Similarly, though America's coastal waters contain an abundance of oil and natural gas, in 1990 President George H. W. Bush issued an executive order that placed a moratorium on offshore leases to oil companies. Today, most of the California coast and all of the Oregon and Washington coasts, the North Atlantic coast, and the Eastern Gulf of Mexico are under this moratorium. While politicians whine about America's dependence on foreign oil, they simultaneously prohibit oil companies from drilling in many oil rich parts of America. And,

---

7. See Raymond C. Niles, "Property Rights and the Crisis of the Electric Grid," *The Objective Standard 3*, no. 2, (Summer 2008): pp.11-27.

8. "What is ANWR and Where is It?" ANWR.org, accessed July 21, 2011, http://www.anwr.org/ANWR-Basics/What-is-ANWR-and-where-is-it.php.

9. "Making the Case for ANWR," ANWR.org, accessed July 21, 2011, http://www.anwr.org/Background/Making-the-Case-for-ANWR.php.

while making empty and impossible promises about creating jobs, those same politicians prevent oil companies from actually creating jobs.

Even when drilling is permitted, oil companies are subject to voluminous environmental regulations that significantly increase costs and stifle investment. For example, to drill offshore, an oil company must comply with the National Environmental Policy Act of 1969, the Clean Air Act of 1970, the Coastal Zone Management Act of 1972, the Endangered Species Act of 1973, and the Clean Water Act of 1977. Or consider the Trans-Alaska Pipeline, which could only open in 1977 after the owners obtained 515 federal permits and 832 state permits.[10] As another example of the burdens placed on energy producers, it took one company, Arizona Clean Fuels, seven years just to get a permit to build a refinery, primarily because of environmental regulations. Planning for the refinery began in 1998, and in late 2011 construction had not yet started because of the delays in securing government permission to build the refinery.[11]

Due to regulations and the threat of lawsuits, *not one* new refinery has been built in the United States since 1976. One commentator states that the reason refineries are not particularly profitable is because "environmentalists fight planning and construction every step of the way and government red-tape makes the task all but impossible."[12] Largely because of expenses imposed by government regulations, between 1981 and 2001 the number of refineries operating in the United States decreased by 52 percent. Even though the remaining refineries regularly operate at more than 90 percent of their capacity, they cannot keep up with demand, and the result is reduced inventories of gasoline.[13] In addition, according to the Government Accountability Office, government requirements for specially formulated gasoline in certain areas of

---

10. "Prudhoe Bay Production," ANWR.org, accessed July 21, 2011, http://www.anwr.org/Background/Prudhoe-Bay-Production.php.

11. "U.S. Oil Refining Capability," FactCheck.org, May 12, 2008, accessed July 21, 2011, http://factcheck.org/2008/05/us-oil-refining-capability/.

12. "US Appears to Have Built its Last Refinery," *Alexander's Oil and Gas Connections*, June 12, 2001, accessed February 2, 2011, http://www.gasandoil.com/goc/news/ntn12966.htm.

13. Ujjayant Chakravorty and Céline Nauges, "Boutique Fuels and Market Power," page 6, accessed January 13, 2011, http://ideas.repec.org/p/emo/wp2003/0511.html.

the country—so-called "boutique fuels"— has "made it more complicated and costly to supply gasoline, elevating the risk of localized supply disruptions."[14] The result is "a tight gasoline market characterized by frequent price spikes, even when the acquisition costs of crude oil did not increase significantly."[15]

Essentially, the government's energy policy consists of making it increasingly expensive and difficult for energy producers to operate, while the nation's businesses and consumers simultaneously demand more energy. The results of this policy are not surprising:

> It causes energy shortages, brownouts, and blackouts that thwart everyone's ability to be productive and enjoy life. And it results in higher prices not only for energy, but for every good and service that depends on energy—which means every good and service in the marketplace, from food to transportation to medical care to sporting events to education to housing.[16]

In short, the government's current energy policy has been an abysmal failure. As we have seen in other industries and fields, government regulations and controls prevent energy producers from acting according to their own judgment and everybody is forced to pay the price. Contrary to the claims of many politicians, the unfettered free market has provided an abundance of increasingly affordable energy. It is government intervention that has created our dependence on foreign oil, high gas prices, and energy crisis after energy crisis.

Increasingly, decisions regarding energy production are made by politicians and bureaucrats who impose their decisions and desires upon the experts in the field—those who own and operate energy companies. Given the number of agencies—on both the state and federal level—that regulate energy producers in one form or another, it is not surprising that the government's energy policy is marked with contradictions. For example, while decrying the nation's dependence on foreign oil, government officials prohibit

---

14. "Gasoline Markets," United States Government Accountability Office, accessed March 27, 2011, http://www.gao.gov/new.items/d05421.pdf.

15. Ibid., p. 7.

16. Brian P. Simpson, "The Assault on Energy Producers," *The Objective Standard 3*, no. 4, (Winter 2008-09): p.1.

domestic drilling in large areas of the country and impede that which is permitted. Further, while more than 75 percent of the citizens of Alaska, the Alaska legislature, the governor, the congressional delegation, and the only permanent residents within ANWR support drilling in ANWR, Congress will not permit it.[17]

As with every issue in which the government regulates businesses, the various agencies controlling the energy industry are a magnet for special interest groups seeking to influence decisions and policies. Environmental groups seek to stop drilling and the construction of power plants. Politically connected businessmen, such as T. Boone Pickens, seek subsidies for alternative energy. Consumer advocates demand price caps and other restrictions on energy producers that make profitability more difficult. Each of these organizations, and more, subject government officials to a steady parade of individuals and groups seeking to shape the nation's energy "plan." And they seek to do so by trampling on the property rights of energy producers when they demand regulations and controls; they trample on your rights as a consumer when they limit your choices and force you to pay higher prices; they trample on your property rights as a taxpayer when they demand subsidies. This last is particularly insulting when we consider the "results."

One example is Range Fuels, which received a $76 million grant in 2007 from the Department of Energy for the purpose of turning wood chips into ethanol. The plant closed in early 2011 without producing a single drop of ethanol.[18] Also in 2011, Solyndra, a manufacturer of solar panels, filed for bankruptcy and stuck taxpayers with $535 million in loans guaranteed by the Department of Energy. Or consider the U.S. Synfuels Corporation, created by Congress in 1980 to provide subsidies to companies seeking to develop alternative sources of energy. After a series of scandals and charges of mismanagement, Synfuels was shut down in 1986 without producing any results other than wasting $1.2 billion of taxpayer money. We can only guess where these tax dollars have gone and whose pockets they have lined. Despite these failures, and

---

17. "Making the Case for ANWR."

18. Timothy P. Carney, "Green-energy Plant Sucks up Subsidies, then Goes Bust," *Washington Examiner*, February 6, 2011, accessed March 27, 2011, http://washingtonexaminer.com/politics/2011/02/green-energy-plant-sucks-subsidies-then-goes-bust.

many others like them, advocates of alternative energy continue to demand a "Manhattan Project" approach to alternative energy—they want the government to throw massive amounts of money at the "problem." They refuse to admit that government "investments" in alternative energy waste money and divert resources. They refuse to acknowledge that decades of government meddling have hampered energy producers and is the true cause of the nation's energy problems.

The advocates of alternative energy schemes ignore the fact that if such energy sources were profitable, private businesses would be utilizing them. Private companies are in business to make money, and they will invest their money where they believe they will achieve the highest return on their investment. The fact is, alternative sources, such as wind and solar, are unprofitable. That is why T. Boone Pickens abandoned his plans for a giant wind farm in Texas. Hence the need for government intervention: subsidies make alternative energy "profitable," while restrictions on traditional energy sources drive up their cost, thereby making alternative sources more cost competitive. As one example, during the 2008 Presidential campaign, while pushing for alternative energy, Obama acknowledged that under his "plan of a cap and trade system, electricity rates would necessarily skyrocket."[19] The immediate result is higher costs to consumers. The long-term result is the inability of energy companies to plan for the future, as they do not know what new regulations and controls will be imposed on them.

Despite the abysmal record of government intervention in the energy industry, many Americans continue to clamor for more government intervention. They believe that the same people who run the post office and our public schools can somehow create an effective energy plan. At the same time, oil company executives—those who have proven that they can provide for our energy needs—are hauled before Congress to defend their actions and their profits.

For example, in 2005, after two hurricanes struck the Gulf Coast—a major oil producing and refining region—gasoline, diesel and natural gas prices soared. Congress then demanded that oil

---

19. Ed Morrissey, "Obama: I'll Make Energy Prices 'Skyrocket'," HotAir.com, November 2, 2008, accessed July 21, 2011, http://hotair.com/archives/2008/11/02/obama-ill-make-energy-prices-skyrocket/.

company executives plod to Washington to explain the dynamics of supply and demand.[20] Then, in 2008, when oil prices were reaching new highs, the Senate Judiciary Committee again grilled oil company executives. Ignoring the government's role in the price of oil, Senator Richard Durbin scolded the executives: "You have to sense what you're doing to us—we're on the precipice here, about to fall into recession. Does it trouble any one of you—the costs you're imposing on families, on small businesses, on truckers?"[21] Then again, in 2011, when gasoline prices approached $4 per gallon, Congress demanded that oil company executives explain the mechanics of pricing.[22] In short, within a five-year period, Congress forced oil company executives to interrupt their efforts to produce energy and instead explain basic economic truths to Senators. One would think that United States Senators would have a better grasp of the science of economics. What is their motivation? Why do these politicians—who cannot even balance the federal budget—think that they have a better grasp of economic truths than executives who run profitable businesses?

Certainly, part of the motivation is to score points with the voters back home who are angry about high energy prices. But the real motivation is much more sinister. Even with their immense power, these politicians cannot control the operations of the market, and they don't like that fact. These politicians want unlimited power over energy companies, and they will use threats, subpoenas, and insults to make it clear who is in charge. As with Mercedes Clemens, John Thoburn, Dan Allgyer, and countless others, politicians view oil executives as mere pawns to be used as government officials decree.

What is the alternative? How can America's growing energy demands be met? The history of the nineteenth century shows what

---

20. Vikas Bajaj, "Oil Executives Defend Profits Before a Critical Congress," *New York Times*, November 9, 2005, accessed July 2, 2011, http://www.nytimes.com/2005/11/09/business/09cnd-energy.html?hp.

21. Steve Hargreaves, "Don't Blame Us for Prices - Oil Execs," CNNMoney.com, May 21, 2008, accessed July 2, 2011, http://money.cnn.com/2008/05/21/news/economy/oil_hearing/index.htm.

22. JoAnn Merrigan, "Oil Execs Called Before Congress Today, Will Defend Record Profits," WSAV.com, May 12, 2011, accessed July 2, 2011, http://www2.wsav.com/news/2011/may/12/oil-execs-called-congress-today-will-defend-record-ar-1835552/.

is possible when energy producers are free to act on their own judgment and keep the profits that they earn.

For centuries, man had sought to overcome the darkness of night with man-made light. Until the early nineteenth century, little had changed from Greek and Roman times—individuals were limited to expensive oil lamps and candles to provide illumination. (In 1823 sperm whale oil—the premium lamp oil—cost forty-three cents per gallon and rose to $2.55 in 1866, or more than $36 in 2011 dollars.)[23] In the 1820s, scientists and entrepreneurs began seeking improved illuminants. Because they had no arbitrary government restrictions, but were instead free to act on their independent judgment, within two decades, three alternative sources of illumination—camphene, stearin oil, and coal gas—were widely available. These new illuminants were better and cheaper than what was previously available, and consumers eagerly bought them.[24]

However, because individuals were free to develop new and better products, these revolutionary, life-enhancing illuminants did not dominate the market for long. In 1846, Abraham Gesner, a Canadian scientist, discovered a process for distilling coal oil into kerosene. Though Gesner's kerosene was 15 percent cheaper than camphene (at the time the lowest priced illuminant), his business venture failed. But other individuals—also free to act as they deemed best—improved on Gesner's process, and by 1860 millions of dollars had been invested into refining coal oil into kerosene.

The discovery of oil in 1859 further revolutionized the energy market. As more discoveries were made, capital flowed into the industry and the number of producers and refiners skyrocketed. The result was an abundance of kerosene and steadily declining prices: from fifty-eight cents a gallon in 1865, the price of kerosene fell to twenty-six cents in 1870. And further declines were to come as efficiencies increased—by 1874 kerosene sold for a mere ten cents a gallon.[25] In a free market, the price of kerosene *declined*

23. Barry W. Poulson, "Technological Change and the Profit Motive," *The Journal of Libertarian Studies 8*, no. 2, (Summer 2008).

24. Alex Epstein, "Energy at the Speed of Thought: The Original Alternative Energy Market," *The Objective Standard 4*, no. 2, (Summer 2009).

25. Alex Epstein, "Vindicating Capitalism: The Real History of the Standard Oil Company," *The Objective Standard 3*, no. 2, (Summer 2008): pp. 35-44.

nearly 83 percent over a nine year period. Compare that to the 100 percent *increase* in energy prices Americans experienced between 2001 and 2010.[26] In the nineteenth century, the freedom of scientists and entrepreneurs to use their property as they judged best—whether drilling for oil or building refineries—allowed even the poorest Americans to illuminate the night and extend their days. And as always happens when men are free, there were more innovations to come.

In the 1870s, Thomas Edison developed the first practical and commercially viable light bulb. At first the cost of electric lighting was more expensive than kerosene, but because men were free to innovate and act on their judgment, by 1932 the price of electricity had fallen by two-thirds and 70 percent of Americans had electricity.[27] Electricity also provided additional benefits—it could be used to power refrigerators, ovens, fans, and many other appliances. Not only did it provide safe, clean, and affordable lighting, it also enhanced lives in a myriad of other ways.

As these examples show, what was once a luxury—illuminating the night—became affordable to everyone because men were free to think and act without arbitrary government controls, regulations, and prohibitions. In less than one hundred years, the energy industry was completely revolutionized—from an expensive prerogative of the wealthy, energy became abundantly and inexpensively available to the masses. And the revolution in energy gave birth to new industries—such as drilling and refining—while also making possible increased productivity on the part of workers. Everyone's life was improved with new life-enhancing values, such as refrigerators, electric stoves, and air conditioning. Scientists and entrepreneurs, each pursuing his own personal profit, made life better for everyone. They did not need a national energy policy or subsidies to develop alternative energy sources. All they needed was freedom. And that is all that today's energy producers need.

We have seen the destructive consequences of government regulations and controls: higher prices, reduced consumer choices, destroyed lives, and energy crises. But if we abolished government

---

26. "Consumer Price Index for All Urban Consumers: Energy," Federal Reserve Bank of St. Louis, accessed February 2, 2011, http://research.stlouisfed.org/fred2/data/CPIENGNS.txt.

27. Niles, "Property Rights and Crisis of Electric Grid," p. 11.

regulations, wouldn't giant corporations monopolize their industry? Wouldn't they manipulate markets and force consumers to pay even higher prices? Don't we need some regulations to ensure a competitive marketplace? Let us now examine the issue of monopolies.

15

Stop Robbing the Barons

Let us say that you start a business. You work long hours to improve your product, maximize your efficiencies, expand your customer base, and market your product. In time, your business becomes very successful and you capture a large portion of the market—let us say, 90 percent. At the same time, you decrease your prices by 83 percent. You are proud of your accomplishment. After years of hard work, you have achieved the success that you dreamed was possible. And then one day, an agent from the Department of Justice visits your office. The Department has received complaints that you have too much market share, that your pricing is anti-competitive, that your market dominance is unfair, and that others cannot compete with you. The Department is going to charge you with violating the antitrust statutes.

You have always operated your business with the utmost honesty and integrity. Sure, you get the best pricing from your suppliers—you are their biggest and best customer. Yes, you cut shrewd deals to get exclusivity in certain stores—that is what astute businessmen do. As you listen to the agent explain the charges against you, you think of all the effort you exerted to produce the best product you could at the lowest possible price. You think of the millions of customers who love your product and buy it willingly. And the result of your efforts is prosecution for being too successful. This is the ultimate result of the antitrust laws—the productive are punished for being "too" productive. This is what happened to John Rockefeller, Bill Gates, and the many other businessmen who have been prosecuted under the antitrust laws.

Without government regulations, it is alleged that businesses would develop into monopolies, or they would combine with competitors to form trusts (as Rockefeller did) and cartels to dominate industries.[1] Absent competition, wouldn't these monopolies charge outrageous prices? And what choice would consumers have but to pay those prices? Don't we need government to "level the playing field" and promote competition? Doesn't the free enterprise system depend on competition? While antitrust laws enjoy widespread support, they are founded on a number of philosophical evasions and historical distortions. Let us begin by looking at the rise of the antitrust statutes.

During the nineteenth century, large-scale business enterprises began to emerge. Improved transportation allowed companies that previously served a local community or a small region to reach a larger customer base. Improved capital markets provided access to the money required to build factories and purchase equipment. Improved technology—fueled by scientific discoveries—permitted mass production and the development of industries that previously did not exist. More abundant and less expensive energy allowed greater mechanization and productivity. Political freedom—including the recognition and protection of property rights—provided a culture in which men could take bold risks and benefit from their successes. That freedom allowed men of unparalleled vision to act without arbitrary government controls and build companies that dominated their industry. In the process, they grew immensely wealthy.

Because of altruism, many viewed these fortunes as an indisputable sign of corruption and immorality. Because the great industrialists put their own personal profit ahead of the needs of others, they were labeled "robber barons," a pejorative term that implied that the industrialists had stolen their wealth. But where did that wealth come from? Did it come from the subsistence farmers who flocked to the factories for jobs? Did it come from the cottage worker who could barely feed his family? In truth, the great industrialists *created* that wealth—they produced the values that others wanted and needed. And they did so on a scale previously

---

1. Trusts are a method of business organization in which a number of firms transfer control of their assets to a third party, generally to achieve greater efficiencies through economies of scale. Cartels are agreements between producers to limit production, fix prices, and set other terms of operation. Monopolies, trusts, and cartels are considered anti-competitive.

thought unimaginable. Wealth does not exist as a fixed pie to be divided up among individuals; wealth must be created, and the potential for creating more wealth always exists. The great businessmen realized that potential, and they provided a better life for millions. For that, they were condemned.

As the nineteenth century came to a close, citizens and politicians began to demand government action to regulate and control large businesses. These efforts were first confined to the state level, but in 1887 the federal government created its first regulatory agency—the Interstate Commerce Commission. Three years later, the Sherman Antitrust Act was passed to "protect" competition. At the time, Congressman William Mason, who supported the act, said:

> trusts have made products cheaper, have reduced prices; but if the price of oil, for instance, were reduced to one cent a barrel, it would not right the wrong done to people of this country by the *trusts* which have destroyed legitimate competition and driven honest men from legitimate business enterprise.[2]

In other words, lower prices for consumers are considered a bad thing if "honest men" are driven from business. The implication being that the only way in which "honest men" can be driven from business is by dishonesty and corruption on the part of their competitors. The fact is, "honest men" can be driven from business for a large number of reasons: an inferior product, poor service, inefficient production, ineffective marketing, or simply not being as good as competitors. Regardless, given that every activity in which a business engages somehow impacts competition, and therefore could drive "honest men" from business, the Sherman Antitrust Act granted the government unlimited power to control businesses.

It is commonly believed that such controls are not only compatible with a competitive market economy, but necessary for competition to thrive: "Because of fears during the late 1800s that monopolies dominated America's free market economy, Congress passed the Sherman Antitrust Act in 1890 to combat anti-competitive practices, reduce market domination by individual corporations, and preserve unfettered competition as the rule of

---

2. Congressional Record, 51st Congress, 1st session, House, June 20, 1890, p. 4100.

trade."[3] Consider the contradiction in this claim. Freedom means an absence of government coercion—the right to act according to one's own judgment. The above quote tells us that, in order to "protect" freedom, some individuals are to be prohibited—by government coercion—from acting on their judgment. In order to "preserve unfettered competition," some individuals are to be fettered in their ability to compete. Government regulations and free markets are incompatible. Indeed, they are polar opposites. To illustrate the absurdity of claiming that government intervention is necessary to protect free markets, let us apply that idea to another realm known for competition—professional athletics.

From 1959 to 1966, the Boston Celtics basketball team won the championship of the National Basketball Association (NBA) a record eight straight times. During the thirteen-year period from 1957 to 1969, they won the championship eleven times. The Celtics dominated their league unlike any professional sports team in history. From 1957 to 1969, the Celtics were "anti-competitive." Based on antitrust theory, the Celtics should have been broken up, fined, and forced to share the secret of their success with other teams. According to antitrust theory, the government should have intervened to "level the playing field." Would that have been just? Would fans have cared to watch, knowing that, if their team was successful, the players might be fined or thrown into jail? Would the players be motivated to perform their best? This sounds ridiculous, yet, this is precisely the threat that hangs over the heads of America's most successful businessmen.

The Celtics succeeded because they were better than their competitors. Businesses succeed when they are better than their competitors; they succeed when they offer a better product or a better price or a better service. Economist Richard Salsman points out that "to compete in a free economy means to create and offer better values to customers than rival firms."[4] Basketball teams that successfully compete collect trophies, and lots of them. Businesses that successfully compete collect money, and lots of it.

---

3. "Antitrust," accessed January 15, 2011, http://topics.law.cornell.edu/wex/Antitrust.

4. Richard Salsman, "'What does Competition Mean Under Capitalism?" January 2, 2000, CapitalismMagazine.com, accessed November 7, 2011, http://www.capitalismmagazine.com/markets/antitrust/241-what-does-competition-mean-under-capitalism.html.

If antitrust laws are obviously absurd when applied to professional sports teams, why are they regarded as necessary when applied to businesses? Why are they regarded as good?

Antitrust laws, like the postal service's universal service obligation, are founded on an arbitrary assertion of how the market *should* operate. When reality does not conform to these arbitrary assertions, government intervention is deemed imperative to correct the "market failure." For mail delivery, imposing arbitrary standards means the universal service obligation is forced upon the postal service. For the market in general, imposing arbitrary standards means "unfettered competition" among competitors who have to be regulated, controlled, and fettered. At the heart of this view of the market is the idea of "pure and perfect competition." Salsman writes that "pure and perfect competition," as described in most economics textbooks, consists of several key elements:

- Every industry must have hundreds of firms and potential entrants, each firm with tiny shares of the overall market.
- Potential entrants must have equal and virtually cost-free access to the industry.
- Each firm must be completely devoid of any power to influence the price of his product or to alter his market share.
- Within each industry the products and services of each firm must be virtually indistinguishable from those of other firms…
- Profits are non-existent; if they exist there is an imperfection…
- Finally, every firm, consumer and investor must have [free] and "perfect information" about the state of prices, production, employment and markets as well as of each others' intentions…[5]

What would this mean for the NBA? Anyone who wants to own a team—and there should be hundreds of teams—should be

5. Richard Salsman, "'Pure and Perfect' Competition? By What Standard?" February 12, 2000, CapitalismMagazine.com, accessed December 20, 2011, http://www.capitalismmagazine.com/economics/271-quot-pure-and-perfect-quot-competition-by-what-standard.html.

able to do so, virtually cost free. Each team must be devoid of the power to influence its market share—its victories. The teams must be indistinguishable. A team cannot win more than it loses—that would be a profit. Each coach and player must have "perfect information" about every other player and coach, including their plans for each game. This would be absurd, yet this is the "ideal" that America's economic policy seeks to achieve, not in a game, but in life.

Consider what this would mean for business owners, employees, and consumers. If you are a business owner, you should have the same market share as your competitors, no matter the merits of your product or service. You cannot advertise, innovate, or improve efficiencies, as these could influence your price, alter your market share, or both. If a new competitor enters the market—and he should have virtually no costs to do so—your market share would decrease. In short, no matter what innovations you develop, no matter what actions you take, no matter how hard you work, your judgment and your effort are meaningless. In this "ideal" market, your market share and your profits are outside of your control. If your thought and effort has no impact on your success, how hard would you work? Would you even bother owning a business?

If you are an employee, you would not be allowed to suggest new products or services—these might influence market share. You should not expect a raise because your boss cannot increase prices. Forget about profit sharing or similar bonuses—there are no profits to share. In short, no matter what innovations you develop, no matter what actions you take, no matter how hard you work, your judgment and your effort are meaningless. How hard would you work under these conditions?

If you are a consumer, you would have no choices when it comes to products and services—they are to be indistinguishable. All personal computers should have the same processor, memory, and software. All restaurants should serve the same cuisine. All automobiles, homes, and clothing should be indistinguishable. In short, you should have no choices regarding products and services. There would be no sales or discounts—businesses that do so would be influencing their price, market share, or both. How enjoyable would your life be?

While declaring that business owners, investors, and consumers should have "perfect information," the advocates of "pure and perfect competition" hold that nobody should be able to act on that information. If a business owner cannot influence prices or market share, if his products are to be indistinguishable from competitors, what is there for him to think about? If there are to be no profits, what do investors have to consider? They can't make money, no matter where they invest. If consumers have no choices, what is the purpose of "perfect information"?

Do these sound like serious ideas or a really bad joke? The sad fact is, these ideas animate much of the government's economic policy. This "ideal" is impossible to achieve, yet it is used to justify government interventions that destroy the lives of individuals. And the greater the attempts to achieve this "ideal," the greater the destruction.

Consider Microsoft as an example. Founded in 1975, the company has spent more than half of its existence under the scrutiny and dictates of antitrust regulators. From 1990 to 2011, Microsoft was under investigation, on trial, or under court orders regarding antitrust issues. Why? When the government finally prosecuted Microsoft for antitrust violations, the judge on the case ruled that Microsoft "had unlawfully tied its Internet Explorer browser to Windows."[6] In other words, the company integrated two of its products for ease of use, and this was deemed unlawful. Microsoft made its products easier to use, and this was considered a crime. When Microsoft's antitrust saga finally ended in May 2011, the government said that it had "leveled the playing field."[7] But independent of the government's persecution, "technology… left the core issue—the browser wars—in the dust. Pervasive broadband has made it irrelevant whether PCs are sold with preinstalled copies of Microsoft's Internet Explorer. Now, anyone can download competing browsers—Mozilla Firefox, Apple Safari, Google Chrome, Opera—in a few minutes, for free."[8] In short, technology, not government intervention, provided consumers with

---

6. Sharon Pian Chan, "Long Antitrust Saga Ends for Microsoft," *The Seattle Times*, May 11, 2011, accessed July 23, 2011, http://seattletimes.nwsource.com/html/microsoft/2015029604_microsoft12.html.

7. Ibid.

8. Ibid.

more options. Despite this, Microsoft had to spend time and money defending itself, not only in America, but also in Europe, where the company was also prosecuted under antitrust laws. And what has Microsoft done since? Consider comments made about Microsoft:

> "Since the antitrust suit, they have become much more cautious and much less aggressive," said Michael Cusumano, a professor at MIT Sloan School of Management, who just wrote about Microsoft in the book "Staying Power."
>
> "They're afraid, it seems. Whether it's antitrust in U.S. or in Europe, they seem to be slowly reacting to the world around them, rather than trying to get in there fast."[9]

In other words, the company that was once a daring innovator has been reduced to playing follow-the-leader for fear of drawing the wrath of government officials. And it appears that Google—another successful innovator—is about to suffer the same fate as Microsoft. In June 2011, word leaked that the Department of Justice is investigating Google for antitrust violations.

Presented as an ideal, antitrust laws are founded on a gross evasion. Those who support antitrust evade the difference between economic power and political power: "[E]conomic power is exercised by means of a *positive*, by offering men a reward, an incentive, a payment, a value; political power is exercised by means of a *negative*, by the threat of punishment, injury, imprisonment, destruction. The businessman's tool is *values*; the bureaucrat's tool is fear."[10] Standard Oil, Microsoft, Google, and every successful business must offer values, or their customers will not willingly buy their products. Contemptuous of the productive genius of successful businessmen, power lusting politicians seek to control the productive through regulations, mandates, and prohibitions. Of course, they insist that their policies are in the "public interest." They argue that they are simply trying to create a "level playing field" on which all businesses can compete. But what is a "level playing field"? What does it mean to compete?

Contrary to the advocates of "pure and perfect competition," a competitive marketplace is not a primary. It is a by-product of a

---

9. Ibid.

10. Ayn Rand, "America's Persecuted Minority: Big Business," in *Capitalism: The Unknown Ideal*, p. 48.

free society. Economist George Reisman writes: "Competition, properly so-called, rests on the activity of separate, independent individuals owning and exchanging private property in the pursuit of their self-interest. It arises when two or more such individuals become rivals for the same trade."[11] In other words, competition results when two or more individuals, each acting on his own judgment and in his own self-interest, offer a similar product or service. And they compete by lowering their prices, producing a better product, offering superior service, or taking some other action that they judge to be a value to consumers and a competitive advantage to their business. Using government force to "level the playing field" means that a businessman must act contrary to his own judgment: he must charge a higher price, produce an inferior product, or take some other action that he believes will harm his business. This means that, in the name of competition, the businessman is prohibited from doing his best. To use force to promote competition is, as Ayn Rand wrote, "a grotesque contradiction in terms."[12] Competition results when someone thinks that he can do something better or faster or cheaper. And that cannot be compelled by government decree—force negates judgment. Freedom sanctions an individual's right to demonstrate his vision. Government coercion renders his vision impotent.

As is *always* the case when government intervenes, the results of antitrust prosecutions are much different than the stated intention. There is great competition today—for government subsidies, tax breaks, special legislation, and other government favors. Government's control over businesses has created a steady parade of lobbyists and special interests competing to gain the unearned. For example, when AT&T announced that it would buy T-Mobile in 2011, "Sprint complained that the deal would dramatically alter the wireless industry, which it said would be 'dominated overwhelmingly' by two companies that have almost 80 percent of U.S. wireless contract customers."[13] Sprint, which had been attempting to buy T-Mobile, would not be one of those two

---

11. George Reisman, "Platonic Competition," *The Objectivist*, Aug. 1968, p. 9.

12. Rand, *Capitalism*, p. 52.

13. "AT&T-T-Mobile Deal May Face Antitrust Test," Reuters, March 21, 2011, accessed July 23, 2011, http://www.msnbc.msn.com/id/42195916/ns/business-us_business/t/att-t-mobile-deal-may-face-antitrust-test/.

companies. Rather than accept the fact that they were out-competed in negotiations, Sprint wants the government to intervene and make it easier to "compete" against its superior rivals. Sprint wants the government to "level the playing field" by using the court room to accomplish what Sprint could not achieve in the board room.

If "leveling the playing field" is to mean anything, it means protecting the rights of each individual to act on his own judgment. It means the freedom to produce to the best of one's ability, without first seeking government permission, filling out Form XYZ in triplicate, or doing anything else to appease government bureaucrats. It means no government regulations, no government subsidies, no government controls, no government intervention. None. Zero. Zip. Nada. It means laissez-faire capitalism. But this is not what the advocates of a "level playing field" call for. They want government to intervene, not to protect individual rights, but to prohibit some individuals from acting as they judge best. They want government to violate the rights of some for the alleged benefit of others. Imagine the outcry if the government had demanded that, in order to "level the playing field," the Boston Celtics had to play with one hand tied behind their backs. This is what government regulations do, whether through occupational licensing, controls on drug makers, private express statutes, taxpayer subsidies to public schools, restrictions on oil companies, or any other control on private companies.

The great industrialists, entrepreneurs, and businessmen of history have always been innovators and visionaries. They are men and women who see an opportunity where others do not, and they have the courage and independence to act on their judgment. For example, John Rockefeller went into competition with the other illuminants that were available at the time. And he later faced a more powerful competitor—Thomas Edison and the light bulb. Bill Gates, Steve Jobs, and Michael Dell each saw opportunities in an industry dominated by giant companies like IBM and DEC. Because each man was free to act on his own judgment (at least in part), he could pursue ideas that others thought silly or doomed to failure. And the results speak for themselves. Freedom, not government controls and mandates, is what fosters competition. How much more could these great innovators achieve if they were not stifled and limited by government controls and regulations?

How much better would our lives be if these great men were really unfettered to compete?

At the same time the government seeks to impose "competition" in some industries, it simultaneously prohibits or greatly stifles competition in others, such as mail delivery, education, utilities, roads, and infrastructure. Ayn Rand wrote:

> By what conceivable standard can [monopolies] be a crime, when practiced by businessmen, but a public benefit, when practiced by the government? ... If [a monopoly] is harmful to competition, to industry, to production, to consumers, to the whole economy, and to the "public interest"—as the advocates of the antitrust laws have claimed—then how can that same harmful policy become beneficial in the hands of the government? Since there is no rational answer to this question, I suggest that you question the economic knowledge, the purpose, and the motives of the champions of antitrust.[14]

What is the purpose? What is the motivation of the advocates of antitrust and other rights-violating legislation?

It should be clear that the real purpose of antitrust, and indeed all government regulations, is not a competitive marketplace, consumer protection, the "public interest," or any other bromide trotted out as justification. The purpose is political power—the power to use government coercion to control the lives and actions of individuals. As evidence: political power has been the result of *every* effort to protect consumers, enhance competition, or promote the "public interest." Without exception, every law that is intended to "level the playing field" or promote the "common good" grants more power to politicians and bureaucrats. But what of monopolies? Can't they gouge consumers? Must we choose between power hungry politicians and price gouging capitalists?

In truth, in a free market, a coercive monopoly—a monopoly that can arbitrarily raise prices independent of supply and demand—is impossible. In a free market, there are no barriers to starting a business, other than those imposed by nature. Consequently, even if a company owns a large share of the market

---

14. Rand, *Capitalism*, p. 59. While Rand was speaking of price fixing, the same principles apply to monopolies.

at any given time, others can enter that market if they judge it to be a profitable use of their money. If a company uses its dominant position to raise prices to outrageous levels, capital will be attracted to the high profits in that industry or related industries, and competitors will drive down prices. If the company refuses to innovate and offer new or better products, others are free to do so and draw off market share. As long as individuals are free to use their property—including their money—as they judge best, no businessman can grow complacent without attracting competition. As one example, consider Henry Ford.

At one time, Ford had 60 percent of the market in automobiles. But he refused to innovate, declaring that customers could have a car in any color they wanted, as long as it was black. Chevrolet began offering consumers more color choices and substantially cut into Ford's market share. Ford had to relent and began offering more color options. Even though Ford dominated the market, he could not prevent Chevrolet from acting on its judgment. Nor could he prevent consumers from acting on theirs.

In the entire history of mankind, the only coercive monopolies that have ever been established were made possible by government intervention, whether by licenses, subsidies, franchises, prohibitions, or some other legislative act or decree. Consider the fact that the coercive monopolies that exist today—such as mail delivery, education, roads, and utilities—are only made possible by prohibitions on competition, taxpayer subsidies, or some other violation of individual rights. Such government intervention is the only means by which a coercive monopoly can maintain its position because political power is used to prohibit or stifle economic freedom.

Absent government intervention, companies that dominate a market do so through superior efficiency, better products, a lower price, or some other benefit to consumers. They offer more value than their competitors, and consumers willingly pay for that value. And because the free market is dynamic, a company must continually seek to increase the value that it offers, or consumers will find other products and services to purchase. This point is amply illustrated by Standard Oil and other companies.

As Standard Oil improved its refining efficiencies, the price of kerosene steadily decreased from fifty-eight cents a gallon in 1865 to ten cents a gallon in 1874. Even though the company was on its way to having 90 percent of the market, its superior efficiency allowed it to sell kerosene more cheaply than competitors and still be enormously profitable. Similarly, even though Ford dominated the automobile market, the price of a Model T decreased from $850 in 1908 to $290 in 1924.[15] Western Union, which dominated the telegraph market during the second half of the nineteenth century, decreased the cost of a telegraph from $1.09 per message in 1867 to thirty cents in 1900.[16] In each instance, and many others, even though a company held a large market share, it continued to innovate and improve efficiencies. The results were lower prices for consumers, not the price gouging alleged of monopolies. These business leaders should be praised rather than vilified. Why are these historical facts ignored and misrepresented? It certainly isn't because of concern for consumers.

In each of the examples above, these companies ultimately lost their dominant position because others remained free to offer new or better products. Standard Oil lost its dominance in illuminants with the invention of the light bulb. And as new competitors entered the market, such as Texaco, Gulf, and Shell, Standard Oil lost market share in refining. Indeed, before it was broken up in 1911 for antitrust violations, Standard Oil's market share in refining had shrunk by nearly one-third. Similarly, Ford lost its dominance in automobiles when Chevrolet and others offered more options; Western Union lost its dominance in communications as the telephone became more widely available.

As long as men are free to act on their judgment without interference from others, they will seek better ways to create the values that we need to live and enjoy our lives. Only government prohibitions, controls, regulations, and other interventions can stop them. Only government intervention can create coercive monopolies. Freedom motivates individuals to compete to produce better values. Government intervention motivates individuals to compete for government favors. Which kind of competition would you prefer?

---

15. Ted Santos, The Power & Paradox of Disruptive Leadership," ChangingMinds.org, accessed February 2, 2011, http://changingminds.org/articles/articles/disruptive_leadership.htm.

16. Tomas Nonnenmacher, "History of the U.S. Telegraph Industry," EH.net, accessed January 15, 2011, http://eh.net/encyclopedia/article/nonnenmacher.industry.telegraphic.us.

In every area we have examined, we have seen how government coercion creates nothing but havoc and harm. We have also seen that free men create the values that we want and need. Does this mean that we should simply abolish government? And if we need government, how can we finance its operations without resorting to coercion, i.e. taxation? Let us now turn to these questions.

16

Government without Taxation

In 2011, the average American worked until April 12 to pay the various taxes that are imposed on him: federal income tax, sales taxes, Social Security, property taxes, state income taxes, and more. In other words, the average American spends more than 25 percent of the year toiling for government policies and services that he does not necessarily want or use. And in fact, he likely finds many of those policies and services abhorrent. Yet, despite his judgment, he is forced to support them financially. "The man who produces," wrote Ayn Rand, "while others dispose of his product, is a slave."[1] Indeed, oppressive taxation was one of the most important complaints America's Founding Fathers voiced against King George III.

We are often told that death and taxes are two inevitable facts of life. While death is a fact of nature, and therefore inescapable, taxes are another issue. It is possible—and moral—to fund government through voluntary means. But before we examine how government can exist without taxation, let us first consider a few facts about the federal income tax.

The federal income tax began as a relatively simple means for raising revenue; it has turned into a labyrinth of seventy-five thousand pages and more than seven hundred different forms. Much of the complexity results from "social engineering"—creating tax incentives for the types of activities that Congress finds acceptable and tax penalties for activities that Congress does not like. For example, tax deductions for the interest on home mortgages encourage Americans to buy homes. Adding to the

---

1. Ayn Rand, "Man's Rights," in *The Virtue of Selfishness*, p. 94 (see Part 1, n.1).

complexity are tax benefits for special interests. As an example, tax credits for investments in alternative energy encourage Americans to invest money as Congress thinks best. Maneuvering through the tax code costs taxpayers more than $265 billion in tax preparation costs each year.[2] In addition, about six billion hours are wasted each year compiling documentation and completing forms—that is the equivalent of three million full-time workers.[3] And even the most diligent and well-intentioned efforts can result in an audit from the most feared and despised federal agency—the Internal Revenue Service.

In response to the increasingly incomprehensible tax code, many have suggested abolishing the current income tax system and replacing it with a flat tax or a national sales tax. While such proposals would likely make taxation less complex and greatly reduce compliance costs, they ignore one important moral fact: taxation is theft.

If your neighbor broke into your home and stole money to pay for his health care, he would be guilty of theft. If an employer withheld wages from an employee in order to pay for his daughter's braces, he would be guilty of theft. Indeed, if a private citizen takes money from another individual by force for any purpose, he is guilty of theft. Neither the status nor the moral nature of an action changes simply because government is doing the taking. In a capitalist society, the initiation of force in any form—including taxation—is prohibited. In a capitalist society, government financing is obtained through voluntary means. How then, does a government in a capitalist society raise the funds that it requires for its legitimate functions? If payment for government services is voluntary, why would anyone volunteer? Don't we need taxation to ensure that everyone pays his "fair share" to support government? After all, government is necessary to protect individual rights, and all individuals benefit from government. These are legitimate questions, and the answers may surprise you.

---

2. Andrew Chamberlain, "Economist Gary Becker on Tax Compliance Costs," Tax Foundation, April 18, 2006, accessed July 25, 2011, http://www.taxfoundation.org/blog/show/1442.html.

3. Charles Riley, "Americans Spend 6.1 Billion Hours on Their Taxes," CNN.com, January 5, 2011, accessed July 25, 2011, http://money.cnn.com/2011/01/05/pf/taxes/IRS_tax_study/index.htm.

Taxation, by its very nature, denies an individual his property, forcing him to dispose of it contrary to his own choices for purposes chosen by others. While few would dispute this point, many believe that taxation is a "necessary evil," for without such coercive measures, government would not receive the funding that it requires. While a completely voluntary system of paying for government has never been attempted, we can observe evidence that clearly demonstrates that individuals *will* voluntarily pay for government.

We see, on a daily basis, individuals voluntarily purchasing the values that they require to sustain and enjoy their lives. From food to cell phones, from housing to vacations, from clothing to flat screen televisions, we witness individuals voluntarily paying for the products and services that they want and need. Individuals make these purchases for their own benefit, to further their own lives (or that of their family, friends, and others that they value). Each individual chooses what is important to his life and pursues those values without coercion or government mandates. The free and independent judgment of individuals—each acting in the pursuit of his self-interest—has not resulted in a shortage of food or clothing or automobiles or "gadgets" or any of the values that humans want and need. Quite the contrary. Americans live in a culture of unprecedented abundance.

What makes that abundance possible is the protection of our rights and the freedom to act on our own judgment (though that freedom is being curtailed each year). The protection of our rights is the only legitimate and moral purpose of government. And, just as individuals voluntarily purchase the values that their lives require, they will (and do) voluntarily pay for the protection of their rights. As Ayn Rand wrote, "Since the proper services of a government—the police, the armed forces, the law courts—are demonstrably needed by individual citizens and affect their interests directly, the citizens would (and should) be willing to pay for such services, as they pay for insurance."[4] Government, when limited to its proper purpose, is a value.

Just as individuals do not need to be compelled to purchase values such as automobiles, computers, and movie tickets, they

---

4. Ayn Rand, "Government Financing in a Free Society," in *The Virtue of Selfishness*, p. 116.

would not need to be compelled to pay for the value offered by a proper government—the protection of their rights. Just as self-interest motivates individuals to buy the values they want and need, self-interest would motivate individuals to pay for the service that makes the pursuit of those values possible in a social setting—the protection of their rights. To argue otherwise is to declare that individuals do not recognize the crucial value offered by a government limited to its proper purpose. It is to argue that individuals must be compelled to take actions that are beneficial and vital to their well-being. This is not true in regard to values such as housing, clothing, and lawn mowers, nor is it true in regard to a rights-protecting government. But how would the federal government raise the trillions of dollars it currently spends? What would happen if citizens did not donate enough to fund the government? To answer this, let us look at government spending.

It is important to understand that a government limited to its proper functions—the police, the courts, and the military—would require a mere fraction of the funding that it currently receives and requires. Limited to the protection of individual rights, government would be much smaller than it is today. When government is limited to its proper purpose, raising the money required for government to fulfill its proper functions is eminently practical. (By historical standards, as a percentage of gross domestic product, government spending in a capitalist society would be approximately 10 percent of what it is today.)

Many of the objections to the idea that government could exist without taxation arise largely because government has grown far beyond its proper purpose. Most taxpayers are rightly incensed when they hear of the many ways government wastes their money. Taxpayers understandably decry $600 toilet seats, programs that pay farmers to *not* grow crops, and welfare fraud. They correctly conclude that nobody would voluntarily support such wasteful spending. However, voluntary financing of government would help end irresponsible government spending. Consider just a few of the consequences of government limited to its proper functions:

- With public schools abolished, you are not forced to pay for the education of children who are not your own. Nor are you compelled to pay for the teaching of ideas that you find immoral. If you wish to provide voluntary assistance to educate others, you are free to do so.

- With "entitlement" programs abolished, you are not forced to provide charity. If you wish to donate to charities, you are free to do so.
- If you do not want to pay for a "bridge to nowhere," you are not forced to do so. If you think that such projects are worthwhile, you are free to invest in them.
- You are not forced to provide subsidies to companies seeking sources of alternative energy. If you want to encourage such activities, you are free to invest in those companies.
- You are not compelled to send aid to foreign nations. If you wish to help those in other countries, you are free to do so.

With government limited to its proper purpose, all services except the police, the courts, and the military are provided by private companies. You are free to spend, invest, and donate your money as you deem best. If you believe that a business or non-profit organization is wasting your money, you are free to withdraw your support. In a capitalist society, if government officials insist on wasting your money, you are also free to withhold your financial support. Try doing that today.

But does this mean that individuals would actually voluntarily support government? Even today, we can find abundant evidence that individuals will, in fact, provide funding for government through voluntary means. We can see that individuals already voluntarily pay for the protection of their rights, whether it is from criminals, to resolve disputes, or to protect them from foreign threats.

According to the Bureau of Labor Statistics, there were approximately 1,007,000 private security guards working in the United States in 2010.[5] This is about 100,000 more than the number of police in 2008.[6] According to the Department of Justice, Americans spend more than $100 billion per year on security

---

5. "Occupational Employment and Wages, May 2010," Bureau of Labor Statistics, accessed February 3, 2011, http://www.bls.gov/oes/current/oes339032.htm.

6. "Occupational Outlook Handbook, 2010-1 Edition," Bureau of Labor Statistics, accessed February 3, 2011, http://www.bls.gov/oco/ocos160.htm#emply.

alarms, security guards, and other security services, which is twice what is spent by federal, state, and local law enforcement departments combined.[7] Clearly, Americans are voluntarily spending money in order to protect their property and persons. And this money is spent in addition to the taxes paid for the provision of police.

(It should be noted that private security companies are not a form of "competing agencies of retaliatory force," which is a term used by many Libertarians. Libertarians advocate "competing governments," which means anarchy. Anarchy is not compatible with freedom.[8] Private security guards must answer to the police when they use force. They must prove that their use of force was objectively justified, and they are subject to criminal penalties if they violate the rights of individuals. In short, they are not competing with the police; they are accountable to the police.)

In addition to private security, individuals also voluntarily provide other financial support to police departments for specific purposes. For example, in Huntington, West Virginia, individuals and businesses donated almost $200,000 to the police department for the purchase of motorcycles, police dogs, and other equipment.[9] In Milwaukee, Wisconsin, private donations in one neighborhood raised $176,000 to help the police pay for overtime and street cameras, which resulted in a decline in crime in that neighborhood.[10]

Further, other organizations successfully engage in ongoing fundraising for police departments. For example, the 100 Club in Houston raises money to support police officers and to provide financial assistance to the families of officers killed in the line of duty. Since 1953, the 100 Club of Houston has raised more than $35 million for special equipment, financial aid, and other disbursements to police officers and their families.[11] Other 100

---

7. "Private Security and Public Law Enforcement," United States Department of Justice, accessed February 3, 2011, http://www.cops.usdoj.gov/Default.asp?Item=2034.

8. See Harry Binswanger's article "Anarchism Vs. Objectivism" at http://www.hblist.com/anarchy.htm for more details.

9. Bryan Chambers, "Donations Help Police Stay Afloat," *The Herald Dispatch*, November 30, 2008, accessed February 3, 2011, http://www.herald-dispatch.com/news/x59589381/Community-donations-help-police-stay-afloat.

10. "Crime Drops in Area That Used Private Donations to Fund Police," *Poe News*, accessed February 3, 2011, http://www.poe-news.com/stories.php?poeurlid=78554.

11. "History," The 100 Club, accessed February 3, 2011, http://www.the100club.org

Clubs operate in more than one hundred communities across the nation, and they have raised millions of dollars to support police officers, firefighters, and their families during times of tragedy.

As another example, private, non-profit foundations exist in more than two dozen American cities for the purpose of raising funds to support local police departments. The Houston Police Foundation was founded in 2005 and raised more than $1 million in its first year. It uses donations by individuals and businesses to "fund special programs, officer safety, training, equipment, and new technology—none of which would be feasible under the City budget."[12] The New York City Police Foundation was established in 1971 "to promote excellence in the NYPD and improve public safety in New York City."[13] The organization has invested more than $100 million in projects for the police department. The Los Angeles Police Foundation has awarded more than $14 million in grants to that city's police department.[14]

These examples, and many more like them, demonstrate that individuals do voluntarily pay for the protection of their rights. Whether it is private security or donations to police departments, individuals recognize the need for such protection and pay for it without coercion. But such payments are only a part of the story of how police departments would operate under a proper government.

In a free society, crimes are properly defined as acts of force; thus, the laws enforced by the police would be substantially reduced as compared to today. Voluntary actions that do not constitute an initiation of force, such as gambling, prostitution, and taking drugs, would be legal, and the police would not spend their precious resources monitoring the voluntary actions of consenting adults. By decriminalizing such activities, the money and time required to enforce these unjust laws would be eliminated. For example, a bulletin issued by the Bureau of Justice Statistics found that 37 percent of the felony cases in the nation's seventy-five most

---

/about.html.

12. "About Us," Houston Police Foundation, accessed February 3, 2011, http://www.houstonpolicefoundation.org/about/about.

13. "Our Mission," accessed February 3, 2011, http://www.nycpolicefoundation.org/NetCommunity/Page.aspx?pid=224.

14. "About Us," Los Angeles Police Foundation, accessed February 3, 2011, http://www.lapolicefoundation.org/about.html.

populous counties involved drug charges.[15] Decriminalizing drugs would reduce the burden, and therefore the costs, on both the police and the courts by more than one-third. This would allow the police and courts to focus on those who actually violate the rights of their fellow citizens—rapists, thieves, murderers, and the like. But if we legalize drugs, prostitution, and gambling, aren't we encouraging such activities? Aren't we giving them a moral sanction?

The fact that an activity is legal does not encourage or sanction that activity. We cannot legislate morality, nor should we attempt to do so. Many actions are immoral—such as having an affair and fathering a child while one's wife is battling breast cancer—but such actions are not and should not be a crime. Legalizing an action simply recognizes the fact that the activity does not violate the rights of other individuals—the activity does not involve the initiation of force. So long as force is not involved, consenting adults should be free to engage in the voluntary activities of their choosing. This does not mean that we should regard all voluntary, consensual activities as moral. It does mean that we recognize the right to engage in such conduct. Those who engage in immoral activities should be ostracized and boycotted, just as racists, sexists, and homophobes should be ostracized and boycotted.[16]

Prohibition, implemented after a Constitutional Amendment was ratified in 1919, provides a compelling example of the evils that result when voluntary activities are banned by government. During Prohibition consumption of alcohol actually increased.[17] Deaths due to alcohol poisoning increased from 1,064 in 1920 to 4,154 in 1925.[18] Crime skyrocketed during Prohibition, and the federal prison population increased 366 percent.[19] Murders increased 78 percent. These trends were reversed upon the repeal of Prohibition—which required another Constitutional Amendment

---

15. Tracey Kyckelhahn and Thomas H. Cohen, Ph.D., "Felony Defendants in Large Urban Counties, 2004", Bureau of Justice Statistics, accessed February 3, 2011, http://bjs.ojp.usdoj.gov/content/pub/pdf/fdluc04.pdf.

16. These points pertain to consenting adults. Restrictions on the actions of minors are proper. Minors are not capable of judging the long-term consequences of their choices and actions.

17. Mark Thornton, "Alcohol Prohibition was a Failure," Cato Institute, July 17, 1991, p. 3, accessed July 10, 2011, http://www.cato.org/pubs/pas/pa157.pdf.

18. Ibid., p. 4.

19. Ibid., p. 6.

ratified in 1933; afterwards the murder rate steadily declined to pre-Prohibition levels.[20] Clearly, Prohibition was impractical. It was impractical because it was immoral; Prohibition criminalized voluntary activities that violated nobody's rights. What caused Prohibition's crime wave? Economist Mark Thorton explains:

> Criminal groups organize around the steady source of income provided by laws against victimless crimes such as consuming alcohol or drugs, gambling, and prostitution. In the process of providing goods and services, those criminal organizations resort to real crimes in defense of sales territories, brand names, and labor contracts. That is true of extensive crime syndicates (the Mafia) as well as street gangs, a criminal element that first surfaced during Prohibition.[21]

Does this sound familiar? Does this sound like the failed "war on drugs"? Prohibition—whether of alcohol or of drugs—simply increases costs to the willing consumers, leads to increased crime, fills our prisons, and diverts the police from activities that truly violate individual rights.

In any free or semi-free country, criminals are a small percentage of the population. While the conviction and punishment of criminals is important, resolving contractual disputes is a much larger and significant aspect of the court system. Long-term interactions between individuals depend upon the cooperation of those involved, and such relationships are typically codified in a contract—a written agreement identifying the responsibilities of each party. Economist Richard Salsman writes that "contracts permit long-range business planning essential to a forward-looking, wealth-building system."[22] A breach of a contract can have significant consequences on the other parties to the contract.

A breach of contract is a form of force—it is the intentional (or negligent) withholding of property or services. For example, if Mike agrees to buy Bob's car, and after receiving the money, Bob refuses to hand over the keys, Bob has deprived Mike of what is rightfully his. Absent the courts, Mike would have to enforce contracts and resolve disputes on his own. He would become judge, jury, and

---

20. Ibid., pp. 6-7.
21. Ibid., p. 7.
22. Salsman, "'What Does Competition Mean Under Capitalism?".

executioner. Consider the simple dispute above: when Bob refuses to give Mike the keys, Mike pulls out a gun and demands what is rightfully his. Bob responds by pulling out a gun. The result is not likely to be a happy ending. To avoid such anarchy and protect their rights, citizens delegate the resolution of disputes to the government. And they willingly pay for that service.

In recent decades, alternative dispute resolution (ADR), such as arbitration and mediation, have gained popularity as efficient and inexpensive methods for resolving disputes. As the court system has become bogged down with frivolous lawsuits, ADR allows for disputes to be resolved quickly and with less cost. Many contracts now call for ADR as the means for resolving any disputes arising from the contract.

For example, arbitration allows all parties to present their case in an informal setting. The arbiter—often an expert in the particular issues in question—will make a legally binding ruling after considering the facts of the case. Similarly, mediation involves a third-party who tries to find an acceptable compromise between the parties in dispute. Upon acceptance by all parties, that agreement becomes a legally binding contract. Interestingly, many courts, such as some small claims courts, are now requiring mediation prior to trial for cases involving lesser dollar amounts. With both arbitration and mediation, the parties in a dispute agree to abide by the results.

ADR services are available from many different organizations. The Better Business Bureau offers both mediation and arbitration services to its members and consumers. The parties to a dispute can select a mutually acceptable third-party, such as an attorney, a retired judge, or an industry expert, to mediate or arbitrate. Private companies, such as the American Arbitration Association and Judicial Arbitration and Mediation Services, offer ADR services, primarily to businesses. Both companies have offices around the world.

While ADR is usually performed outside the auspices of the courts, the rulings of arbiters and the agreements reached through mediation are legally binding and enforceable in court. As with security guards, private dispute resolution is not competing with government, but rather, it offers an alternative method. In each instance—private security and ADR—those involved are ultimately held accountable by government. ADR is a private means of resolving a disagreement; however, individual rights are ultimately protected by government.

While the police and courts deal with domestic threats to individual rights, the military protects the rights of individuals from foreign threats. And Americans also voluntarily support the military.

Perhaps the best known organization providing support for American troops is the United Services Organization (USO). Founded during World War II, the USO provides care packages, phone cards, and entertainment for American troops stationed abroad. Charities such as the Fisher House Foundation, the Intrepid Fallen Heroes Fund, and National Military Family Association and nearly three hundred other organizations raise millions of dollars to provide equipment, financial aid, education, and other assistance to soldiers and their families. During the Iraq war, numerous charities, such as the Armor 4 Troops Foundation, were established to provide armor and other protective equipment for deployed soldiers. And many businesses have donated equipment to troops stationed overseas. One business, efi Sports Medicine, a San Diego-based exercise equipment manufacturer, donated more than 150 of its Total Gym machines to troops stationed in Iraq and Afghanistan.[23]

Just as a government limited to its proper functions would reduce the burden on the police and the courts, in a capitalist society, the burden on the military would also be reduced. A proper foreign policy would eliminate "peace keeping," food distribution, and "nation building." The military would be used to kill and destroy the enemies of America—those who threaten the freedom of Americans. The result would be fewer military expenses and fewer American casualties.[24]

We have seen that Americans willingly donate money or otherwise voluntarily provide financial support for the legitimate functions of government. In addition to direct, voluntary contributions, government can use other methods to raise the funds required to protect our rights, without resorting to coercion or the seizure of private property. The methods discussed below are not

---

23. "Equipment from Home Boosts Troops Abroad", Aug 18, 2006, accessed February 3, 2011, http://clubindustry.com/military/equipment_home_troops/.

24. For more information on a proper foreign policy, see Elan Journo, *Winning the Unwinnable War* and Peter Schwartz, *The Foreign Policy of Self-Interest.*

necessarily exhaustive, but merely an indication of how government can finance its operations while respecting the rights of individuals.

Lotteries have long been used by governments to raise revenues. Forty-four states and the District of Columbia have lotteries. According to the North American Association of State and Provincial Lotteries, state lotteries generated revenues of nearly $18 billion (after expenses) in 2010.[25] Lotteries are played voluntarily, and thus represent a non-coercive method for government to raise money. However, lotteries do have their critics.

Opponents of state-run lotteries argue that they are a form of regressive taxation—that the poor are more likely to play lotteries, and that they promote gambling. Whether these claims are true or not is irrelevant—individuals should be free to act on their own judgment, even when others think that their judgment is poor. In a free society, individuals have no restrictions on their actions, so long as they respect the mutual rights of others. Those who want to play the lottery are free to do so.

Another way for government to raise money is by selling land and other property. In a capitalist society, virtually all property would be privately owned. Government would not own parks or forests or museums or large tracts of undeveloped land. Government would only own the few parcels needed to house the police, the courts, and the military. Limited to its proper functions, government would divest itself of all unnecessary property. The federal government is the largest property owner in the nation. Indeed, the federal government owns nearly 30 percent of the land in the United States, including nearly 85 percent of Nevada and nearly 70 percent of Alaska.[26] Selling this land would raise hundreds of billions of dollars, if not trillions. (And we have seen that selling the national parks will not result in fast food chains, strip malls, and condominiums in Yellowstone.) While selling assets is a one-time generation of funds, the money raised would be substantial. And taxpayers would no longer be forced to pay for the maintenance of parks and museums.

---

25. "Lottery Sales and Profits," North American Association of State and Provincial Lotteries, accessed February 3, 2011, http://www.naspl.org/index.cfm?fuseaction=content&menuid=17&pageid=1025.

26. "How Much Land Does the Federal Government Own?," AllVoices.com, accessed February 3, 2011, http://www.allvoices.com/contributed-news/914109.

Other non-coercive methods could provide ongoing funding. For example, Pennsylvania Correctional Industries (PCI) is a program that employs inmates at fifteen state prisons while they serve their sentences. Inmates produce garments, soaps and degreasers, and forms for the state government. Inmates receive credits for their work, which can be spent at the prison commissary or applied towards fines and restitution. PCI Director Tony Miller told an interviewer that "some inmates, after serving their time and being released, have written letters of thanks for the skills they learned through their PCI jobs that helped them get jobs when they left prison."[27] For the fiscal year that ended in June 2007, PCI made $1 million in profit on $34 million in gross sales. In fiscal 2008-09, the California Prison Industry Authority had sales of $234.2 million from products such as clothing, textiles, fine-ground optics, and bedding.[28]

Supreme Court Justice Warren Burger was a vocal proponent of "factories with fences," as he called them. His efforts in the 1980s and 1990s led to the expansion of Federal Prison Industries (FPI), which produces furniture, textiles, electronics, and other items. But don't these prison factories have an advantage over private companies?

Critics of prison factories argue that this is the case. They argue that prison factories have an unfair competitive advantage over private sector industries because inmates are paid substantially less than private sector workers. But prison factories are less efficient and, not surprisingly, must contend with significantly higher security costs. As Robert Q. Millan, a former member of FPI's Board of Directors, once said:

> As a former banker, I am well aware of the operations of a variety of businesses. In private sector business, it is of primary importance to eliminate all inefficiencies possible in order to maximize profit. I could not recommend to my former bank, or

---

27. Kari Andren, "Prison Factories Produce a Range of Items, Including Hope," *The Pittsburgh Post-Gazette*, August 17, 2008, accessed February 3, 2011, http://www.post-gazette.com/pg/08230/904703-454.stm.

28. Thomas R. Harris, George G. Goldman, and Shannon Price, "The Economic Impact of the California Prison Industry Authority on the California Economy for FY 2008/09," p. 3, California Prison Industry Authority, December 2010, accessed October 30, 2011, http://pia.ca.gov/public_affairs/pdfs/CALPIA%20Economic%20Impact%20Study%2008-09.pdf.

any bank, that it make loans to a business that… had the inherent inefficiencies that handicap FPI.[29]

In other words, prison factories do not have a competitive advantage, and in fact, must contend with factors that render them inefficient. That, however, does not make them unviable as a means of supporting the costs of operating prisons.

In 2009, FPI had gross sales of $885 million. Fifty percent of the money earned by inmates was used to pay fines, restitution, and child support. Without a prison job, these payments would not be possible. During its more than seventy-five year history, FPI has been self-sustaining, and indeed, it has turned over more than $80 million to the federal treasury. This has eliminated any cost to the taxpayer.

While the primary purpose of prison is punishing criminals, prison factories provide side benefits, such as opportunities for inmates to learn job skills, which reduces recidivism and provides a means for inmates to make restitution to their victims. In addition, prison factories can provide inmates with a means to improve their standard of living while in prison. In this sense, life in prison should be no different than life outside—each individual should be responsible for his own welfare. The only difference is that inmates should be provided with the bare necessities, and any amenities they wish to enjoy while in prison should be purchased with money earned in prison.

While these examples demonstrate that government can be funded without resorting to coercive taxation, what of those who refuse to voluntarily support government? Won't they receive the benefits of government—the protection of their rights—even though they pay nothing? This is the so-called "freeloader problem."

The fact that some individuals will not voluntarily support government is hardly an argument against government without taxation. If we recognize the sanctity of individual rights, that the initiation of force is immoral, then we cannot force individuals to act contrary to their own judgment, no matter the issue. Morally, each individual has a right to act according to his own judgment, so

---

29. "Factories with Fences," p. 6, accessed February 3, 2011, http://www.unicor.gov/information/publications/pdfs/corporate/CATMC1101_C.pdf.

long as he respects the mutual rights of others. This precludes the use of force, even when that compulsion would be used in an individual's "self-interest." Each individual has a moral right to choose his values and his means for attaining them, and others have no right to compel him to act otherwise. To compel an individual to act in his "self-interest" is a contradiction.

The number of individuals who will freeload is irrelevant. We have already seen that millions of Americans voluntarily pay to protect their rights and their property. They will continue to do so whether others contribute or not. In other words, individuals pay to protect their rights because it is in *their* self-interest, and this fact does not change simply because others do not recognize that their self-interest includes supporting legitimate government functions. Those with the most to lose—e.g., businesses and the wealthy—will not subject themselves to anarchy merely because a neighbor refuses to contribute to the police department. Further, it is in the self-interest of all citizens to protect the rights of other citizens. A threat to the rights of one individual is a threat to the rights of all. A thief, rapist, or murderer may victimize a "freeloader" today, but he might victimize you tomorrow.

We have previously seen that, when men are free, rational ideas supplant irrational ideas. Just as boycotts and ostracism will motivate a racist to change his ways or suffer economically, individuals can boycott and ostracize those who refuse to voluntarily support government. Consider further the social custom of tipping service providers, such as waiters, valets, and bell boys. Tips are voluntary payments above and beyond the advertised price, and most patrons willingly make these payments. If millions of Americans voluntarily tip their waitress for keeping their coffee cup full, why should we believe that they won't voluntarily pay the police for protecting their life and their property?

As we have seen, funding government through voluntary means is practical. Recognizing the value of protecting their rights, individuals pay for that protection when they hire security services. And they do so without the need for coercive taxation, which itself violates the very purpose of government—the protection of individual rights. Which would you prefer: to work for the government until mid-April or to live free and spend your money as you choose? Wouldn't one of your choices be to pay a small amount for the protection of your freedom?

Part 3

Conclusion

"That is not a just government," wrote James Madison, "nor is property secure under it, where the property which a man has in his personal safety and personal liberty, is violated by arbitrary seizures of one class of citizens for the service of the rest."[1] Whether government seizes an individual's property or restricts his free use of it, the principle remains the same. Whether government takes your money through taxes, takes your land through eminent domain, or controls the use of your property through regulations, property is not secure.

The Founding Fathers recognized that the rights to life and property are inseparable—that to deny a man his property is to deny him the means of sustaining and enjoying his life. They recognized that "[g]overnment is instituted to protect property of every sort,"[2] no matter the cause and no matter the number of citizens who advocate seizing it or controlling its use.

Today, your right to property is routinely violated by government. You must work more than a quarter of the year to pay your taxes. You are subject to a myriad of controls and regulations on the use of your property, from what you can build to how you can invest. You are forced to pay for cleaning up pollution on "public property," prohibited from draining your swamp, and prosecuted if your business is "too successful." Your property is

1. James Madison, *The Papers of James Madison*. Edited by William T. Hutchinson et al. Chicago and London: University of Chicago Press, 1962--77 (vols. 1--10); Charlottesville: University Press of Virginia, 1977--(vols. 11--), accessed February 3, 2011, http://press-pubs.uchicago.edu/founders/documents/v1ch16s23.html.

2. Ibid.

not yours to use as you judge best, but often can be used only with the permission and approval of government officials.

The right to property is the practical implementation of individual rights. Property rights recognize the fact that material values are necessary to live.

> Man has to work and produce in order to support his life. He has to support his life by his own effort and by the guidance of his own mind. If he cannot dispose of the product of his effort, he cannot dispose of his effort; if he cannot dispose of his effort, he cannot dispose of his life. Without property rights, no other rights can be practiced.[3]

By now, the importance of property rights should be clear. If you are not free to use your property as you judge best, you are not free to produce and earn the values that your life requires. You cannot live your life as you choose. Your life becomes a means to the ends of politicians, bureaucrats, or "the community." Without property rights, you cannot pursue the values that bring satisfaction, joy, and happiness to your life.

No individual has a right to take your property or threaten you for refusing to obey his demands. No individual acquires this right by being elected to public office, no matter how many citizens vote for him. No group of elected officials acquires this right, no matter how large their majority. The only moral and proper purpose of government is the protection of individual rights, including property rights. A government that controls or seizes your property for the service of others is neither moral nor just.

America's moral and economic greatness was built on the recognition and protection of property rights. America's re-birth must be as well.

---

3. Ayn Rand, "What is Capitalism?" in *Capitalism: The Unknown Ideal*, p. 18.

Part 4

The Pursuit of Happiness

What does happiness mean to you? Does it mean a career that you love? Does it mean a family? Does it mean discovering a cure for some horrible disease? Does it mean building your dream house? No matter your answer, only you can determine what will bring you satisfaction, joy, and happiness. Only you can determine what values make your life worth living.

The right to the pursuit of happiness means just that. You have a moral right to take the actions you deem necessary to achieve the values that will bring you happiness. The right to the pursuit of happiness is not a guarantee that you will achieve the values that you desire, but the freedom to pursue your values as you judge best. Just as the right to property does not mean that others must provide you with a home, an automobile, a flat-screen television, or any other material value, so the right to the pursuit of happiness does not mean that others must ensure your satisfaction and joy.

The Founding Fathers regarded the right to the pursuit of happiness to be as important as the rights to life and liberty; indeed, these rights are inseparable. To live your life as you choose, you must have the liberty to pursue the values that bring you happiness. You must be free to choose both the ends—your values—and the means—the actions you will take to achieve those values.

As we have seen, government force can stop you from pursuing your values. Through regulations, controls, prohibitions, and mandates, government can compel you to act contrary to your judgment. Government can force you to abandon your values; it can erect outrageous obstacles in your path. Occupational licensing laws can force you to abandon a career unless you meet arbitrary standards. The Food and Drug Administration can prohibit you from selling (or taking) medications that it has not approved. Land-use regulations can prevent you from building your dream house. Government—the agency that is supposed to protect your right to the pursuit of happiness—can, and often does, stop you from doing just that.

Government intervention is founded on the premise that you have a moral obligation to serve others. According to altruism, you have a duty to place the welfare and interests of others before your own. In other words, you must sacrifice your values and your happiness for the values and happiness of others. If you cannot live as you choose, if you are not free to act on your own judgment, if your property may be seized for the use of others, you are not free to pursue your own happiness.

By now, the impracticality of government intervention should be clear. Government intervention violates your right to life, liberty, property, and the pursuit of happiness. It should also be clear that private, non-coercive alternatives exist. But does this mean that *all* government intervention is evil? Does it mean that individuals should be free to do anything they desire? Wouldn't a capitalist society turn into "dog-eat-dog" competition and "survival of the fittest"? Is a capitalist society even possible? These are the questions we will now answer.

17

Are You Selfish?

If you are a student, should you benefit from your studies? Or should your good grades be taken from you and shared with your beer-drinking classmates because they need better grades in order to pass? If you are a business owner, should you benefit from working long hours, developing more efficient production methods, and creating innovative marketing? Or should some of your profits be taken from you and given to a competitor because he needs the money in order to avoid bankruptcy? If you are an employee, should you benefit from attending training seminars, improving your skills, and working into the evening? Or should the raise that you have earned be given to a less-deserving co-worker because he needs it more?

In other words: Who should properly be the beneficiary of *your* actions?

Altruism says that others should benefit from your actions. Altruism holds that service to others is your moral obligation. According to altruism, you have a duty to help your less industrious classmates, business competitors, or co-workers by sharing your grades, your profits, or your raise. You must put aside your own self-interest to promote the interests and welfare of others.

You probably agree that the hard working student, business owner, and employee should benefit from his efforts. You probably reject the notion that the needs of lazy students, less innovative businessmen, or less industrious employees justify penalizing those who work harder and are more successful. That is, you probably reject the most blatant examples of altruism. However, have you ever said or agreed with the following: Everyone has a responsibility to give back to their community. Or, all of us must pay our fair share of taxes. Or, we have a duty to help those who are less fortunate. Or, we all must sacrifice for the common good? All of these clichés, and many more like them, are founded on altruism. All hold that you must place the welfare of others before your own welfare. All are founded on the premise that you have a moral obligation to place the interests of others before your self-interest.

Most Americans regard selfishness—the pursuit of one's self-interest—as bad and immoral. Yet, most Americans also believe that individuals should pursue their self interest: they should study diligently, they should work hard at their job, they should save for their future, and they should take responsibility for their actions. Why does this contradiction exist? The answer can be found in altruism.

Altruism also says that its antithesis is "selfishness." According to altruism, "selfishness" means sacrificing others to oneself. Altruism, as philosopher Leonard Peikoff writes, holds that "some men are mere means to the ends of others; that somebody's throat must be cut. The only question then is: your life for their sake or theirs for yours?"[1] Is this the only alternative? Must we choose between sacrificing ourselves for others or sacrificing others for ourselves? Doesn't life require sacrifice? Before we answer these questions, let us first look at the meaning of sacrifice.

Sacrifice does not mean forgoing an immediate pleasure, gain, or value for a greater value in the future. Sacrifice means giving up a greater value for a lesser value or a non-value. If you are a student and you spend Friday night studying for an important exam while your friends party, it is not a sacrifice; it is in your self-interest to study. If you are a business owner and you pay yourself a modest salary in order to invest in your business, it is not a sacrifice; it is in your self-interest to invest in your business. If you are an employee and you miss dinner one evening to complete a presentation for an important client, it is not a sacrifice; it is in your self-interest to do well by your clients. In each instance, you are pursuing your self-interest by forgoing a short-term benefit or gain in order to achieve a greater long-term value. In doing so, you gain what you believe to be in your self-interest—better grades, more customers, or a promotion. And a gain is not a sacrifice.

---

1. Leonard Peikoff, *Objectivism: The Philosophy of Ayn Rand*, (New York: Dutton, 1991), p. 235.

Life requires choices, and often, those choices are between the short-term and the long-term. Often, those choices are between what is less important versus what is more important. Giving up a short-term, less important value in order to attain a long-term, more important value is not a sacrifice. Such actions demonstrate perseverance, dedication to your goals, and acting on principle. Such actions are in your self-interest because they help you achieve your most important values.

If you value your grades and the career you are pursuing, it would be a sacrifice to go partying with your buddies to the neglect of your studies. If you desire to build your business, it would be a sacrifice to pay yourself an exorbitant salary at the expense of investing in your company. If you are seeking a promotion or raise, it would be a sacrifice to improperly prepare for a presentation and risk losing an important client. In each instance, you are giving up the long-term, highly important value for some immediate benefit or gain. In each instance, giving up what you highly value *is* a sacrifice. Sacrificing your values is not in your self-interest; sacrifice is the renunciation of the values that would have brought you happiness. With this understanding of sacrifice, let us look at the consequences of sacrifice.

In previous chapters, we have seen the results when individuals are forced by government to sacrifice their self-interest for the "public interest"—higher costs, fewer choices, and destroyed lives. When individuals cannot act on their own judgment, their lives become the property of others. Their means for pursuing happiness—their own independent judgment—is rendered irrelevant. But what are the results when an individual sacrifices others to himself?

Criminals are frequently cited as examples of "selfish" people. They do not hesitate to do harm to others, purportedly for their own personal benefit. Clinical psychologist Dr. Stanton E. Samenow writes, "Despite a multitude of differences in their backgrounds and crime patterns, criminals are alike in one way: *how they think*."[2] To the criminal, other people are pawns to be used as he desires. He believes that "[o]ther people and their property exist

---

2. Dr. Stanton E. Samenow, *Inside the Criminal Mind*, (Times Books: New York, 1984), p. 20.

for his benefit."[3] Whether through deceit, intimidation, or outright coercion, the criminal believes that he is justified to use any means necessary to fulfill his desires. As one criminal told Samenow, "All the people there [in the bar where he worked] were pawns or checkers waiting for me to deal with them as I wished and to sacrifice any I wished."[4] The altruist declares that individuals must sacrifice for the "public interest"; the criminal declares that individuals must sacrifice for his "interest." But do criminals benefit by sacrificing others? Are they really pursuing their own self-interest?

Consider Barry Minkow as an example. As a sixteen-year-old, Minkow started a restoration business in his parent's garage. Over the next five years, he rapidly expanded the "business," took it public, and became a media darling, even appearing on "The Oprah Winfrey Show." But the "business" was nothing more than a Ponzi scheme, and in 1988, Minkow was sentenced to twenty-five years in federal prison for defrauding investors and lenders of more than $100 million. While Minkow "enjoyed" immense wealth—he was "worth" $110 million at the age of twenty-one—his con left him in constant psychological turmoil. One reporter who interviewed Minkow wrote: "Ironically, Minkow said the end of a Ponzi scheme can be the most psychologically therapeutic. 'The first good night sleep I got was in prison,' said Minkow. 'Because it was over, I didn't have to lie anymore.'"[5] And Minkow isn't alone. Another reporter tells of comments made by Bernie Madoff: "'It was a nightmare for me,' he told investigators, using the word over and over, as if he were the real victim. 'I wish they caught me six years ago, eight years ago.'"[6] Madoff later said that he was happier in prison than he had been in years. "I lived the last twenty years of my life in fear," he said.[7] While these criminals might have appeared successful, confident, and happy, they were extremely tormented.

---

3. Ibid., p. 98.

4. Ibid., p. 99.

5. Lauren Cox, "What Was Madoff Thinking?" *ABC News*, December 15, 2008, accessed February 5, 2011, http://abcnews.go.com/Health/MindMoodNews/story?id=6452520&page=1.

6. Steve Fishman, "Bernie Madoff, Free at Last," *New York Magazine*, June 6, 2010, accessed February 5, 2011, http://nymag.com/news/crimelaw/66468/.

7. "Bernie Madoff Prison Interview with Barbara Walters," YouTube, accessed October 29, 2011, http://www.youtube.com/watch?v=ZT19ULcowhc.

They may have fooled others, but they could not, and did not, fool themselves. In the short-term, they were a psychological wreck. In the long-term, they lost everything—their money, their prestige, and their freedom. Was this in their self-interest?

These criminals, and others like them, may achieve the material trappings of success. They may have a large bank account, eat in the finest restaurants, and drive expensive cars. But their "success" is an illusion, and they know it. Their "success" is built on an increasingly precarious web of lies. And lying takes a toll. Psychologist Dr. Michael Hurd writes that "lying can be hazardous to your mental health.... Let's face it: It takes enough energy to keep up with the things that are real, much less having to keep track of things that are fictitious and untrue!" Hurd calls this an "emotional time bomb," and the liar never knows when it will go off. Hurd concludes that most people "understand that once they lie to somebody else, they become dependent on that person's ignorance of the truth in order to maintain the lie. Relying on the ignorance of others doesn't sound very healthy to me!"[8] Minkow, Madoff, and countless others confirm Hurd's assessment.

Similarly, an individual can sacrifice others for his own personal gratification, even though he commits no crime. For example, golfer Tiger Woods engaged in a string of sexual adventures outside of his marriage. Woods deceived his wife, his sponsors, and his fans. In confessing his transgressions, Woods said that he had been "selfish." But was he? In the end, he lost his marriage, his reputation, numerous sponsors, and the respect of millions of fans. Was this in his self-interest?

Woods, Minkow, and Madoff were not selfish. Each pursued some irrational desire while ignoring the long-term consequences of his actions. Each willingly sacrificed others for his own personal desires. And in the end, each wound up actually sacrificing his *own* well-being. This illustrates the fact that deception, fraud, and the initiation of force is destructive to both the victim and the victimizer.[9] This fact is true of individuals and of societies. The

---

8. Dr. Michael Hurd, "Lying is Hazardous to Your Mental Health," DrHurd.com, accessed June 24, 2011, http://www.drhurd.com/index.php/Life-s-a-Beach/Published-Columns/Lying-is-hazardous-to-your-mental-health.html.

9. Fraud is an indirect form of force, in that it deprives an individual of his values without his consent. It is the use of lies and deception, rather than a gun, to obtain the material values of others.

initiation of force is immoral, impractical, and destructive, whether one is seeking personal goals or "social" goals. It destroys individuals who seek to use force to achieve their "self-interest," and it destroys nations that seek to use force for the "public interest."

The advocates of altruism would have us believe that we have one of two choices: to live a life of self-denial or a life of hedonistic gluttony. We can be Mother Teresa or we can be Bernie Madoff. But this is a false alternative. Human beings can live together peacefully and cooperatively, with each pursuing his own values and self-interest. When individuals are free to associate and contract as they judge best, individuals interact and trade to the mutual benefit of all. We have seen examples in mail delivery, libraries, employment, education, energy, and more. When individual rights are respected and protected—when force is prohibited in human relationships—individuals pursue their self-interest by producing and trading values.

In a capitalist society, an individual can be altruistic if he so desires. If he wants to give his property to the poor and the needy, morally nobody has a right to stop him. His rights protect his freedom to act as he deems best for his life. But he cannot impose his choices on others. In a capitalist society, the altruist cannot force others to sacrifice *their* property. He cannot force others to act contrary to their own judgment. And the same is true of those who choose to be selfish. In a capitalist society, neither the altruist nor the selfish individual can use force. Neither can impose his values or his morality on others. Each is free to act on his own choices, so long as he respects the mutual rights of others. But what if everyone were selfish? What if everyone put his own self-interest first? Before we answer this, let us first be clear on the meaning of selfishness.

As we have seen, the actions of Madoff, Minkow, and Woods were not in their self-interest. Rational selfishness, or self-interest, writes Ayn Rand,

> holds that *human* good does not require human sacrifices and cannot be achieved by the sacrifice of anyone to anyone. It holds that the *rational* interests of men do not clash—that there is no conflict of interests among men who do not desire the unearned,

> who do not make sacrifices nor accept them, who deal with one another as *traders*, giving value for value.[10]

According to Rand, rational selfishness is not the pursuit of any momentary desire. It is not the fraud of Madoff or the hedonism of Woods. Rational selfishness requires an intransigent recognition of, and devotion to, your highest values. It requires identifying the long-term consequences of your actions and acting accordingly.

The fact that a person desires something does not mean that it is in his long-term interest. A "career" of defrauding investors might bring in millions, but if the perpetrator's soul is tortured and he winds up in prison, it does not serve him well. A night of partying with call-girls might be "fun," but if it destroys a person's marriage and his career, it does not serve him well. An individual cannot achieve his long-term self-interest if he ignores the consequences of his actions. Referring to those who act on whim, author Craig Biddle writes:

> To the extent a person allows irrational desires to dictate his choices and actions, he *will* be unhappy. To the degree he does whatever he feels like doing without regard to both the short-range and the long-range consequences—including both the physical and the spiritual effects—he *will* suffer.[11]

Life is not a series of disconnected actions. One's choices and actions today determine tomorrow's results. To ignore this fact is to risk one's physical and emotional well-being, as Woods, Madoff, and others, have demonstrated.

Your self-interest—the pursuit of your happiness—does not require coercion, fraud, or deceit, nor can happiness be achieved by such methods. Your self-interest is served by producing values and trading with other producers, to the mutual benefit of all.

Consider the great businessmen of the past and present. They do not use deceit or coercion to obtain their customers. They are not promoting the "public interest." They are pursuing their self-interest; they are seeking a profit. And a profit is earned by producing values that others want or need. John Rockefeller, for

---

10. Ayn Rand, "The Objectivist Ethics," in *The Virtue of Selfishness* (New York: Signet, 1964), p. 31.

11. Biddle, *Loving Life*, p. 28.

example, was able to dramatically reduce the price of kerosene and make it affordable to the masses. He exchanged value for value. He brought illumination to millions, allowing them to extend their days and enhance their lives. Henry Ford improved the efficiency of manufacturing an automobile, thereby making motorized transportation affordable to millions. Michael Dell and Steve Jobs created affordable personal computers, allowing everyone to be more productive. These men grew wealthy, not through conquest, fraud, or coercion, but by offering something new, better, or less expensive. They were motivated by a selfish purpose—their own personal benefit. And so are their customers.

The customers of Rockefeller, Ford, Dell, and Jobs are not motivated by the "public interest" or a desire to make these businessmen wealthy. Their customers are motivated by what they gain by purchasing the products offered. Rockefeller's customers bought his kerosene because they wanted nighttime illumination—in their judgment this would be a good thing. Ford's customers bought his products because they believed that being able to travel when and where they desired was a good thing. Dell's customers buy his computers because they want the benefits that come from owning a computer, not because it will promote some noble cause.

To the extent that they are rational, both the businessman and his customers are being selfish. Each acts for his own well-being, based on his own independent judgment and based on his own values. Neither uses force to impose his judgments on others. If you do not like Fords, you can buy a Chevy, a Honda, a Toyota, a BMW, or any number of other automobiles. If you do not like Dell computers, you are free to buy a product from Hewlett Packard, Acer, Toshiba, Apple, or any number of other manufacturers. If you do not like Google, you can use Bing, Lykos, or Yahoo! In a free society, nobody can morally stop others from offering or seeking better values.

John Rockefeller could not stop Thomas Edison from producing a better illuminant. Henry Ford could not stop Chevrolet from offering more color choices. Steve Jobs could not stop Michael Dell from offering a less expensive computer, just as the makers of the Blackberry could not stop Jobs from making the I-Phone. Jerry Yang (Yahoo!) could not stop Sergey Brin (Google) from developing a competing search engine. When force is prohibited, individuals cannot use threats, clubs, or guns; they use reason and persuasion. When force is prohibited, individuals do not seize wealth by pilfering and pillaging; they create wealth by producing the values that others want and need. In a capitalist society, businesses pursue their self-interest by helping others pursue *their* self-interest. Businesses succeed by producing values that enhance the lives of their customers. And competition motivates producers to create better values.

In a free market, wealth is accumulated "democratically," with each consumer "voting" with his wallet. Each consumer spends his money on the values that he believes will be best for his life. And he can vote as often as his desires and circumstances will allow. The producers who attract the most "votes" amass the most wealth, and it is done with the voluntary consent of consumers. Both producer and consumer act according to their own independent judgment, and each pursues his own self-interest.

The extent to which you pursue your own personal values is the extent to which you are selfish. If you own a business, you seek to offer a product that is better or cheaper. You do not do this for the "public interest," but for the profit you will earn—your self-interest. You don't take the risk, endure the headaches and frustrations, and work hard in order to create jobs for others. You do it for your own personal benefit. If you are an employee, you do not work late, take additional courses, or improve your skills in order to contribute to the "public interest." You do it to advance your career and make more money. You do it for your own self-interest. You do not save and invest in order to stimulate the economy. You do it so that you can buy a house, take a vacation, send your children to college, or live comfortably in retirement. You do it for your own personal benefit. The pursuit of your values—your self-interest—is the pursuit of your happiness.

Certainly, others often derive benefits from your actions. Your business does provide jobs and offers products that others desire. Your employer earns a bigger profit when you perform well. Your savings and investments are used by others to build their businesses. But these benefits are secondary; they do not serve as your primary motivation. Your primary motivation is the benefit that *you* will derive.

Selfishness does not entail callous disregard for others or pursuing any momentary desire. It means the refusal to sacrifice your values. It means recognizing that your life and your happiness are your responsibility. It means living your life for yourself. That is good. That is moral. That is your right.

If everyone were selfish, wouldn't individuals lack benevolence? Doesn't altruism really mean kindness and good-will towards others? Let us examine societies that have implemented altruism consistently, and contrast them with a society that recognized and protected the right of each individual to pursue his own happiness.

18

Feeding the Hand that Bites You

We are told that altruism is an expression of good-will toward other men. For example, Altruists International, is an organization dedicated to "encouraging people to think more about the welfare of others, not about what they can get *from* other people, but what they can give *to* them."[1] Their website states that

> Altruists choose to align their well-being with others—so they are happy when others thrive, sad when others are suffering. Essential in establishing strong relationships, most societies acknowledge the importance of altruism within the family. By motivating cooperation rather than conflict, it promotes harmony within communities of any size.[2]

Is this true? Does altruism really promote "cooperation rather than conflict"?

We are also told that selfishness and capitalism lead to "cut-throat" competition and an absence of benevolence. As an example, Altruists International claims that, "The inherent conflict in conventional money establishes zero-sum (competitive) relationships between people and organizations—so that those who help others necessarily disadvantage themselves."[3] Is this claim true?

---

1. "What Is Altruists International?" *Altruists International*, accessed July 2, 2011, http://www.altruists.org/about/.

2. "What is Altruism?" *Altruists International*, accessed July 2, 2011, http://www.altruists.org/about/altruism/.

3. Ibid.

Does capitalism promote relationships that benefit one individual at the expense of others?

To answer these questions, let us re-examine the words of Auguste Comte—who coined the term altruism: "All honest and sensible men, of whatever party, should agree, by a common consent, to eliminate the doctrine of rights.... Rights, then, in the case of man, are as absurd as they are immoral."[4] To Comte, we are to dispense with the entire notion of rights. Rights, remember, sanction your freedom of action in a social context. Rights protect your freedom to act according to your own judgment. According to altruism, this is absurd and immoral; according to altruism, you should not be free to act on your own judgment.

Many altruists would reject Comte's claim, arguing that we can have both individual rights and altruism. If this were true, then why is every altruistic government program and policy implemented with coercion? Why are public libraries and parks, government schools, "entitlement" programs, and every other government intervention ultimately backed by government force? If altruism and individual rights are compatible, why does the political implementation of altruism always result in the violation of individual rights? Philosopher Leonard Peikoff explains:

> Altruism demands the initiation of physical force. When the representatives of the needy use coercion, they regularly explain that it is obligatory: it is their only means of ensuring that some recalcitrant individual, whose duty is self-sacrifice, carries out his moral obligations—of ensuring that he gives to the poor the unearned funds that he is born owing them, but is trying wrongfully to withhold.[5]

If, as altruism holds, you have a moral obligation to help the needy, your refusal to do so denies the needy of what is "rightfully" theirs. According to altruism, taking your money to give to the poor is an act of "justice"—it is returning to the needy what is "morally" theirs.

If altruism demands the violation of individual rights, what would government be like if it embraced Comte's "ideal"? Sadly,

---

4. Auguste Comte, *The Catechism of Positive Religion*, trans. Richard Congreve (London: John Chapman, 1858), pp. 332-33.

5. Peikoff, *Objectivism: Philosophy of Ayn Rand*, p. 320.

many leaders in the twentieth century have provided an answer. As one example, the leader of one European nation explained his moral philosophy:

> It is thus necessary that the individual should finally come to realize that his own ego is of no importance in comparison with the existence of his nation…
>
> This state of mind, which subordinates the interests of the ego to the conservation of the community, is really the first premise for every truly human culture…. The basic attitude from which such activity arises, we call—to distinguish it from egoism and selfishness—idealism. By this we understand only the individual's capacity to make sacrifices for the community, for his fellow men.[6]

The nation was pre-World War II Germany and the leader was Adolf Hilter. Hitler brought altruism to its logical conclusion: he extinguished individual rights, forcing individuals to serve others. And Hitler was not alone.

Vladimir Lenin, the first dictator of the Soviet Union, declared, "Unquestioning submission to a single will is absolutely necessary for the success of the labour process...the revolution demands, in the interests of socialism, that the masses unquestioningly obey the single will of the leaders of the labour process."[7] Lenin's successor, Josef Stalin, similarly remarked, "Ideas are more powerful than guns. We would not let our enemies have guns, why should we let them have ideas?"[8] Both Lenin and Stalin demanded that the individual sacrifice his judgment to that of their leaders. And like Hitler, they backed their demands with guns. The mountains of corpses that resulted testify to their willingness to use those guns to get the sacrifice they demanded, one way or another. In a totalitarian regime, the individual is to sacrifice everything—his

---

6. Quoted in Leonard Peikoff, *The Ominous Parallels* (New York: Stein and Day, 1982), p. 3.

7. Quoted in Maurice Brinton, "The Bolsheviks and Workers Control 1917-1921," AnarchyIsOrder.org, p. 99, http://www.anarchyisorder.org/CD%234/Lay-outed%20texts/PDF-versions/Brinton,%20Maurice%20%20The%20bolsheviks%20and%20workers%20control%20%28%2717-%27.pdf.

8. Robert G. Torricelli (Editor), *Quotations for Public Speakers: A Historical, Literary, and Political Anthology* (New Brunswick: Rutgers University Press, 2000), p. 121.

rights, his property, his independent thoughts, and his life—to the state.

Some might argue that Nazi Germany and Soviet Russia were aberrations, that the resulting misery and death were simply the work of madmen. They might argue that Hitler and Stalin took a good idea—altruism—too far. But did they? Did they distort altruism, or did they, as Comte advocated, "eliminate the doctrine of rights"? The truth is, these brutal dictators did not distort altruism; they took altruism seriously. They eliminated all rights. They demanded that individuals "give" to others. They demanded "co-operation" and sacrifice to others. And they got it at the point of a gun. The rivers of blood that resulted are the most visible evidence of the destruction wrought by altruism.

Others might argue that Hitler and Stalin are not examples of what they mean by altruism. They might argue that their intention is not dictatorship. However, one's intentions do not change the consequences of one's ideas. For example, the advocates of minimum wage laws would likely argue that they do not intend to destroy jobs, yet job destruction is the result. Those who advocate expanding regulations on oil companies would likely argue that they do not intend to drive up the price of energy or foster dependence on imported oil, yet those are the consequences. Results are not determined by one's intentions but by the nature of the ideas one advocates and acts upon. The same principles lead to the same results, regardless of one's intentions. This is true whether one is advocating for an increase in the minimum wage or advocating altruism.

Political principles ultimately derive from moral principles. Morality defines the proper conduct for the individual; political principles define the proper conduct of individuals in a social setting—the interaction between individuals. A code of morality that upholds rational self-interest will advocate a political system in which individuals are free to act according to their own judgment in the pursuit of their own values, that is, the protection of individual rights and capitalism. A code of morality that upholds self-sacrificial service to others will advocate a political system that violates individual rights, that is, as system that forces individuals to sacrifice their desires, judgment, and self-interest. If a culture embraces altruism, it must ultimately advocate the use of government coercion, and with it, increasing government control over the lives of individuals.

Dictators seek complete control over the lives of citizens, and they build police states to achieve their end. However, in a totalitarian state, the police cannot be everywhere. They cannot monitor every conversation or activity, yet the authorities must maintain complete control. They accomplish this by enlisting citizens to inform on one another. In the Soviet Union, for example, a vast network of citizens was recruited to spy on their fellow citizens. It is estimated that as many as 60 percent of the Soviet citizens were informants in one way or another.[9] These informants were used by the government to collect information regarding criminal activities, as well as reports of domestic abuse, excessive drinking, and political "crimes."[10] The Nazis used similar tactics in Germany:

> The problem for the average citizen was that no one ever knew for sure just who those informants were. It could be anyone, your milkman, the old lady across the street, a quiet co-worker, even a schoolboy. As a result, fear ruled the day. Most people realized the necessity of self-censorship and generally kept their mouths shut politically, unless they had something positive to say.[11]

Do you think that fear of your fellow citizens engenders good-will and benevolence towards them? The Germans and the Russians viewed their fellow citizens with suspicion, wondering which one might report a passing remark to the authorities. Is this the kind of society in which the pursuit of happiness is even possible? Under such conditions, would you engage in idle discussion—or any discussion—with your paper boy, the mail man, or the clerk at the supermarket? The Germans and the Russians wondered what comment might result in a visit from the police, and therefore, suppressed thoughts that might be taken as criminal. When citizens self-censor, when they do not speak their mind for fear of governmental reprisal, freedom has been eliminated, and with it,

---

9. Louise I. Shelley, *Policing Soviet Society* (New York: Routledge, 1996), p. 114.

10. Ibid., p. 117.

11. "The Gestapo is Born," The History Place, http://www.historyplace.com/worldwar2/triumph/tr-gestapo.htm, accessed February 10, 2011.

"the doctrine of rights." This is what altruism advocates, and it is what altruism "achieves" when practiced consistently.

While America has not yet reached such a state, during the debate over health care reform, the Obama Administration asked citizens to report "disinformation," and set up a website for that purpose:

> There is a lot of disinformation about health insurance reform out there, spanning from control of personal finances to end of life care. These rumors often travel just below the surface via chain emails or through *casual conversation*. Since we can't keep track of all of them here at the White House, we're asking for your help. If you get an email or see something on the web about health insurance reform that seems fishy, send it to...[12] [emphasis added]

Ostensibly, the Administration sought to refute this "disinformation." Allegedly, the Administration only wanted to make citizens aware of the facts. But we must remember that, according to President Obama, we are our brother's keeper. According to Obama, we have a duty to others. He has demonstrated no hesitancy to "eliminate the doctrine of rights" by forcing you to pay for the health care of others, or by imposing more strangulating regulations on the financial industry, or by seeking "cap and trade" legislation. The fact is, when government asks citizens to report casual conversations, the difference between that regime and a totalitarian state is only one of degree, not one of principle.

When the government openly asks for informants, the fear of governmental reprisal is tangible. When government controls and regulations touch every corner of your life, that reprisal can take many forms—the denial of a permit or license, an inspection by OSHA or the EPA, an audit by the IRS, or some other action by the myriad agencies and bureaus assigned to oversee your activities. John Thoburn was thrown in jail for defying an arbitrary edict by zoning officials to move ninety-eight trees. Dan Allgyer's farm was raided by armed federal agents because he had the audacity to sell

---

12. "Facts are Stubborn Things," White House, August 4, 2009, accessed February 5, 2011, http://www.whitehouse.gov/blog/Facts-Are-Stubborn-Things/.

raw milk to consenting customers. The message in these cases, and many more, is obey, or else. No matter your judgment, no matter your values, you are forced to sacrifice both.

Totalitarian governments seek to control both what you say and what you do—they seek total control over your life. These controls spawn government agents to issue permits, check paperwork, and ensure that you are conforming to their edicts, decrees, and mandates. Informants are simply a part of the enforcement apparatus, and they create fear, suspicion, and ill-will towards fellow citizens. While America has not reached such a state, the trend is towards greater government control and everything that that implies. If you think that dictatorship is not possible in America, twenty years ago did you think ObamaCare was possible? Did you think that bailing out Wall Street, taking over General Motors and Chrysler, and the mortgaging of your children's future was possible? Did you think annual deficits of $1.5 trillion were possible?

As government control over the lives and actions of individuals grows, elected officials battle to secure government programs, favors, and projects for their constituents as a means of being re-elected. Money is collected from taxpayers across the nation, sent to Washington, and then re-distributed as deemed to be in the "public interest" by representatives and senators. While taxpayers from Arkansas and Michigan are paying for sorghum research in Texas and berry research in Alaska,[13] taxpayers from Georgia and Ohio are paying for the conservation of Old Tiger Stadium in Detroit and a water taxi service in Connecticut.[14] While taxpayers from Oregon and Virginia are paying for bus service in Missouri and Mississippi, taxpayers from Maine and Florida are paying for water and sewage infrastructure in Washington and West Virginia.[15] Remember this the next time you tell your children that you can't afford some treat, or deny yourself some small pleasure. Remind yourself that you must put aside your own self-interest—a vacation, a new car, or

---

13. "2008 Pig Book Summary," Citizens Against Government Waste, accessed April 10, 2011, http://www.cagw.org/reports/pig-book/2008/#I_Agriculture.

14. "Earmarks Rise to $19.6 Billion in CAGW's 2009 Pig Book," Citizens Against Government Waste, accessed April 10, 2011, http://www.cagw.org/newsroom/releases/2009/earmarks-rise-to-196.html.

15. "2008 Pig Book Summary," Citizens Against Government Waste, accessed April 10, 2011, http://www.cagw.org/reports/pig-book/2008/#XII_TransportationHousing_and_Urban_Deve.

private school for your children—so that others can enjoy bus service or tours of an old sports stadium.

The battle to get a piece of this government largesse is a primary reason for the growing number of lobbyists. Eager to secure a share of your money, special interest groups seek to convince government officials that their cause serves the "public interest," while competing groups make similar claims. Those groups represent environmentalists, consumer organizations, the states, trade associations, labor unions, and virtually every conceivable collective. They represent everyone but individuals. The result is a form of civil warfare. It is a civil war cloaked in the niceties of Congressional hearings, where the "weapons" are cocktail parties, inside financial deals, campaign donations, and other perks for government officials. Each group agrees on the means—government coercion—and they simply disagree on the ends. Whether they are demanding money for the poor or more benefits for the elderly, whether they seek to restrict drilling or want more regulations on financial institutions, whether they want subsidies to grow rice or subsidies for producing alternative fuels, special interests insist that they represent the "public interest." And to make matters worse, they advocate the use of government coercion to take your money, control your life, or both. They are vultures fighting for the scraps of flesh left on the once vibrant American economy.

Special interest politics is creating a culture of animosity and vitriol, all in the name of the "public interest." The degree to which a government violates individual rights, wrote Ayn Rand,

> is the degree to which it breaks up the country into rival gangs and sets men against one another. When individual rights are abrogated, there is no way to determine who is entitled to what; there is no way to determine the justice of anyone's claims, desires, or interests. The criterion, therefore, reverts to the tribal concept of: one's wishes are limited only by the power of one's gang. In order to survive under such a system, men have no choice but to fear, hate, and destroy one another; it is a system of underground plotting, of secret conspiracies, of deals, favors, betrayals, and sudden, bloody coups.

> It is not a system conducive to brotherhood, security, cooperation, and peace.[16]

It is a system in which individuals gang together to determine who will be forced to sacrifice. It is a system of "dog-eat-dog" and cut-throat competition in which each gang competes to engage in legalized extortion. Lobbyists and the politically connected compete to secure bailouts for automakers, subsidies for alternative energy companies, or legislation that protects the snail darter. And competing groups demand bailouts for Wall Street, subsidies for farmers, or legislation that protects unions. But it hasn't always been this way. Americans haven't always been scavengers seeking to plunder others.

Prior to the early twentieth century, America was a nation of great benevolence. For the first one hundred years of the republic, the federal government was largely limited to its proper purpose—the protection of individual rights—and special interests were limited in number and impact. Because government intervention was minimal, the incentive to influence government officials was also minimal. As a result, Americans did not fight one another over the use of federal tax dollars, tax breaks, controls on other citizens, or similar government interventions. When problems and needs arose, citizens generally did not rush to Washington demanding that Congress "do something." Instead, they did what free and independent individuals do—they took care of the problem.

We have already seen that throughout colonial America individuals banded together to form private libraries. Unable to afford books on their own, individuals pooled their money to solve a mutual problem. This type of mutual-aid was common throughout the nineteenth century and early twentieth century. And that aid took many forms.

For example, the Independent Order of Saint Luke and the United Order of True Reformers were all-black societies comprised of ex-slaves. Both were established to provide medical and burial insurance for members. While this was a common benefit of many mutual-aid (i.e., fraternal) societies, they also provided educational opportunities for members and provided charitable services for the community. The Ladies of the Maccabees taught managerial,

---

16. Ayn Rand, "The Roots of War," in *Capitalism: The Unknown Ideal*, pp. 36-7.

financial, and other business skills to women. The Loyal Order of Moose became well-known for its orphanage—Mooseheart—near Aurora, Illinois. The Security Benefit Association operated both an orphanage and a home for the elderly.[17]

In Ybor City, Florida, five mutual-aid societies were established by workers in the cigar industry in the last decade of the nineteenth century.[18] While these societies were formed along racial lines, such as separate societies for Italians and Cubans, they often "rallied to each others aid, shared medical services, hosted dances, organized sporting and cultural events…."[19] Because most members were immigrants, the societies also provided English and citizenship classes. Like many such societies, medical benefits were an important part of membership. The El Centro Asturiano society, built a hospital that had a pharmacy, six active doctors, and thirty specialists. At the time, it was regarded as "the most modern and well equipped hospital in the city of Tampa and perhaps the entire American South."[20] Dues for the Italian society—L'Unione Italiana—were sixty cents a week (about sixteen dollars in 2011), which included unemployment benefits and medical coverage.

Unfortunately, government intervention—in several forms—drove these societies out of business. In the early 1900s, the government, spurred by lobbying from the medical profession, began tightening licensing requirements on doctors. As we saw in chapter six, occupational licensing is often used to reduce competition and increase the income of the licensed professionals, and this was no exception. As licensing decreased the supply of doctors, the profession sought to penalize doctors who accepted contracts with the mutual-aid societies. The medical profession then "launched an all-out war against fraternal medical services by imposing manifold sanctions, including denial of licenses against doctors who accepted these contracts."[21] In response, some

17. David Beito, "From Mutual Aid to Welfare State: How Fraternal Societies Fought Poverty and Taught Character," The Heritage Foundation, July 27, 2000, accessed February 5, 2011, http://www.heritage.org/research/lecture/from-mutual-aid-to-welfare-state.

18. "Cigar makers & the Mutual Aid Societies," CigarsofTampa.com, accessed February 5, 2011, http://www.cigarsoftampa.com/mutual-aid.html.

19. Ibid.

20. Ibid.

21. Beito, "Mutual Aid."

societies, such as the Security Benefit Association, built their own hospitals. But additional government intervention, such as special tax benefits for businesses that paid for insurance for employees, put further pressure on the mutual-aid societies. In short, government intervention in the form of licensing and special treatment under the tax code made it economically unreasonable to continue the voluntary fraternal societies.

A final government intervention was the rise of the welfare state. The lure of "free" benefits from the government was an enticement that led to declining memberships in the fraternal societies. Just as bad money drives out good money (Gresham's Law), bad social programs—those backed by government coercion—drive out good social programs—those that are voluntary and consensual. When citizens could get "free" benefits from the government, they no longer saw a need to pay for them. Rather than working together to solve common problems, many citizens increasingly turned to government to solve their problems. Rather than engaging in voluntary, cooperative efforts to address common concerns, citizens increasingly sought to use government coercion to force others to pay for their problems. Rather than respecting the rights of others, citizens increasingly sought to violate individual rights in the name of the "public interest."

As these examples show, altruism and government intervention breed animosity towards one's fellow citizens, and the greater the intervention the greater the animosity. Altruism does not create co-operation, as its advocates claim; it creates competition to violate individual rights. Intervention turns individuals into warring factions, each fighting to get a piece of a pie that belongs to someone else. In contrast, the recognition and protection of individual rights promotes good-will, and citizens willingly work together to the mutual benefit of all involved. In a free society, citizens do not view one another as threats but as fellow travelers in the pursuit of happiness.

While some concede that government regulations sometimes go too far, they argue that society needs some rules of conduct. Don't we need rules to prevent anarchy? Aren't some controls and regulations necessary for a society to function? Are all government regulations evil? We will now turn to these questions.

19

Chains, Whips, and Guns

In 1960, the Code of Federal Regulations (CFR) contained 22,877 pages.[1] By 2007, the CFR had swelled to 145,816 pages, an increase of more than 530 percent.[2] Seemingly, no detail is too small to escape the attention of regulators. For example, federal regulations stipulate that textile manufacturers follow certain labeling requirements, even in their advertisements: "If a written ad for a textile product makes any statement about a fiber, or implies the presence of a particular fiber, the fiber content information required on the label—except for percentages—also must appear in the ad."[3] If an American fails to conform to regulations controlling the smallest detail of his business, he may be subject to fines, imprisonment, or both. Americans are expected to plan their businesses and their lives, never knowing when the law might be changed, why, or for whose benefit. James Madison warned of the danger inherent in such government power in *The Federalist #62*:

> It will be of little avail to the people, that the laws are made by men of their own choice, if the laws be so voluminous that they cannot be read, or so incoherent that they cannot be understood;

---

1. Clyde Wayne Crews, "Ten Thousand Commandments: An Annual Snapshot of the Regulatory State," Competitive Enterprise Institute, p. 12, accessed January 22, 2011, http:// http://cei.org/sites/default/files/Wayne%20Crews%20-%2010,000 %20Commandments%202006.pdf.

2. James Gattuso, "Red Tape Rising: Regulatory Trends in the Bush Years," Heritage Foundation, accessed January 22, 2011, http://www.heritage.org/research/regulation /bg2116.cfm.

3. "Threading Your Way Through the Labeling Requirements Under the Textile and Wool Acts," Bureau of Consumer Protection, accessed September 12, 2011, http://business.ftc.gov/documents/bus21-threading-your-way-through-labeling -requirements-under-textile-and-wool-acts#ads

> if they be repealed or revised before they are promulgated, or undergo such incessant changes that no man, who knows what the law is to-day, can guess what it will be to-morrow. Law is defined to be a rule of action; but how can that be a rule, which is little known, and less fixed?[4]

Of course, Madison was correct.

As one example, Abner Schoenwetter was arrested in 1999 and ultimately spent six years in federal prison for violating the Lacey Act. The act allows American government officials to indict and prosecute anyone who imports "fish or wildlife taken, possessed, transported, or sold in violation of...any *foreign* law [emphasis added]".[5] Schoenwetter was considered a criminal because he imported some lobsters that were less than 5.5 inches long, they were in plastic bags rather than cardboard boxes, and because he deposited the proceeds of his sales into a bank, which was considered money laundering. While the federal government was busy prosecuting Schoenwetter for allegedly breaking a Honduran law, the attorney general of Honduras wrote to United States Attorney General John Ashcroft to explain that there was no violation. Even when Honduran officials filed a "friend of the court" brief in defense of Schoenwetter, the federal government did not relent. It is bad enough that an American businessman must operate under the oppressive, detailed regulations of the federal government; it becomes virtually impossible when he may be prosecuted for "breaking" foreign laws. A businessman cannot operate a successful business if he must spend his time satisfying the demands of politicians and regulators rather than satisfying the demands of the marketplace. How can anyone pursue his values—his happiness—with such threats and controls?

For example, at the end of 2010, tax cuts from the Bush Administration were set to expire. Republicans wanted to extend the lower rates, while Democrats wanted to allow tax rates to rise. As Congress and the White House debated the issue, financial markets and businesses were paralyzed. Not knowing what their tax rates would be in just a few weeks, investors and entrepreneurs did

---

4. James Madison, "The Federalist No. 62," February 27, 1788.

5. Paul Rosezweig and Ellen Podgor, "Eight Years for Bagging Lobsters?" The Heritage Foundation, December 31, 2003, accessed September 1, 2011, http://www.heritage.org/research/commentary/2003/12/eight-years-for-bagging-lobsters.

not know what actions to take. Even the Internal Revenue Service was in limbo—it could not finalize tax tables until the issue was resolved.

The growing number of regulations requires increasing numbers of agents and bureaucrats to issue permits, monitor operations, check paperwork, and ensure that you are in compliance with government dictates. In 1960, the various federal regulatory agencies employed 57,109 people. In 2009, an estimated 263,989 people were employed at the federal level to oversee the activities of you and your fellow citizens, an increase of more than 360 percent.[6] The growth in the number of regulators has far exceeded population growth: In 1960, there was one regulator for approximately 3,165 citizens; in 2009, there was one regulator for about 1,144 citizens. And, to add insult to injury, you must pay the expenses and salaries of those who are controlling your actions—spending by federal regulators was an estimated $51 billion in 2009.[7]

The cost of increased control over your activities is not limited to the expenditures of the regulatory agencies. Indeed, a greater cost is imposed in meeting the mandates issued by those agencies. A report by the Competitive Enterprise Institute found that the cost of meeting federal regulations was $1.751 trillion in 2008.[8] State and local regulations add another $446 billion in expenses to Americans each year. In total, the various federal, state, and local regulations impose on each person more than $6,600 per year in regulatory compliance costs.[9] These are hidden taxes on every product you purchase. As one example, the Obama Administration proposed fuel-economy standards that auto makers estimated would add $1,300 to the cost of an average car.[10] Those additional costs would

---

6. Veronique de Rugy and Melinda Warren, "The Incredible Growth of the Regulators' Budget', *Mercatus Center at George Mason University*, No. 08-36, September 2008, p. 4, accessed January 22, 2011, http://mercatus.org/publication/incredible-growth-regulators-budget.

7. Ibid, p. 2.

8. Clyde Wayne Crews, Jr., "Ten Thousand Commandments, 2011 Edition," *Competitive Enterprise Institute*, p. 2, accessed June 19, 2011, http://cei.org/sites/default/files/Wayne%20Crews%20-%2010,000%20Commandments%202011.pdf.

9. Michael Hodges, "Government Regulatory Compliance Cost Report," accessed January 22, 2011, http://grandfather-economic-report.com/regulation.htm.

10. Stephen Power and Christopher Conkey, "U.S. Orders Stricter Fuel Goals for Autos", *The Wall Street Journal*, May 19, 2009, accessed January 22, 2011, http://online.wsj.com/article/SB124266939482331283.html.

price many families out of the new car market and damage an already beleaguered domestic auto industry.

While many regulations prohibit or mandate certain actions, other regulations are intended to simply make some activities economically unfeasible. For instance, during the 2008 Presidential campaign, Barack Obama said, "So if somebody wants to build a coal-powered plant, they can; it's just that it will bankrupt them because they're going to be charged a huge sum for all that greenhouse gas that's being emitted."[11] In other words, Obama wants to eliminate coal-powered plants, but he won't be straightforward about it and simply ban them. Instead, he will achieve his ends by imposing outrageous fees on those who dare to act differently than he desires. Whether through outright prohibitions, mandates, or large fees, government regulations make nearly every activity and product more expensive. What could you do with an extra $6,600 per household member each year?

Government regulations impose other costs as well. We have previously seen that regulations imposed by the Food and Drug Administration add as much as 85 percent to the cost of medicines. Business owners and managers must waste time defending themselves against frivolous complaints filed with the Equal Employment Opportunity Commission. Energy companies must contend with endless regulations imposed on drilling, refining, and transporting petroleum products. Overall, producers spend an increasing amount of time filling out paperwork and complying with government mandates, and less and less time actually producing.

Further, the costs of regulations are not always computable in terms of time or dollars. Restrictions on activities stifle innovation and prevent many products, efficiencies, and other developments from ever reaching the market. Because that which does not exist cannot be measured, the costs to consumers and businesses cannot be computed. For example, for years the federal government essentially prohibited fish farms (giant enclosed feed lots for fish) in federal waters. Even though these farms are viable industries in Norway, Chile, Canada, and other nations, this industry barely exists

---

11. Steve Mufson, "The Last Minute Obama-McCain Coal Debate ," *The Washington Post*, November 3, 2008, accessed May 30, 2011, http://onfaith.washingtonpost.com/postglobal/energywire/2008/11/the_last_minute_obama-mccain_c.html.

in the United States because of federal regulations. As a result, many businesses are not started, fewer jobs are created, and the consumers of seafood have fewer options and must pay higher prices. Government intervention in oil drilling, nuclear power plants, land-use, medicines, mail delivery, education, and virtually every industry, stifles innovation.

Despite the pretense of protecting Americans, regulations also reduce our health and safety. We have already seen that delays in drug approval by the Food and Drug Administration have led to the deaths of hundreds of thousands of Americans. The National Research Council has found that fuel efficiency standards—which mandate smaller cars—have contributed to thousands of deaths in automobile accidents.[12] And again, many new products and innovations—developments that might save lives—are never created because of the restrictions and mandates imposed by politicians, bureaucrats, and regulators. By every measure, and in every industry, regulations are destructive.

Consider the fact that technology companies, which generally have fewer regulations than other industries, produce the most innovation. Consider the spectacular advances in computers, televisions, phones, video games, and cameras in the past twenty years. In contrast, when was the last time *any* noticeable advance was made in mail delivery, education, infrastructure, or any other service dominated by government? Further, two of the most heavily regulated industries—health care and the financial sector—are routinely regarded as "broken." Why are government monopolies and heavily regulated industries the objects of derision, scorn, and contempt, while those industries that are the most free continue to amaze and delight us with their innovations?

By now, the answer should be clear: regulations force individuals to satisfy the decrees and edicts of politicians and bureaucrats, rather than act on their own judgment. Who do you think is more likely to develop new and innovative products: Jeff Bezos (Amazon.com), Bill Gates, and Steve Jobs, or Harry Reid, Nancy Pelosi, and Barney Frank?

---

12. See National Research Council, Transportation Research Board, *Effectiveness and Impact of Corporate Average Fuel Economy (CAFE) Standards* (Washington, D.C.: National Academy Press, 2002), accessed January 22, 2011, http://books.nap.edu/openbook.php?record_id=10172&page=R1.

A number of justifications are offered for regulations, but they all mean the same thing: regulations are necessary for society to function in a civilized manner. As one commentator argues:

> Regulations are simply a list of rules, guidelines and codes of ethics created to establish a baseline of behavior in the interest of every participant's safety and well-being, and a list of consequences that will be enforced on people choosing to violate those guidelines and thereby risk jeopardizing everyone's safety and well-being.[13]

This is a common view of regulations. But is this true?

Guidelines are a *suggested* course of action; regulations are *mandatory*. Guidelines allow for discretion; regulations do not. Guidelines allow you to exercise your own judgment; regulations render your judgment irrelevant. Regulations carry the authority of law, and those who refuse to obey are subject to fines, jail, or both. Regulations compel you to place the judgment of others before your own, even when those others are wrong. If you take an unapproved drug, massage horses, marry someone of the same gender, sell raw milk, or plant trees in the "wrong" place, you do not "risk jeopardizing everyone's safety and well-being." The only individuals impacted are those who are voluntarily involved. Regulations are not guidelines; they are chains that restrict your freedom, and they are backed by the whips and guns of government. No matter the particular argument offered, "justifications" for regulations ultimately mean that you must put aside your self-interest for the "public interest."

Some argue that regulations are actually in our self-interest because they prevent anarchy. Without regulations, the argument goes, individuals would be free to do anything they pleased, and the result would be chaos. Certainly, society needs laws regarding social conduct—how individuals are to interact with others. Morally, those laws must be guided by the principle of individual rights—the moral right of each individual to act according to his own judgment in the pursuit of his own happiness, as long as he respects the

---

13. Tina Dietz, "The Case for Just Enough Regulations", *The Ronoake Times*, November 11, 2008, accessed January 22, 2011, http://www.roanoke.com/editorials/commentary/wb/183755

mutual rights of others. That is, you may not initiate force to interfere with the actions of others, just as others may not initiate force to interfere with your actions. Just as it is immoral and criminal for your neighbor to steal your money in order to pay for his health care, it is immoral and criminal for government to do so. It is immoral and criminal for your neighbor to threaten you for selling products that don't meet with his approval; likewise, it is immoral and criminal for government to do so. Regulations prevent you from acting as you judge best. Regulations force you to place the "public interest" before your own interests. As a matter of principle, the initiation of force—including government regulations—is immoral and criminal.

While many—particularly conservatives and businessmen—concede that regulations sometimes go "too far," they accept the premise that regulations are proper. For example, Thomas J. Donohue, President and CEO of the U.S. Chamber of Commerce, wrote in 2010, "Business supports sensible and effective regulation, but it doesn't buy the premise that more is necessarily better." Donohue went on to write that "there is an obvious and legitimate need for regulation."[14] What is a sensible regulation? By whose standard? Lysander Spooner did not find Congressional prohibitions on private mail delivery to be sensible. Mercedes Clemens didn't find it sensible that she needed to attend veterinary school in order to massage horses. Abigail Burroughs and her family did not find the Food and Drug Administration's refusal to allow her to take an experimental drug to be sensible. John Thoburn did not find it sensible to move ninety-eight trees. Dan Allgyer did not find it sensible that armed government agents raided his farm because he was selling raw milk to willing customers. What Donohue—or anyone else—finds sensible, others may not. There is no moral reason that the judgment of Donohue or some petty bureaucrat should supersede the judgment of those whose lives are involved. There is no moral reason that the happiness of Burroughs, Thoburn, Allgyer, or anyone else should be sacrificed because Donohue thinks some regulation is "legitimate" and "sensible."

---

14. Thomas J. Donohue, "When Is It Too Much Regulation?" U.S. Chamber of Commerce, July 2010, accessed January 22, 2011, http://www.uschambermagazine.com/article/when-is-it-too-much-regulation.

Motivated by altruism, Donohue believes that the "public interest" supersedes the rights and interests of businessmen. He accepts the violation of individual rights as legitimate, and then can only quibble over whose rights should be violated and to what extent. He grants to politicians and bureaucrats the moral authority to dictate to businessmen, and then meekly complains that some regulations go "too far." What he does not understand is, if he concedes his rights at any time, on any issue, the game is over—his rights are no longer inviolate.

Consider the following scenario: you confront a burglar in your home. He suggests a compromise. Rather than take all of your jewelry and cash, which he intended to do, he will take only half of it. "Don't be selfish," he might say. "You have a moral obligation to put the needs and interests of others before your own. And I need your stuff." Would you recognize his "right" to take 50 percent of your property, whereas taking all of it would be going "too far"?

To compromise with the burglar is to abandon your right to your property. It is to declare that, as a matter of principle, the burglar has as much right to your property as you do, and the only issue is how to divide that property. The same applies to all rights. To compromise on the principle of individual rights is to declare all rights null and void. All that is left is to negotiate the extent to which your rights will be violated.

Many believe that if all government regulations were repealed, businesses and individuals would cheat and connive to gain unearned profits. They believe that, without government regulations, the marketplace would turn into a competition to defraud others. It is certainly true that individuals are capable of fraud. Bernie Madoff, Richard Stanford (who ran a scheme similar to Madoff's), Enron, and others have demonstrated this fact quite clearly. However, Madoff, Stanford, and Enron were subject to regulation by the Securities and Exchange Commission (SEC), which repeatedly failed to discover their frauds. According to the SEC's website, the "mission of the U.S. Securities and Exchange Commission is to protect investors…."[15] The failure of the SEC to protect investors in these cases are but a few examples of the failure

15. "The Investor's Advocate: How the SEC Protects Investors, Maintains Market Integrity, and Facilitates Capital Formation," U.S. Securities and Exchange Commission, accessed July 1, 2011, http://www.sec.gov/about/whatwedo.shtml.

of regulations to achieve their stated purpose. While an unregulated market would not prevent fraud, the heavy hand of the SEC is clearly not doing it either. What does a capitalist society offer as an alternative?

As economist Alan Greenspan once wrote:

> The attempt to protect the consumer by force undercuts the protection he gets from incentive. First, it undercuts the value of reputation by placing the reputable company on the same basis as the unknown, the newcomer, or the fly-by-nighter. It declares, in effect, that all are equally suspect...Second it grants an automatic...guarantee of safety to the products of any company that complies with its arbitrarily set minimum standards...The minimum standards, which are the basis of regulation, gradually tend to become the maximums as well...A fly by night securities operator can quickly meet all the S.E.C. requirements, gain the inference of respectability, and proceed to fleece the public. In an unregulated economy, the operator would have had to spend a number of years in reputable dealings before he could earn a position of trust...
>
> Protection of the consumer by regulation is thus illusory. Rather than isolating the consumer from the dishonest businessman, it is gradually destroying the only reliable protection the consumer has: competition for reputation...Government regulations do not eliminate potentially dishonest individuals, but merely make their activities harder to detect or easier to hush up.[16]

As evidence, consider the time it took for the frauds of Charles Ponzi (for whom "Ponzi Scheme" is named), Enron, Stanford, and Madoff to be discovered. Enron's fraud took eight years to unravel, Stanford went undetected for nearly fifteen years, and Madoff's fraud lasted decades. And don't forget, Enron, Stanford, and Madoff all had to file regular reports with the SEC. How long did it take to discover Ponzi's fraud in 1920? Operating in an unregulated market prior to the SEC, Ponzi was exposed in about eight months. In a free market, the truth was exposed in less than a year, and countless victims were saved. Clearly, the SEC did not protect

---

16. Alan Greenspan, "The Assault on Integrity," in *Capitalism: The Unknown Ideal* (New York: Signet 1967), pp. 119-20.

investors. Instead, Enron, Madoff, Stanford, and their ilk hid behind the skirt of the SEC to gain legitimacy and thereby more easily defraud a greater number of investors.

As further evidence of the importance of reputation, consider the effort and money that businesses invest in developing and protecting their brand name—their reputation. Businesses understand that consumers can quickly lose trust and confidence if the company markets an inferior product or service, presents the wrong image, or in any way damages its reputation. And damage to its reputation can occur even when the company does nothing wrong. For example, in 1982, seven people died in Chicago after a product tampering incident in which Tylenol was laced with cyanide. Sales of Tylenol across the nation immediately plummeted from a 37 percent market share to 7 percent. The makers of Tylenol, Johnson & Johnson, faced a crisis, as Tylenol was a respected brand that dominated its category. The company had a tremendous challenge to overcome the bad publicity relating to the product tampering. It responded by pulling all Tylenol from the market, a move that cost the company $100 million. When Johnson & Johnson brought Tylenol back to the market months later, the company introduced triple-seal tamper-resistant packaging and sent more than 2,250 sales people to speak to the medical community.[17] These efforts restored confidence in the product, and Tylenol regained its market share. While this is an extreme example, it demonstrates that businesses recognize the importance of their reputation and will go to considerable lengths to protect it.

Additionally, in the absence of government regulations, consumers are accountable for their own decisions. They are free to act according to their own judgment and cannot use government coercion to impose the consequences of their choices upon others. For instance, those who live in flood plains cannot force others to rebuild their homes when flooding occurs. Those who take out mortgages that are beyond their means cannot compel taxpayers to bail them out when they face foreclosure. But the absence of government regulations does not mean that individuals have no means for making wise decisions. Even in today's heavily regulated

---

17. "The Tylenol Crisis, 1982," Effective Crisis Management, accessed June 19, 2011, http://iml.jou.ufl.edu/projects/fall02/susi/tylenol.htm.

market, consumers have many sources of information regarding companies they seek to do business with.

Underwriters Laboratories (UL) is one example. UL is a private product safety testing and certifying organization. Founded in 1894, their website states:

> UL has developed more than 1,000 Standards for Safety. These are essential to public safety and confidence, reducing costs, improving quality and marketing products and services. Millions of products and their components are tested to UL's rigorous safety standards with the result that consumers live in a safer environment than they would have otherwise.[18]

Products that meet UL standards are allowed to display the UL logo as long as the product remains compliant. As an example of the importance of reputation in a free market, UL's reputation is such that failure to meet its standards can mean the death of a product:

> [I]t may be extremely difficult to sell certain types of products without a UL Mark. Large distributors may be unwilling to carry a product without UL certification, and the use of noncertified equipment may invalidate insurance coverage. It is common practice in many fields to specify UL Listed equipment or UL Recognized materials.[19]

Unlike government regulations, which are imposed on producers and consumers regardless of their individual choices, UL certifications are entirely voluntary. A manufacturer can choose to market a product that does not meet UL standards, and consumers are free to purchase such products if they choose. While both assume certain risks on the basis of their choices, each remains free to act according to his own judgment. UL is only one example of private companies offering testing and consumer information.

MET Laboratories offers a service that competes with UL, offering further choices to consumers and manufacturers. MET's

---

18. "Standards for Safety," Underwriters Laboratory, accessed January 22, 2011, http://www.ul.com/global/eng/pages/corporate/standards/.

19. "Underwriters Laboratories," *Wikipedia*, accessed January 22, 2011, http://en.wikipedia.org/wiki/Underwriters_Laboratories#About_UL.

website describes the difference between its service and that of UL: "The main difference between these two marks is with the level of involvement and partnership between the manufacturer and the test lab."[20] Whether this difference is worthwhile to a particular manufacturer or not is a judgment that each company can make. But unlike government regulations, the market is providing manufacturers with options—each can voluntarily choose the testing company that suits his needs or none at all.

Similarly, *Good Housekeeping* has been testing and approving products since 1909. The magazine first began testing products "to study the problems facing the homemaker and to develop up-to-date, firsthand information on solving them."[21] In 1910, the magazine built the *Good Housekeeping* Institute in Springfield, Massachusetts, to test products. The Institute included a model kitchen, a domestic science laboratory, and stations for testing products under household conditions. As with the UL mark, the *Good Housekeeping* Seal of Approval has become an important aspect of marketing and brand recognition for many products.

Interestingly, both UL and the *Good Housekeeping* Seal of Approval were started during the Progressive Era—a time when businesses were unjustly under attack for the safety of their products. At the time, new consumer products were appearing in abundance, and consumers were uncertain how to judge the quality and safety of these products. Recognizing the need for independent evaluation of products, these two private companies moved to satisfy the concerns of consumers without government coercion. And they are not alone in providing the ultimate in consumer protection—information.

For example, Consumers Union (CU) tests products and publishes the *Consumer Reports* magazine. Its mission

> is to work for a fair, just, and safe marketplace for all consumers and to empower consumers to protect themselves. The organization was founded in 1936 when advertising first flooded the mass media. Consumers lacked a reliable source of

---

20. "MET vs. UL," *MET Labs*, accessed January 22, 2011, http://www.metlabs.com/pages/AsGood.html.

21. "The History of the Good Housekeeping Seal," GoodHouseKeeping.com, accessed January 22, 2011, http://www.goodhousekeeping.com/product-testing/history/good-housekeeping-seal-history?click=main_sr.

> information they could depend on to help them distinguish hype from fact and good products from bad ones. Since then [*Consumer Reports*] has filled that vacuum with a broad range of consumer information.[22]

Unlike government regulations, which impose standards across an industry regardless of the judgments of those involved, the CU mission statement respects the judgment of both manufacturers and consumers. CU reports its findings and allows the consumer to make the decision that is best for him. To insure its independence and impartiality, CU accepts no advertising or free products. In addition to its laboratory testing, the organization also conducts extensive surveys with its readers, which results in numerous product reliability reports from the actual users of the products. These reports add to or detract from a product's reputation, again illustrating the crucial role of reputation in a free market.

The old adage "buyer beware" can be more aptly stated as "buyer be aware." Each of the examples above demonstrates that the private sector can and does provide consumers with the information that they require to make an informed decision. However, consumers must take responsibility for their buying decisions. They must research the products and services that they are considering and accept the consequences of their choices. The freedom to choose and personal responsibility are inseparable.

Certainly, some individuals do make irrational decisions. But regulations do not prevent this from occurring. Regulations simply make it more difficult, or impossible, for the rational person to act on his judgment. Regulations punish the rational and often protect the irrational from the consequences of their choices and actions. Because some individuals might abuse drugs, you must secure government permission to obtain treatment for a disease. Because some individuals might take out mortgages that they cannot afford, you must meet tighter government restrictions to obtain a home loan. Because some individuals put their money into investments that they do not understand, you are permitted to invest your money only in ways approved by government officials. Your

---

22. "Our Mission," ConsumerReports.org, accessed January 22, 2011, http://www.consumerreports.org/cro/aboutus/mission/overview/index.htm.

choices are controlled and restricted—not because of your actions—but because of the choices and actions of others.

We have seen that the free market rewards rationality. Government intervention stifles and prevents rationality.

The issue isn't one of intelligence but virtue.[23] A person must take responsibility for his own decisions, and that includes knowing the limitations of his own knowledge. If an individual doesn't understand a particular investment, he shouldn't invest in it. If he doesn't understand what a contractor or doctor recommends, he should seek additional information. If an individual surrenders the responsibility of making his own decisions, he surrenders control over his own life, and with it, the pursuit of his own happiness.

Government regulations restrict or eliminate personal choice. They force individuals to act in accordance with the demands and mandates of government officials, rather than according to their own judgment. Regulations foster dependence on government officials to make decisions, and thereby diminish personal responsibility. Despite the pretense of protecting the "public interest," regulations prevent individuals from pursuing the values that will bring them personal happiness.

Benevolence and good-will can only be achieved when individuals do not treat their neighbors as sacrificial animals. Prosperity can only be achieved when individuals can act on their own judgment. Happiness is possible only when individuals are free to pursue their own values. We have seen that the growing power of government is making benevolence, prosperity, and the pursuit of happiness increasingly difficult. Is the solution to place more power in "the people"? Let us now turn to the topic of democracy.

---

23. This issue was raised by Dr. Harry Binswanger through his moderated discussion group, the Harry Binswanger List.

20

Democracy versus Individual Rights

Ronald Reagan, America's fortieth President, said, "Democracy is worth dying for, because it's the most deeply honorable form of government ever devised by man."[1] John Adams, America's second President, said that "democracy never lasts long. It soon wastes, exhausts, and murders itself. There never was a democracy yet that did not commit suicide."[2] These two Presidents have vastly different ideas about democracy. Which one, if either, is correct?

Most Americans believe that the "will of the people as expressed in democratic elections, should reign supreme. But "the people" do not speak with one voice. They have different opinions, desires, and values, as even the most cursory examination of any political issue will reveal. Some want their children taught evolution while others prefer creationism. Some want more money spent on welfare programs while others want more spent on the police. Some want more controls on businesses while others think that regulations kill jobs. Some want government to invest in alternative energy while others want government to allow drilling in the Arctic National Wildlife Refuge. On each of these issues and many others, there is a wide disparity of opinion. But at the end of the day, most Americans accept the premise that the majority may properly use the coercive power of government to impose its views and values on the rest of society, including the minority.

---

1. "Ronald Reagan on the 40th Anniversary of D-Day," The History Place, accessed September 11, 2011, http://www.historyplace.com/speeches/reagan-d-day.htm.

2. John Adams, letter to John Taylor, (April 15, 1814).

Contrary to the views of many, America was not founded as a democracy. Democracy is unlimited majority rule. Democracy means that the majority may do as it chooses, simply because it is the majority. The Founding Fathers understood that a democracy is a tyranny of the masses and is as much a threat to individual liberty as the tyranny of a monarch. James Madison, America's fourth President, wrote, "There is no maxim, in my opinion, which is more liable to be misapplied, and which, therefore, more needs elucidation, than the current one, that the interest of the majority is the political standard of right and wrong."[3] A quote often attributed to Benjamin Franklin succinctly and eloquently captures the essence of the issue: "Democracy is two wolves and a lamb voting on what to have for lunch. Liberty is a well-armed lamb contesting the vote!" The Founders sought to protect the liberty of the minority, recognizing that the individual is the smallest minority, by creating a constitutional republic. They created a government with limited, specific, and enumerated powers.

In a constitutional republic, the actions of the majority are limited. The majority, no matter how large, may not violate the rights of individuals. Under such a government, individuals are free to act on their own judgment, as long as they respect the mutual rights of others, no matter how many citizens disagree with their actions. In a constitutional republic, government is limited to the protection of individual rights. Consider America's Constitution, which enumerates, defines, and limits the actions of government. The Bill of Rights, for example, specifically states actions that government may not take, such as limiting free speech or prohibiting gun ownership. The genius of the Founding Fathers was their ability to translate the principles of individual rights into a practical, workable government.

In theory and in practice, democracy means that the "will of the people" supersedes the rights of individuals. Democracy means that if enough citizens agree, then your rights may be violated at any time. It means that citizens can petition government to stop the construction of a building they do not like or to prohibit smoking in private businesses. It means that your neighbors can vote to tax you to pay for new schools or to modernize infrastructure. They can

---

3. James Madison, letter to James Monroe, (October 5, 1786).

vote to force private businesses to pay a higher minimum wage or to prohibit restaurants from using trans fats. Citizens can vote to deny certain individuals the right to marry or to prohibit gun ownership. Democracy means that your "rights" are merely permissions, which may be withdrawn any time the "will of the people" declares that doing so will serve the "public interest." Democracy means anything, and everything is open to a vote.

To illustrate this, let us say that your neighbor needs an operation, but he cannot afford to pay for it. If he broke into your home and stole the money from you, his action would be a violation of your rights. The nature of his action does not change if your town holds a referendum and your neighbor convinces 51 percent of your community to support robbing you. An action does not become proper and moral simply because a majority supports it. The violation of individual rights is not justified merely because a majority favors a particular action. Stealing your money is theft, whether it is done by a lone robber or by a vote of your neighbors. And it doesn't matter whether that vote is taken in your town, in your state capital, or in Washington, DC.

In response to the growing power of the federal government, many conservatives advocate for "states' rights." In 2009, Texas Governor Rick Perry said, "I believe the Constitution does not empower the federal [government] to override state laws without restraint."[4] Former Massachusetts Governor Mitt Romney said, "I respect the rights of states to come up with their own answers and their own solutions to compete with one another."[5] Both Perry and Romney express the contemporary view of "states' rights": states should not be restricted by the federal government in the laws that they enact. But this is only one part of "states' rights."

Others argue that states should be able to nullify federal laws, which, advocates claim will restrain an out of control federal government. As an example, the Tenth Amendment Center (TAC) argues, "Jefferson himself introduced the word 'nullification' into the American political lexicon, by which he meant the indispensable

---

4. "Gov. Perry Speaks in Support of States' Rights," *State of Texas*, April 9, 2009, accessed June 30, 2011, http://governor.state.tx.us/news/speech/12228/.

5. James Hamby, "Romney's South Carolina Debut: States' Rights, Medicare and Barbecue," CNN.com, May 21, 2011, accessed June 15, 2011, http://politicalticker.blogs.cnn.com/2011/05/21/romneys-south-carolina-debut-states-rights-medicare-and-barbecue/.

power of a state to refuse to allow an unconstitutional federal law to be enforced within its borders."[6] And who is to decide which laws are unconstitutional? TAC is clear on its answer:

> If the people of your state want to allow Homosexual marriages, which I am against on moral grounds, so be it. Either fight to repeal it or move. How dare the Federal government and Nancy Pelosi tell me and my neighbors that I have to have Homosexual marriage or not.
>
> Abortion? Same thing, I am against it, however, if you are not willing to effect change in your own state, how dare you tell others how to run their lives. Prayer in school? If my neighborhood school wants to say a prayer each morning to thank God, who is some atheist in New Jersey to say we cannot?
>
> How dare anyone expect the federal government to act like a bully and force change in your neighborhood whether you want it or not.[7]

In other words, it is wrong if the federal government allows gay marriages and abortion or prohibits prayer in school, but it is proper for state governments to do so. These are matters for each state to decide. It is wrong for "the federal government to act like a bully and force change in your neighborhood," but it is perfectly acceptable if the state government is a bully and forces such change. It is wrong if Congress issues mandates and prohibitions, but it is acceptable if the state legislature does so.

Fundamentally, the advocates of "states' rights" are arguing that the Constitution should not be the supreme law of the land. They claim that the states should be permitted to supersede the Constitution, either by passing laws that violate the Constitution or by nullifying federal laws at their own discretion.

Consider what this would mean if implemented. If a majority of Ohioans voted to seize all of the wealth of millionaires within the state, they should be allowed to do so without restraint from the federal government. If the citizens of California want to outlaw private ownership of guns, the Second Amendment should not stop

---

6. Thomas E. Woods Jr., "Nullification: Answering the Objections," *Tenth Amendment Center*, accessed June 30, 2011, http://www.tenthamendmentcenter.com/2011/02/01/nullification-answering-the-objections/.

7. Rick Montes, "What is a Tenther?" *Tenth Amendment Center*, accessed June 30, 2011, http://www.tenthamendmentcenter.com/2010/05/06/what-is-a-tenther/.

them. If the people of Massachusetts want to enslave doctors with mandated universal health care, as Mitt Romney did, the federal government should not stand in the way of their "solution." If Alabamans decide to re-institute Jim Crow laws, they have a "right" to ignore the Constitution. If the people of Maryland choose to deny Catholics the right to vote, as they did in 1718,[8] the federal government has no voice in the matter. Each state should be allowed to "experiment." Each state should be allowed to enact any laws desired by its citizens, including those that violate individual rights. As the term is used today, "states' rights" means that state legislatures should have no restrictions. "State's rights" is not a defense of individual rights; it is their negation. "State's rights" simply means democracy on the state level.

Interestingly, progressives also advocate democracy. As one example, in 2000 then Senator-elect Hillary Clinton said, "I believe strongly that in a democracy, we should respect the will of the people…."[9] And, as one website dedicated to progressivism states, "To coin a phrase, progressivism champions government 'of the people, by the people, for the people.'"[10] If both progressives and conservatives champion democracy, what is their difference? Why do they seem to disagree on so many issues?

The difference between progressives and many conservatives[11] is one of detail, not principles. The use of government regulations, prohibitions, and mandates is accepted by both progressives and conservatives. Progressives want those controls and regulations to emanate from Washington; conservatives want them to be issued from the state capital. For example, as governor of Texas, Rick Perry issued an executive order forcing young girls to be vaccinated for the human papillomavirus (HPV).[12] Progressives and

---

8. Matthew E. Bunson, "America's Catholic Colony," *Catholic Answers Magazine*, accessed September 25, 2011, http://www.catholic.com/magazine/articles/america%E2%80%99s-catholic-colony.

9. "Hillary Calls For End To Electoral College," CBSNews.com, accessed September 17, 2011, http://www.cbsnews.com/stories/2000/11/10/politics/main248645.shtml.

10. "What is Progressivism?" Progressive Living, accessed June 16, 2011, http://www.progressiveliving.org/progressivism.htm.

11. Conservatives fall into different camps, such as fiscal conservatives and social conservatives. They are not monolithic on every issue. I am speaking of conservatives in general.

12. Perry later rescinded that order, but in issuing the original order he demonstrated his willingness to use government coercion.

conservatives agree that government intervention is the proper means for solving virtually any problem, real or imagined. Progressives want to restrict drilling for oil, force you to buy health insurance, and tax the wealthy to pay for their welfare schemes. Conservatives want to penalize those who hire illegal aliens, restrict pornography, and mandate the teaching of "intelligent design" in government schools. Individuals across the political spectrum support bans on smoking, regulations on property use, the "war on drugs," and saving Medicare. Politicians from both parties run for office promising grand results founded on government intervention, and when the promised results do not materialize, either they or their successors propose further controls, regulations, and programs to correct the problems caused by earlier interventions. Virtually nobody, progressives and conservatives alike, questions the use of government coercion.

Why is government intervention regarded as the solution to nearly every problem? Why is it so widely accepted that some individuals must put aside their self-interest—their pursuit of happiness—for the alleged "public interest"? The answer can be found in the morality that "justifies" government coercion—altruism.

Neither progressives nor conservatives nor moderates question altruism. Barack Obama argues that if "everybody took an attitude of shared sacrifice…we can solve our deficit and debt problem next week, and it wouldn't require radical changes."[13] Former Alaskan Governor Sarah Palin states that "real solidarity means everyone being willing to sacrifice."[14] Former Utah Governor and Presidential candidate Jon Huntsman states that if elected President, "I wouldn't hesitate to call on a sacrifice from all of our people, even those at the very highest end of the income spectrum."[15] Progressives believe that you should sacrifice for the poor, the

---

13. "Obama Hits Optimistic Note at end of Midwest Swing," CNN.com, August 17, 2011, accessed September 25, 2011, http://articles.cnn.com/2011-08-17/politics/obama.bus.tour_1_president-barack-obama-deficit-reduction-spending?_s=PM:POLITICS.

14. "Palin: Wis. Unions Must Be 'Willing to Sacrifice'," FoxNews.com, February 19, 2011, accessed September 25, 2011, http://www.foxnews.com/politics/2011/02/19/palin-wis-unions-willing-sacrifice/#ixzz1YyHPPiy8.

15. "Huntsman: I Wouldn't Hesitate to Call on Rich to Sacrifice," PBS.org, August 25, 2011, accessed September 25, 2011, http://www.pbs.org/newshour/rundown/2011/08/huntsman-i-wouldnt-hesitate-to-call-on-rich-to-sacrifice.html.

needy, and the polar bears. Conservatives believe that you should sacrifice for family, country, and God. Progressives and conservatives agree that you must sacrifice your rights for the "public interest." They simply disagree on what constitutes the "public interest."

The result is the slow erosion of individual rights, no matter which party is in control. Progressives force you to bail out Detroit, while conservatives force you to bail out Wall Street. Progressives force you to pay for your neighbor's health care, while conservatives force you to pay for your neighbor's prescriptions. Both force you to provide financial support for government schools, pay for hospitals in Iraq, and provide subsidies for farmers. Both progressives and conservatives believe that they have a right to dispose of your money, and therefore your life, as they judge to be in the "public interest." Both believe that they are justified to use government coercion to compel you to act contrary to your own judgment. Both have plunged the nation deeper and deeper into debt. Both are leading us ever closer to the realization of John Adams' prediction: "There is never a democracy that did not commit suicide." If we wish to reverse this trend, we must reject the idea that government should force individuals to sacrifice their self-interest for the "public interest." And we must do so consistently, completely, and without exception. We must oppose government intervention on every level and on every issue. We must oppose government intervention on principle.

Individual rights prohibit the use of force in dealing with other individuals. Your rights protect your freedom to act as you choose without interference from others, so long as you respect their mutual rights. In a capitalist society, your interactions with others must be based on the voluntary consent of each individual, just as their interactions with you must be based on your voluntary consent. All interactions must be based on the trader principle:

> A trader is a man who earns what he gets and does not give or take the undeserved. He does not treat men as masters or slaves, but as independent equals. He deals with men by means of a free, voluntary, unforced, uncoerced exchange—an exchange which benefits both parties by their own independent judgment.[16]

---

16. Ayn Rand, "The Objectivist Ethics," in *The Virtue of Selfishness*, p. 31.

The trader principle recognizes your right to contract as you deem best. It recognizes your right to associate with whom you choose, on terms and conditions that are mutually acceptable. It recognizes your right to use, keep, and dispose of your property as you determine best. The trader principle recognizes your right to take the actions that you believe are best for your life, and it simultaneously recognizes the mutual rights of others to do the same.

We have seen the existential consequences of the trader principle—and its negation—in a myriad of ways. We saw it when Lysander Spooner offered a mail service that consumers preferred over the United States Postal Service. Spooner believed that he could offer better mail service than the government. Because he was free to act on his decisions—until Congress passed additional postal regulations—he was able to prove the truth of his claim. And consumers were also free to act on their judgment. They could choose to use his service, an alternative, or none at all.

We saw the trader principle in action when John Rockefeller improved the efficiency of refining and distributing kerosene to such an extent that he could cut the cost 83 percent and still make a fortune. Rockefeller believed that he could improve efficiencies and make kerosene dramatically more affordable. Because he was free to act—until Congress passed antitrust statutes—he was able to demonstrate that he was correct. And consumers were also free to act on their choices. They were free to buy his kerosene, purchase an alternative, or continue to burn candles.

We saw the trader principle applied when Henry Ford doubled the wages of his workers. Ford believed that his company would increase efficiencies by paying workers more. Because he was free to act as he deemed best, he proved his critics wrong. When he refused to offer more color choices, his competitors were also free to act on their judgment. And consumers were free to buy a Ford, a competitor's product, or use a horse and buggy.

We saw the trader principle in action when Mercedes Clemens massaged horses, until she was stopped by occupational licensing laws. The trader principle was applied when Dan Allgyer sold raw milk to willing customers, until his farm was raided by armed federal agents. In every issue that we have examined, we have seen that individuals and private businesses produce and trade the values that others want and need, unless they are prohibited from doing so by government coercion.

If we wish to return America to its glory, we must abandon the ideas that have led us to our present condition. We must reject democracy, "states' rights," and the morality upon which they are founded—altruism. We must remember the words of John Adams, that democracies inevitably commit suicide, as America is doing today. We must defend individual rights and the morality upon which they are founded—rational selfishness. We must declare that each individual has a moral right to live his life for his own self-interest; that *is* the meaning of the right to life, liberty, and the pursuit of happiness.

How do we return America to a nation that respects and protects individual rights? Is there a political party that supports individual rights? These are the questions we will now answer.

21

The Tea Party to the Rescue?

On February 19, 2009, Rick Santelli, a commentator for CNBC, launched into a rant on the floor of the Chicago Board of Trade. Incensed at the direction the government was taking, Santelli called for a protest, similar to the Boston Tea Party of 1773, to denounce the government's policies. And thus was born a grassroots movement—the Tea Party. This unique movement has the potential to dramatically change American politics. Indeed, the 2010 mid-term election was heavily influenced by the movement, with many "Tea Party candidates" winning election. But will this influence last, or will the Tea Party become an interesting footnote to history, like the Bull Moose and the Greenback Parties? To answer this, we must examine the ideas that animate the movement.

As a grassroots movement comprised of hundreds, if not thousands, of separate organizations, those who align themselves with the Tea Party hold a wide variety of positions on various issues. However, three basic positions are widely embraced by members of the movement: fiscal responsibility, free markets, and limited government. While these positions are consistent with the theme of this book, will the ideas advocated by the Tea Party actually lead to fiscal responsibility, free markets, and limited government? Let us begin by looking at the mission statement of the largest organization within the Tea Party movement, the Tea Party Patriots:

> We believe that it is possible to know the original intent of the government our founders set forth, and stand in support of that intent. Like the founders, we support states' rights for those powers not expressly stated in the Constitution. As the government is of the people, by the people and for the people, in

all other matters we support the personal liberty of the individual, within the rule of law.[1]

Certainly, we can identify the intent of the Founders. They left us a rich library of writing, from the Declaration of Independence to James Madison's notes on the Constitutional Convention, from *The Federalist Papers* to the letters of the Founders, from speeches and pamphlets to the Constitution itself. From these documents and speeches we can identify the fundamental intent of the Founders—the protection of individual rights. Indeed, many heroes of the Revolution, such as Patrick Henry and George Mason, refused to endorse the Constitution because they feared that a strong federal government would soon usurp individual rights. Even among the Founding Fathers, there was confusion as to the meaning and application of individual rights; therefore, it is not surprising that there was disagreement on the meaning and intent of the Constitution.

These confusions and disagreements prevented the Founders from fully implementing the principles of individual rights in the Constitution. In 1776, the Declaration of Independence set forth the principles of the American Revolution, stating that all men possess certain rights, namely to life, liberty, and the pursuit of happiness; further, the Declaration states that the purpose of government is to protect these individual rights. But in writing the Constitution in 1787, the Founders did not apply this principle consistently, with the legalization of slavery being the most obvious example. As another example, Article I, Section 8 of the Constitution grants Congress the authority to seize money from the citizens against their will: "Congress shall have power to lay and collect taxes, duties, imposts and excises." The same section authorizes Congress to dictate how businesses may operate, that is, "To regulate commerce with foreign nations, and among the several States, and with the Indian tribes."[2] The Fifth Amendment grants

1. "Tea Party Patriots Mission Statement and Core Values," Tea Party Patriots, accessed June 11, 2011, http://www.teapartypatriots.org/Mission.aspx.

2. At the time of the Constitutional Convention, many of the states had enacted legislation limiting trade with other states. The Founders sought to eliminate these barriers by giving Congress the sole power to regulate trade between the states. While the intention of the Founders was the facilitation of free trade, the authority to regulate commerce was eventually used as "justification" to regulate virtually every economic activity.

Congress the power to seize private property: "No person shall be… deprived of… property, without due process of law; nor shall private property be taken for public use, without just compensation." (Taking private property, even with compensation, forces an individual to act contrary to his own judgment and thereby violates his rights.) For all its brilliance, the Constitution grants Congress the authority to legally violate individual rights. To insist that Congress be guided by the Constitution without addressing these issues is to leave that authority in place.

The Founding Fathers were giants among men. Their achievements are not diminished by these inconsistencies. However, these inconsistencies, coupled with the influence of altruism and growing demands for government intervention, allowed for the gradual growth of government power. Given the power to tax and regulate, Congress slowly and steadily exercised that power, justifying each expansion of government as necessary to promote the "public interest." For example, the broad powers given to the Food and Drug Administration are for the purpose of "protecting the public health."[3] Similarly, the powers vested in the Environmental Protection Agency are to ensure that "all Americans are protected from significant risks to human health and the environment where they live, learn and work."[4] As we have seen, these two agencies and others like them control virtually every aspect of our lives under the guise of regulating commerce between the states and promoting the "general welfare."

The Tea Party can only return government to its proper role—the protection of individual rights—by addressing these issues. Americans cannot limit the powers of government by blindly following the Founding Fathers. To do so is to embrace their errors and inconsistencies. Nor can Americans simply hold Congress accountable to the Constitution, for that too means embracing those errors and inconsistencies. Americans must complete the work of the Founding Fathers. And that means rejecting some of the ideas advocated by the Founders and codified in the Constitution.

---

3. "What Does FDA Do?" Food and Drug Administration, accessed September 25, 2011, http://www.fda.gov/AboutFDA/Transparency/Basics/ucm194877.htm.

4. "Our Mission and What We Do," Environmental Protection Agency, accessed September 25, 2011, http://www.epa.gov/aboutepa/whatwedo.html.

To complete the work of the Founders, the principles of individual rights must be applied completely and consistently. Americans must recognize and defend the *moral* right of each individual to his own life, his own liberty, his own property, and the pursuit of his own happiness, no matter his race, gender, sexual orientation, or nation of birth. The defense of individual rights is the only way for the Tea Party to achieve its goals of limited government, free markets, and fiscal responsibility. To understand this, let us examine each of these in turn.

First, to speak of limited government is to imply that government is limited by something, versus a government that can act without restriction. As we saw in the last chapter, neither democracy nor "states' rights" places limits on government. Both sanction unlimited government powers, as long as the majority agrees. Individual rights, as we have seen, place boundaries on the actions of government. Individual rights prohibit others, including government, from using force to compel anyone to act contrary to his own judgment, as long as he respects the mutual rights of others. Only the principle of individual rights properly limits government. Only the principle of individual rights defines what actions are proper for government to undertake. A government limited to the protection of individual rights will not compel a person to obtain a government permit to repair his neighbor's computer. It will not prohibit a farmer from selling raw milk to willing customers. It will not jail a business owner because he refuses to move trees on his driving range. If the Tea Party wishes to achieve limited government, it must defend individual rights.

Similarly, a free market requires the recognition and protection of individual rights. A free market means the right of each individual to produce and trade as he deems best. As we have seen, government regulations, controls, and mandates prevent a person from doing so. Government coercion can prevent someone from operating a private mail delivery service, manufacturing (or taking) life-saving drugs, or building his dream house. Occupational licensing can prevent a person from entering the profession of his choosing; anti-discrimination laws and labor legislation prevent him from associating and contracting as he judges best. The operative word in free market is "free"—the absence of government coercion. Only the principle of individual rights prohibits government intervention in economic activities. Only the principle of individual rights creates a free market. If the Tea Party wishes to achieve free markets, it must defend individual rights.

Finally, only individual rights allows individuals to hold government fiscally responsible. With government limited to its proper purpose—the protection of individual rights—the alphabet soup of government agencies would not exist. There would be no FAA, SEC, OSHA, EPA, HUD, SSA, FEMA, FDA, or IRS. Individuals would not be forced to financially support programs and policies that they oppose. Politicians would not have the power to legally take your money without your consent. They could not compel you to support government schools, road construction, "green" energy, or a war that you oppose. Every dollar that you earn would be yours to spend as you choose, including financially supporting government. You would have complete control of your finances. What better way is there to hold politicians fiscally responsible than to make them acquire your money through your voluntary consent?

Embracing the principle of individual rights is also practical, for it will differentiate the Tea Party from Democrats and Republicans. Without individual rights as the unifying principle of the Tea Party, the movement will simply offer re-packaged versions of the same ideas (such as "states' rights") advocated by the major political parties. The Founding Fathers did not respond to the abuses of King George III by proposing a variation of monarchy. They did not seek to replace one form of tyranny with another. They rejected the entire idea that anyone—the king or "the people"—should control the lives of individuals. The Founding Fathers put forth a radical new idea: each individual has a right to live his life free from the arbitrary restrictions of government, whether government is controlled by a single person or by "the people." The Tea Party must deliver that same radical message.

This message offers something for every rational, hard-working American who does not desire government handouts but only the freedom to pursue his own dreams. In today's political environment, the concept of "rights" is seldom used to mean freedom of action; instead, "rights" is used to mean an entitlement to an object, such as a job, shelter, education, or health care. And those "entitlements" must be provided by the responsible, hard-working Americans who are trying to make their own lives better. If the Tea Party wishes to have a long term impact on America, it must reject this perverted view of rights and defend the proper view—the freedom of each individual to live his life as he thinks best. This message will have practical benefits for the Tea Party.

In embracing and defending individual rights, the Tea Party will not only provide a compelling and consistent message to all Americans, it will provide an unanswerable response to critics of the movement. Critics of the Tea Party have leveled many charges. Critics claim that the Tea Party is racist and dominated by political insiders and corporate interests. They also claim that Tea Party members are misrepresenting the Constitution and that their positions are contradictory. Let us examine these criticisms and see how a consistent application of individual rights addresses them.

Because it materialized shortly after America's first black President took office, many have viewed the Tea Party as a racist reaction to Barack Obama. In August 2011, Indiana Representative Andre Carson (who is black) proclaimed, "Some of them in Congress right now with this tea party movement would love to see you and me—hanging on a tree."[5] Others have claimed that the Tea Party would like to return to the days of Jim Crow, citing negative comments made by Senator Rand Paul regarding the Civil Rights Act of 1964.[6]

As we saw in chapter seven, in a capitalist society a person is free to hold irrational ideas, including racism. He is free to discriminate against blacks; he is not free to initiate force against anyone, including blacks. A person is free to refuse service to anyone; he is not free to burn a cross in their yard or lynch them. We also saw that after the Civil War and prior to the passage of Jim Crow laws, both plantation owners and streetcar companies put aside any racist ideas they held. Plantation owners put their self-interest before their racism and negotiated employment agreements that were beneficial to both the land owners and black laborers. Streetcar companies put their self-interest before their racism and refused to segregate customers on the basis of race. It took government intervention, in the form of Jim Crow laws, to

---

5. "Indiana Lawmaker's Lynching Reference Riles Tea Party," IBJ.com, August 31, 2011, accessed September 11, 2011, http://www.ibj.com/indiana-lawmakers-lynching-reference-riles-tea-party/PARAMS/article/29268.

6. In 2010, Paul said that the government should not prohibit individuals from discriminating on the basis of race.

institutionalize racism and violate the rights of blacks, plantation owners, and streetcar companies. In a capitalist society, the law is truly colorblind. In a capitalist society, the rights of all individuals—black, brown, yellow, and white—are recognized and protected. If the Tea Party defends individual rights, the claim of racism is refuted.

Others have claimed that the Tea Party is not a grassroots movement, but what House Minority Leader Nancy Pelosi called an "astroturf" movement; that is, the movement is controlled by political insiders and corporate interests. For example, an article titled "A Marxist Analysis of the Tea Party Movement" the following claim:

> Influential capitalist interests have been deeply involved with the organization and political direction of the movement since its inception. Take the supposedly spontaneous rant by Santelli. It turns out that months before his performance, a "Chicago Tea Party" website was registered by Zack Christenson, Republican producer for Chicago right-wing radio host Milt Rosenberg. Almost immediately after Santelli spoke, the website was activated and became part of a broad internet protest that got the Tea Party rolling.[7]

The vast majority of Tea Party members, the argument holds, are simply pawns. In short, the Tea Party is just another example of the rich and powerful manipulating the citizenry in an attempt to maintain the status quo.

Certainly, there are some wealthy individuals, such as the Koch brothers, who support the Tea Party. There are some politicians and former politicians, such as Rick Perry, Sarah Palin, and Dick Armey, who align themselves with the Tea Party. So? Such facts do not refute the positions held by the Tea Party. To make an issue of who supports the Tea Party is to evade the ideas and positions of the movement. It is an attempt to discredit the movement, not by refuting its arguments, but by fallacious attacks: if "capitalist interests" support the Tea Party, then surely the movement is intellectually bankrupt. While such arguments merit little

---

7. "A Marxist Analysis of the Tea Party Movement," League for the Revolutionary Party, accessed September 11, 2011, http://www.lrp-cofi.org/statements/teaparty.html.

consideration, they do present an opportunity to address the real issue.

Freedom of speech and freedom of association apply to all individuals, including former politicians, the wealthy, and Marxists. Each has a right to spend his money in support of his values, and that includes donating to the causes of his choice.

As we saw in chapter eleven, the dominance of money in the political process is a consequence of the vast economic powers held by government. Those powers are a magnet for campaign contributions and lobbying, as individuals, businesses, and organizations seek to influence policies that impact their lives and activities. Those powers also provide incentive for individuals to become career politicians and political insiders and thereby benefit from their political power and connections.[8] A government limited to the protection of individual rights would not have the power to destroy businesses or grant unearned benefits. It would not have the power to force taxpayers to bail out a bank, outlaw incandescent light bulbs, or provide taxpayer subsidies to companies making solar panels—"crony capitalism" is an oxymoron.[9] The fundamental problem is not the role of money in politics, but the role of government in our lives. By embracing and defending individual rights, the Tea Party can make this crucial point while advancing its positions of limited government, free markets, and fiscal responsibility.

Other critics, such as the Constitutional Accountability Center (CAC), argue that the Tea Party is misrepresenting the Constitution and the intent of the Founding Fathers:

> Tea Partiers and their friends have made a great many bold statements about the Constitution and the role of the federal

---

8. This is not to say that those who hold political office for a prolonged period are necessarily corrupt or seeking to use their position for personal gain. However, the vast powers held by government officials does attract such individuals.

9. "Crony capitalism" refers to a system in which government intervention is the source of business success. That intervention can take many forms: preferential legislation, protectionism, subsidies, or other forms of intervention. But capitalism is a system in which government does not intervene in the economy in any form. A system in which government intervention is the source of business success is properly called fascism—a system in which "private property" is controlled and regulated by government. It is not capitalism, no matter which adjectives are used.

government. While Tea Party activists and their conservative friends and allies do not agree on everything, they are united in their view that the federal government is exercising powers today that are beyond the limits of our Constitution.[10]

Among the examples cited are civil rights laws, environmental protection, corporate regulations, and Social Security. The CAC goes on to argue that the Founding Fathers

> established the federal government to act whenever the states were "separately incompetent" and granted the federal government broad power to, among other things, regulate interstate commerce and tax and spend to promote the general welfare. To be sure, our Constitution established a national government of enumerated and not unlimited powers... But while these powers are enumerated, they are also broad and substantial.[11]

On these points, the CAC is accurate. Tea Party supporters do claim that the federal government has expanded far beyond its Constitutional limits. It is also true that the Constitution grants Congress the power to regulate commerce and levy taxes. And this, the CAC argues, is a problem for the Tea Party—if the Constitution authorizes Congress to regulate commerce and levy taxes, how can the Tea Party claim that Congress is exceeding its Constitutional authority when it does so?

There are, in fact, two separate issues here: what is and what should be. Or, what is in the Constitution and what should be in the Constitution. The failure to make this distinction can, as we have already seen, present a significant obstacle to the Tea Party.

We have seen that the Constitution is not a perfect document. If the Tea Party wants Congress to abide by the Constitution, it must recognize the errors in the Constitution. The fact that government is granted a power does not make it right. The fact that

---

10. Elizabeth Wydra and David Gans, "Setting the Record Straight: The Tea Party and the Constitutional Powers of the Federal Government," Constitutional Accountability Center, July 16, 2010, Issue Brief No. 4, accessed September 17, 2011, http://www.theusconstitution.org/upload/fck/file/File_storage/Setting%20the%20Record%20Straight%20Issue%20Brief%20formatted.pdf.

11. Ibid.

government has the authority to tax and regulate does not mean that it should have that authority. If the Tea Party wants limited government and free markets, it cannot argue that regulations have gone "too far" or that taxation is excessive. As we saw in chapter nineteen, such arguments are simply a compromise. Such arguments abandon the principle of individual rights, and the debate shifts to a discussion of whose rights will be violated and to what extent. The Tea Party must oppose all regulations and all taxation as a violation of individual rights. To do otherwise is to argue that regulations and taxes that promote Tea Party issues and causes are proper, but regulations and taxes that promote progressive issues and causes are improper. That will appear inconsistent and hypocritical, and rightly so. Defending individual rights completely and consistently addresses the errors in the Constitution, and more importantly, presents a proper view of government.

And that brings us to the final criticism that we will examine: the positions of some Tea Party members are sometimes contradictory. For example, while Tea Party supporters decry "entitlement" programs and runaway government spending, polls have found that Tea Party members are opposed to cuts to two of the largest government programs—Social Security and Medicare. Because Tea Party supporters are generally older, it appears that Tea Party members oppose government programs that benefit others, but support government programs that benefit them. The fact is, both Social Security and Medicare violate individual rights. Both programs force a person to provide financial support for these programs regardless of his own desires or judgment. Defending individual rights means calling for the end of every improper government program, including Social Security and Medicare.

The method for ending Social Security and Medicare is beyond the present discussion. But as one example of the proper approach, both programs should be phased out over a period of time, such as thirty or forty years. Individuals should be immediately allowed to opt out of the program—they would give up any claims to future benefits and would also no longer have to pay taxes to fund the programs. Phasing out these programs allows individuals to take responsibility for their own lives and plan for their future, while also keeping promises that have been made. While there are many options on how to end Social Security and Medicare, anyone who supports individual rights must advocate that they be abolished.

The Tea Party arguably represents America's last hope to save the nation from financial ruin and tyranny. But the movement will not succeed if it simply recycles the same stale ideas as the Democrats and Republicans. It must offer new ideas—ideas founded on and in the defense of individual rights. Not only will that provide a consistent and compelling message to the American public, it is the only principled defense of limited government, free markets, and fiscal responsibility. It is the only principled defense of capitalism.

Is a capitalist society possible? Can we rescue America from the precipice of financial ruin? Can we establish a society that completely and consistently protects individual rights? Let us conclude by answering these questions.

22

The Moral is the Practical

Throughout history, individuals have been forced to live for the benefit of others, whether the king, the clan, or the community. On July 4, 1776, America's Founding Fathers rejected this premise, taking an unprecedented step in human history and declaring to the world "that all men are created equal, that they are endowed by their Creator with certain unalienable rights, that among these are life, liberty and the pursuit of happiness." However, for all its significance, the Declaration of Independence was only a mid-point; it was both a culmination and a beginning.

The Declaration culminated what John Adams would later call the "real American Revolution." To Adams, "The Revolution was effected before the war commenced. The Revolution was in the minds and hearts of the people"[1] in the fifteen years prior to the start of the War of Independence. During that period, the nation witnessed a "radical change in the principles, opinions, sentiments, and affections of the people."[2] From loyal subjects of the British king, the American people turned into revolutionary intellectuals, willing to fight the most powerful military on earth.

The Declaration also marked the beginning of another journey, one that concluded with the ratification of the United States Constitution in 1788. Prior to war with Britain, the colonies had been separate and independent political entities. They had united for a common cause—the protection of individual rights—but the Articles of Confederation under which they operated during and

---

1. John Adams "Letter to H. Niles," February 13, 1818, TeachingAmericanHistory.org, accessed July 5, 2011, http://teachingamericanhistory.org/library/index.asp?document=968.

2. Ibid.

after the Revolutionary War proved insufficient to address numerous problems that arose, such as the many interstate conflicts that were developing. Ostensibly meeting in Philadelphia in the summer of 1787 to revise the Articles, the delegates to the Federal Convention soon agreed to write a new governing document. The delegates sought to construct a federal government that was sufficiently powerful to wage war, enter treaties, and resolve interstate disputes, while simultaneously allowing for state independence and the protection of individual rights. It was a delicate balance to strike, and despite the issues raised in the previous chapter, they brilliantly accomplished their goal.

Wanting to be liberated from the chains of tyranny, millions of individuals from around the world flocked to America during the nineteenth century. The recognition and protection of individual rights allowed the tired, the poor, and the huddled masses to pursue their own happiness. They built steel mills and railroads. They invented the telegraph, the light bulb, and the automobile. They produced an abundance of food and consumer goods. In pursuing their own self-interest, millions of people raised the standard of living of all Americans to unrivaled heights. But the freedom of the nineteenth century did not last.

Today, government is no longer the protector of individual rights. Individuals are prohibited from freely entering the profession of their choosing; they are forced to support public institutions, such as government schools, regardless of their own desires and values. Zoning and taxation prevent individuals from using their property as they judge best; the growing number of regulations and controls coercively interfere with the moral right of individuals to live their lives in the pursuit of their values and their happiness. We have seen the destructive consequences of government intervention on the lives of individuals, such as Lysander Spooner, Abigail Burroughs, Mercedes Clemens, Dan Allgyer, John Thoburn, and others. And they are not the only victims. The rights of every American living today are violated by government intervention. Regulations, controls, and prohibitions prevent each of us from living our lives as we choose. Just as sadly, government programs and policies also violate the rights of future generations.

A child born in America in 2011 inherits a portion of the national debt exceeding $45,000. And if we include unfunded liabilities, such as Social Security and Medicare, that number climbs to more than $175,000![3] Add to that number the debts of state and local governments, and a child born today starts life with an enormous financial obligation in which he had no voice. And before that child can even talk, present generations continue to add to his burden. In this sense, the father of altruism—Auguste Comte—was right: "We are born under a load of obligations of every kind, to our *predecessors*, to our successors, to our contemporaries. After our birth these obligations increase or accumulate, for it is some time before we can return any service [emphasis added]." Though Comte was not speaking of national debt, government spending has given truth to his words. A child born today is presumed to have an obligation to pay the debts of his predecessors.

It is a gross injustice to force an individual to act contrary to his own judgment. But to impose obligations on an individual before he has even been born is a monstrous evil. No matter his eventual judgment of government schools and parks, government's monopoly on mail delivery and infrastructure, welfare programs, or any other government policy or program, his judgment will be irrelevant—he will be forced to pay for such indecencies. Regardless of his choice of career, he will be forced to abide by the licensing and labor laws of previous generations. No matter his values, his judgment will be superseded by that of his ancestors—the past will restrict, control, and regulate his life. Thomas Jefferson, in a letter to James Madison, declared "that the earth belongs in usufruct[4] to the living." Jefferson went on to write:

> Then no man can by natural right oblige the lands he occupied, or the persons who succeed him in that occupation, to the payment of debts contracted by him. For if he could, he might during his own life, eat up the usufruct of the lands for several generations to come, and then the lands would belong to the dead, and not to the living, which would be reverse of our principle. What is true of every member of the society

---

3. "US Debt Clock," USDebtClock.org, accessed September 13, 2011, accessed September 25, 2011, http://www.usdebtclock.org/.

4. Usufruct means "the right to use and derive profit from a piece of property belonging to another."

> individually, is true of them all collectively, since the rights of the whole can be no more than the sum of the rights of individuals.[5]

Isn't this what the nation's soaring debt is doing? Are we not "eating up the usufruct of the lands for several generations to come"? Are we not obligating our children, and their children, to pay for the debts contracted by the dead? Those not yet born will come into the world with their future earnings spoken for. Without choice or voice, they will be forced to pay for the profligacy of past and present generations. This is the legacy we are leaving our children, their children, and future generations. Their lives and their happiness will be sacrificed for the dead.

Every rational parent wants to leave his children a better world than he inherited. Every rational parent wants his children to be free to pursue their own dreams, their own personal happiness. But how can a person do this if he is beholden to the past? How can he be free when the bread he has not yet baked is being eaten today? How can he pursue his happiness when the use of the property he does not yet own is being controlled and regulated? He will be forced to live, not for the profligacy of an arbitrary king, but for the profligacy of his ancestors. Is this the legacy that we want to leave our children?

Fortunately, we can change this. "We have it in our power," as Thomas Paine wrote in *Common Sense*, "to begin the world over again."[6] To do so, we must complete the work of the Founders. We must complete the American Revolution. As in the 1760s and 1770s, this will require a "radical change in the principles, opinions, sentiments, and affections of the people." It will require an intellectual revolution. It will require a revolution fought with ideas rather than muskets. If we want to change history and the direction our nation is headed, we must change the ideas that shape our culture.

In 1776, the American people faced a grave choice: They could continue their allegiance to King George III, or they could defend their rights as free and independent individuals. They could accept

---

5. Thomas Jefferson, "Letter to James Madison," September 6, 1789, accessed September 25, 2011, http://classicliberal.tripod.com/jefferson/mad02.html.

6. Thomas Paine, *Common Sense*, USHistory.org, accessed October 5, 2011, http://www.ushistory.org/paine/commonsense/sense6.htm.

the increasing power of the British government, or they could reject the premise that they must live their lives to satisfy the arbitrary decrees of the king. They could deliver their children and future generations into servitude, or they could fight for freedom and individual rights. Our situation today is no less grave, and the choices that we face are, in principle, no different.

In 1776, the Founders faced the greatest military power on earth. Their chances of victory were slim, given the rag-tag collection that comprised the American army. We do not face a potent army, but rather, an impotent idea—altruism. Though altruism is widely accepted and deeply held, its power—and everything that it makes possible—comes only from our sanction. It is only through our voluntary acceptance of altruism that government control of our lives has grown. If we withdraw that acceptance, if we reject the idea that we must put aside our self-interest for the "public interest," what "justification" can be offered for ObamaCare, "cap and trade," restrictions on drilling, or any other government intervention? What other "justification" can be offered to those who are prohibited by government from selling raw milk, starting a mail delivery company, or building his dream house?

The "real American Revolution" was fundamentally a revolution of ideas; completing the work of the Founders must be equally so. Just as the Founders fought for the principle of individual rights, so must we. But we must carry their battle one step further. We must defend the rights of each individual to his own life, his own liberty, and the pursuit of his own happiness, not just politically, but also morally.

The Founders recognized the fact that individuals do not easily reject the old and familiar. As Thomas Jefferson wrote in the Declaration,

> all experience hath shewn that mankind are more disposed to suffer, while evils are sufferable than to right themselves by abolishing the forms to which they are accustomed. But when a long train of abuses and usurpations, pursuing invariably the same object evinces a design to reduce them under absolute despotism, it is their right, it is their duty, to throw off such government, and to provide new guards for their future security.

The same is true of ideas. Altruism, like King George III, has a "long train of abuses." It has sanctioned the growth of government, compelling individuals to sacrifice their own self-interest and happiness for the "public interest." It has pursued "invariably the same object"—self-sacrificial service to others. In declaring that individual rights are "absurd and immoral," altruism has delivered mankind into "absolute despotism." Altruism is the moral foundation of Nazism, communism, socialism, fascism, and the welfare state. Each demands that the individual sacrifice his own self-interest for others; the only difference between these social systems is the degree of government control and the slogans used. It is our right, it is our responsibility to ourselves as individuals, to throw off the idea that our lives must be lived for others and to declare our independence as individuals.

For the Founders to throw off the chains of a tyrannical king was an act of utmost courage. It required the conviction that their cause was just. It required an intransigent devotion to the principles for which they fought. They did not take their actions lightly, pledging to one another "our Lives, our Fortunes, and our sacred Honor." Thomas Jefferson, James Madison, George Washington, and the other Founding Fathers knew that if they were captured, they would be hanged as traitors. During the war, many Founding Fathers lost their lives, their fortunes, or both. But none lost their sacred honor. They fought for the most noble cause the world has ever witnessed—the inviolate rights of the individual.

To throw off the self-sacrificial chains of altruism, to challenge long-held ideas, also requires courage. And the cause of freedom and individual rights requires no less. "These are the times that try men's souls," as Thomas Paine wrote in the bleak winter of 1776. "Tyranny, like hell, is not easily conquered; yet we have this consolation with us, that the harder the conflict, the more glorious the triumph. What we obtain too cheap, we esteem too lightly: it is dearness only that gives every thing its value."[7]

The task of completing the work of the Founders will try our souls. The Founding Fathers identified the ideas necessary to create this great nation. It is now our turn to fight the battle of ideas. We, who love America, can restore America to its glory and its

---

7. Thomas Paine, "The Crisis," USHistory.org, accessed October 5, 2011, http://www.ushistory.org/paine/crisis/c-01.htm.

greatness. Can we win? Can we turn America back from the brink of self-destruction?

Even though a completely capitalistic society has never existed, America came close in the nineteenth century. Even with a growing number of government controls and regulations, America blossomed from a nation of subsistence farmers into the world's most powerful economic producer. The examples in this book have shown what is possible when men are free. Free men, unshackled by arbitrary government controls and regulations, can and do create an abundance of material values that enable us to sustain and enjoy our lives. From the inexpensive and abundant kerosene of John Rockefeller to the I-Pad of Steve Jobs, from the affordable automobiles of Henry Ford to the life-enhancing production unleashed by Bill Gates, freedom—the absence of government coercion—makes everyone's life better. We have seen examples from India, Britain, France, and America. We have seen examples that span centuries. Whenever men are free to act on their own judgment, in the pursuit of their own values, extraordinary things happen. Freedom is universally practical and moral—it is proper for all men, in all nations, in all eras.

The examples of freedom's practicality are not limited to this book: the unprecedented economic progress of nineteenth century America is an undeniable historical fact. Even today, the contrast between North Korea and South Korea, or the innovations of technology companies versus the stagnation of our public schools, demonstrate the practical benefits of freedom. Such evidence is available to anyone who cares to honestly assess history or look at the world today. With few exceptions, nearly everyone agrees that capitalism delivers "the goods." Why then are capitalism and America so despised?

The answer lies in morality. Capitalism and America are despised because they are regarded as immoral. Capitalism is despised because it is founded on the idea that each individual has a moral right to put his own interests, welfare, and personal happiness before the "public interest." And so long as capitalism is regarded as immoral, it will be despised. So long as individuals accept altruism as the moral ideal, they must regard capitalism as immoral.

Only one social system is founded on the idea that each individual has a moral right to his own life, his own liberty, and the pursuit of his own happiness. Only one social system prohibits the use of physical force in human relations, and thereby makes possible individual freedom. Only one social system recognizes and protects individual rights. That system is capitalism. America, which has come closest to realizing the moral ideal of capitalism, is despised for that fact.

The battle to save capitalism and America can be won. To do so, we must, as occurred in the years prior to the War of Independence, change the "minds and hearts of the people." Those who love America must do more than protest the latest government "stimulus," bailout, or "entitlement" program. We must protest against the ideas that make such policies possible. More importantly, we must spread the right ideas, not variations of the same worn out ideas that have led us to where we are today. America will not be saved by debating over the beneficiaries of government largesse. Capitalism and America will only be saved by defending the idea that government regulations and controls violate individual rights and are never moral, no matter the cause. America will only be saved by defending the idea that each individual has a moral right to his own life, his own liberty, his own property, and the pursuit of his own happiness.

More fundamentally, those who love America must reject the idea that the individual must place the "public interest" before his own self-interest. To quote John Galt, the hero of Ayn Rand's *Atlas Shrugged*:

> The world you desired can be won, it exists, it is real, it is possible, it is yours.
>
> But to win it requires total dedication and a total break with the world of your past, with the doctrine that man is a sacrificial animal who exists for the pleasure of others. Fight for the value of your person. Fight for the virtue of your pride. Fight for the essence of that which is man: for his sovereign rational mind. Fight with the radiant certainty and the absolute rectitude of knowing that yours is the Morality of Life and that yours is the battle for any achievement, any value, any grandeur, any goodness, any joy that has ever existed on this earth.
>
> You will win when you are ready to pronounce the oath I have taken at the start of my battle—and for those who wish to know the day of my return, I shall now repeat it to the hearing of the world:

> I swear—by my life and my love of it—that I will never live for the sake of another man, nor ask another man to live for mine.[8]

America was the first nation in the history of mankind to recognize and protect the right of each individual to live his life for his own sake. The Founding Fathers fought an intellectual battle for that ideal. Now it is our turn.

---

8. Ayn Rand, *Atlas Shrugged* (New York: Signet, 1992), pp. 983-84.

Recommended Reading

Alexander Hamilton, James Madison, and John Jay, *The Federalist Papers.* Three Founding Fathers explain the meaning and intent of the United States Constitution.

Ayn Rand, *Atlas Shrugged.* Rand's classic novel dramatizes the role of the mind in man's life.

———— *Capitalism: The Unknown Ideal.* Rand examines the intellectual roots of capitalism and its practical consequences.

———— *The Virtue of Selfishness.* The morality of rational self-interest is defined and defended.

Capitalism Magazine.com. An extensive collection of articles and commentary on capitalism, current events, and politics.

Craig Biddle, *Loving Life.* An easy-to-read overview of Ayn Rand's philosophy, Objectivism.

Henry Hazlitt, *Economics in One Lesson.* Hazlitt refutes common economic fallacies.

John Locke, *Two Treatises on Government.* Locke's writings on the nature of rights and the purpose of government had a profound influence on the political philosophy of the Founding Fathers.

Leonard Peikoff, *The Ominous Parallels.* Nazi Germany was the result of the ideas present in the culture. Those same ideas are shaping America today.

The Objective Standard. A quarterly journal on current events and issues.

Index

About the Author

Brian Phillips has been actively defending individual rights for the past twenty-five years. He has successfully helped defeat attempts to implement zoning in Houston, Texas, and Hobbs, New Mexico. His writing has appeared in *The Freeman*, *Reason*, *The Orange County Register*, *The Houston Chronicle*, *The Objective Standard*, and dozens of other publications.

Brian has been a small business owner since 1986, and he has seen how government regulations and controls impede the ability of business owners to grow their business. He has written and lectured on the principles and ethics of business for trade publications and trade associations.

Brian resides in Houston, Texas, with his wife, Elaine, and three cats.